# Praise for
## *Understanding Everyday Incivility*

"Shelley Lane frames a theoretical 'why' for civility as she acknowledges increasing cases of incivility in the public domain. Her work outlines a basic presupposition: people must be heard, not dismissed by pejorative statements. She reclaims civility as a pragmatic democratic foundation in this historical moment."

**—Ronald C. Arnett, Duquesne University; author of *Levinas's Rhetorical Demand: The Unending Obligation of Communication Ethics***

"*Understanding Everyday Incivility* offers a thorough, informed, and readable examination of the many forms that incivility can take and the various contexts in which it occurs. Lane's numerous thought-provoking examples of behavior that might be labeled uncivil keep her analyses concrete and relevant to contemporary life. Her strategies for promoting civility are both sensible and timely."

**—Emrys Westacott, Alfred University**

"Meticulously researched and written with lucidity, this book provides deep insights into our civility crisis. Rather than prescribe a set of rules, Lane explains what we need to consider if we are to build a truly lasting civility. A gem of a book that ranks with the best literature on civility."

**—Benet Davetian, University of Prince Edward Island; author of *Civility: A Cultural History***

# Understanding Everyday Incivility

## *Why Are They So Rude?*

Shelley D. Lane

ROWMAN & LITTLEFIELD
Lanham • Boulder • New York • London

Published by Rowman & Littlefield
A wholly owned subsidiary of
The Rowman & Littlefield Publishing Group, Inc.
4501 Forbes Boulevard, Suite 200, Lanham, Maryland 20706
https://rowman.com

Unit A, Whitacre Mews, 26-34 Stannary Street, London SE11 4AB,
United Kingdom

British Library Cataloguing in Publication Information Available

**Library of Congress Cataloging-in-Publication Data**
Names: Lane, Shelley D., author.
Title: Understanding everyday incivility: why are they so rude? / Shelley D. Lane.
Description: Lanham : Rowman & Littlefield, a wholly owned subsidiary of The Rowman
    & Littlefield Publishing Group, Inc., [2017] | Includes bibliographical references and
    index. |
Identifiers: LCCN 2017006080 (print) | LCCN 2017024284 (ebook) | ISBN
    9781442261860 (electronic) | ISBN 9781442261853 (cloth : alk. paper)
Subjects: LCSH: Courtesy.
Classification: LCC BJ1533.C9 (ebook) | LCC BJ1533.C9 L35 2017 (print) | DDC 177/
    .1—dc23
LC record available at https://lccn.loc.gov/2017006080

∞ ™ The paper used in this publication meets the minimum requirements of American
National Standard for Information Sciences Permanence of Paper for Printed Library
Materials, ANSI/NISO Z39.48-1992.

Printed in the United States of America

To my father, Simon M. Lane, D.P.M., M.S.Ed. (1924–2017), a podiatrist, college dean, interim university president, risk management specialist, professor, author, amateur historian, community organizer, and most importantly, loving father, who was a model of civility.

# Contents

# Preface

I write this preface only four days before president-elect Donald Trump's inauguration and after what may be described as one of the most divisive and uncivil campaign seasons in our nation's history. While American presidential campaigns have been noted for acrimony since our country's inception, the overwhelming amount of incivility in the 2016 election and the speed at which it was disseminated is unprecedented. Politics aside, President Trump's campaign included too many examples of uncivil words and behavior to include in this preface. Trump began the road to the White House by naming his opponents "Lying Ted, Crooked Hillary, Little Marco, Crazy Bernie," and "Low-Energy Jeb." He labeled Mexican immigrants "criminals" and "rapists," and at one point, called for a blanket ban on Muslim immigration (but later suggested that Muslim immigrants be identified in an official registry). Trump retweeted comments made by white supremacists and disparaged congressman John Lewis, an icon in the civil rights movement, as a man of "all talk" and "no action." Trump also acknowledged that he had assaulted women by "grabbing them by the p—sy." He mocked a disabled reporter; stated that Senator John McCain is not a war hero because he was captured; and alleged that his "long and beautiful fingers" are similar to his sex organ.

The 2016 campaign is notable not only for the rapid dispersal of uncivil rhetoric (thanks to Trump's use of Twitter and social media in general), but also for the political incivility that is influencing our everyday encounters throughout the United States. Approximately 879 real-world (i.e., non-digital) hate incidents were reported to the Southern Poverty Law Center just ten days after the election. The Council on American-Islamic Relations also experienced an escalation in hate incident reports—an increase greater than those that happened immediately after the 9/11 attacks. While most hate-related situations and uncivil behaviors occurred on sidewalks and streets, colleges and universities experienced an increase in uncivil acts, many of which were directly tied to Trump. A Trump sign with a swastika drawn over it was left near the Hillel office at the University of Virginia. The name "Trump" was written on the door to a Muslim prayer room at New York University. A Marshall University student tweeted that "As soon as Trump hits 270 electoral votes I am grabbing the first girl I see by the p—sy. #MAGA" (this hashtag was used by Trump supporters and is the acronym of "Make America Great Again," Trump's campaign slogan). Even more disheartening is the uncivil campaign rhetoric that has made its way into K–12 classrooms. Teachers have reported an increase in bullying behaviors and children, who are American citizens, cry at their desks in fear that they and their families will be deported. The slogan "Black Lives Suck" has been scrawled on high school bathrooms and benches, and Latino children have been taunted by students who shout, "Build the wall!"

It is important, now more than ever, to understand everyday incivility, its causes and consequences, and the need to promote civil communication. Everyday incivility is a destructive force that results in psychological, emotional, and even physical harms. But just as words can threaten, offend, and obfuscate, they can also be used to comfort, clarify, and remind us that we're all human beings who deserve to be treated with respect. I feel uplifted when I remind myself of the Seattle mother who started the Facebook group, "Dear President Trump: Letters from Kids about Kindness." One six-year-old girl wrote a letter in which she advised: "Be nice to things. Do not say mean things. . . . Good luck with your new job! Let me know if I can help." Another six-year-old wrote: "Dear Mr. Trump, Kids in my class are very scared. Please don't kick them out. In my school we get sent to the wall when we're in trouble. My friends did not do anything wrong."

I am also hopeful when I recall that Justin Normand, looking like the quintessential Texan in a cowboy hat, checkered shirt, and cowboy boots, stood in front of a local mosque and held a sign that urged Muslims to stay strong because we are all Americans. Normand's intent was to show support for the local Muslim community and counter President Trump's anti-Muslim comments. I am similarly hopeful when I read about UT Austin student Amina Amdeen, a *hijab*-wearing Muslim, who put herself in harm's way to protect another. Amdeen threw herself in front of Trump supporter Joseph Weidknecht, to shield him from anti-Trump protesters who threatened him with violence. The encounter ended with Amdeen and a number of anti-Trump protesters supporting Weidknecht's expression of free speech.

The children's letters, Justin Normand, and Amina Amdeen help move me from cynicism about the state of humanity in our country to hope for the future, which is one outcome of "conversational civility." Conversational civility includes a balanced approach to the good and bad that people can do, and encourages us to keep a conversation going in an attempt to solve the problems we share. Conversational civility reminds us to communicate in a respectful manner and to refrain from using words and actions that are harmful to our community. It is my hope that *Understanding Everyday Incivility: Why Are They So Rude?* will increase your understanding of both the benefits and costs associated with civil behavior and enable you to find your own way to promote civility.

*Understanding Everyday Incivility* would merely be a book idea without the support and kindness of my family, friends, and additional significant others. I want to thank my spouse, Lawrence "Loren" Miller, PhD, for allowing me to "hijack" the computer room and for his proofreading and editorial comments. My adult children, Ethan Lane-Miller, Elizabeth and Chris Shuma, and Ariana Lane-Miller, deserve praise for their patience and understanding when I worked on this book rather than joining them at the movies or at a restaurant. My parents, Simon M. Lane and Rita A. Lane, have been a constant source of support, and my best friend, Helene Cohen Gilbert, is a soul sister whose wisdom and unconditional love sustain me.

I also want to thank the editors at Roman and Littlefield for believing in my project; Dr. Deborah Cohn, associate professor of marketing at New York Institute of Technology, for providing me with her prepublication manuscript, "Thanks, I Guess: What Consumers Complain about When They Complain about Gifts"; and Elisabeth A. Lambert, for her copyediting skills. Additionally, I am grateful for the *Minding the Workplace* and *Ethics Alarms* blogs, and extend thanks to their authors, Dr. David Yamada and Jack Marshall, respectively. *Minding the Workplace* and *Ethics Alarms* have provided me with thoughtful commentary about dignity and bullying, the study of right and wrong, and numerous examples of civil and uncivil behavior.

Finally, I must express my gratitude to former student and current colleague and friend, David Leitnick. David once was my "nontraditional" (i.e., "adult") student in an evening public speaking course that I taught at a community college. He and I had numerous discussions after class about public speaking and other topics, and as I listened to him present a speech on workplace bullying, I realized that he was describing our community college president. Workplace bullying was a new area of research at the time, and David was passionate about it in that it had affected him personally. I began to research the topic for the same reason as David; we both were targeted by workplace bullies.

David and I have stayed in contact during the fifteen-plus years we have known each other. He received a master's degree in humanities and literary studies from the University of Texas at Dallas, where I began teaching in 2006. I broadened my research from workplace bullying to civility in general, and found that while there is much research about political incivility, the few studies of day-to-day incivility are scattered among journals in urban studies, sociology, business, and philosophy, to name a few. David moved to the Mideast to teach English as a foreign language and became a dual citizen of the United States and Great Britain. I became an associate dean at UT Dallas and wrote a memoir and textbooks with a civility theme. Although I needed a break from researching and writing, I couldn't stop thinking about *Understanding Everyday Incivility*, and finally gave in to the compulsion to write the book. And in the end, I realize that *Understanding Everyday Incivility* would not have become a reality if it weren't for David Leitnick and his workplace bullying speech. Thank you, David; I hope to meet with you over a pint in London someday!

Shelley D. Lane, PhD
January 16, 2017
The University of Texas at Dallas

# Foreword

## David C. Yamada

Paths sometimes cross in wonderfully odd ways. In the case of Dr. Shelley Lane, it was via my discovery of her memoir reflecting upon a formative junior year abroad. It so happens that our respective overseas study experiences in the United Kingdom have given us a shared interest in this topic, and a couple of years ago I was researching online for first-person accounts by other collegiate sojourners. This led me to Shelley's book, *A Stirling Diary: An Intercultural Story of Communication, Connection and Coming-of-Age* (Lane, 2010), which drew heavily upon the personal journals that she kept during her time overseas.

For someone who gets soggy at the mere memory of his own semester in England, Shelley's account of her time at Stirling University in Scotland inspired no small amount of nostalgia on my part. Now, this alone would've prompted a friendly e-mail of appreciation to the author. But my connection with Dr. Lane was destined to become a more enduring professional one when I read, in the Preface, an explanation of what prompted her to unearth her undergraduate journals and to write her remembrance:

> Soon thereafter fate provided me with two reasons why I should read them again: a new president at the community college where I worked who made Attila the Hun appear weak and timid, and foot surgery that had me in crutches for four months. I finally returned to the journals to keep my mind away from the workplace bully and to forget that I wasn't easily mobile.

Shelley's words jumped off the page for me: *She wrote this memoir in part as a healthy distraction from being bullied at work!* As a law professor specializing in employment law and policy, I have been researching, writing, and talking about workplace bullying and workplace dignity for nearly twenty years. It made eminent sense to me that someone experiencing a toxic work situation might seek to mentally escape from it by revisiting a special chapter in her past and writing about it.

I contacted Dr. Lane to thank her for *A Stirling Diary* and to discuss her work experiences. Our exchanges revealed that she had since left the school that hosted her workplace tormenter and moved on to a new and exciting position at the University of Texas at Dallas. I could tell—yes, simply by the tenor of her e-mails(!)—that she was literally and figuratively in a much better place.

I am equally delighted that Shelley has written this book. *Understanding Everyday Incivility: Why Are They so Rude?* is an informed, wide-ranging, and provocative examination of a topic that carries everyday significance. As Dr. Lane points out in the first chapter, this is not a volume about manners and etiquette. Rather, here we find civility and incivility observed and interpreted through the lens of a communication scholar and teacher who happens to be a thoughtful human being.

Some may be drawn initially to this book due to the current state of American political discourse, especially in the aftermath of a contentious and often vulgar presidential campaign. Shelley acknowledges that political behavior is likely to come up in many discussions about civility, but she urges us to take our examination of this topic beyond news headlines and tweets. After all, questions and concerns about civility and incivility permeate our private and public lives. In the pages that follow, you'll read about family disputes, road rage, online behavior, relationship issues, workplace tensions, school dynamics, community relations, and more—all framed by a communication perspective.

As I mentioned above, my original interest in this topic stems primarily from my longtime focus on workplace interactions. Workplace incivility is a significant problem that undermines both employee well-being and organizational morale and productivity. In some cases it may manifest itself in more serious types of abuse, such as bullying, mobbing, and discriminatory harassment. Some of these behaviors violate established employment protections; too many escape liability and accountability. In any event, the various forms of incivility at work should not be regarded equally or yield identical organizational responses. Even a very heated argument between co-workers is not the same as a targeted campaign to destroy someone's self-confidence and livelihood. Distinctions matter.

Indeed, variations of incivility can be nuanced and complex. Of course, civility is a good thing and incivility is not, and we should strive for the former in terms of how we interact with others. Ah, if only it was that easy! This baseline is a mere starting point, and *Understanding Everyday Incivility* takes us to the next levels of understanding by shedding light on our behaviors, what motivates us, and how we might do better. With that in mind, I have several pieces of advice for those engaging the pages that follow:

First, understand that this book is neither a breezy self-help manual nor a heavy academic tome. Written in an accessible style, it is backed by research and insight that lift our overall grasp of the topic. Its content should be contemplated, not simply galloped through, in attempting to comprehend how we relate to each other.

Second, do accept Dr. Lane's invitation to put yourself in the roles of various actors described in these stories and scenarios and to ask what you would do under like circumstances. Depending on your self-image, don't assume that you are always the "good" person or the "bad" person! Also, while at times "taking sides" is the necessary and right thing to do, here I suggest trying to withhold judgment while striving for understanding.

Finally, consider this volume to be a humane and stimulating invitation for all of us to navigate this challenging world with more heart quality. Agree with it, disagree with it (civilly, of course!), and learn some life lessons from it. I'm sure Dr. Lane would be justly pleased if this book has that effect.

David C. Yamada, J.D.
Professor of Law and Director, New Workplace Institute
Suffolk University Law School
Boston, Massachusetts

## REFERENCE

Shelley D. Lane, *A Stirling Diary: An Intercultural Story of Communication, Connection and Coming-of-Age* (Lane, 2010).

*Part I*

# Understanding Everyday Incivility

# Chapter One

# Introduction to
# Everyday Incivility

*Things are pretty bad—there's a lot of general rudeness, inconsideration, a me-first attitude.*
*—A St. Louis man whose comments are included in "Aggravating Circumstances: A Status Report on Rudeness in America"*[1]

Forty-seven-year-old software developer Michael Dunn just wanted to gas up the car during his stop at a Florida gas station. Instead, he fired approximately ten shots into a car of four teenagers, one of whom, Jordan Davis, was killed. The reason? Dunn's attorney stated that Davis verbally threatened Dunn and that Davis was armed with a weapon. This caused Dunn to shoot in self-defense. However, no weapon was found in the teen's car. The prosecution maintained that after pulling up beside the teens, Dunn told his girlfriend, "I hate thug music." Although Dunn wasn't threatened, the prosecutor described him as feeling "disrespected" because the volume of the music increased during an exchange of "F-bombs." In the end, Dunn was convicted of attempted second-degree murder.[2]

Thankfully, few incidents involving uncivil communication result in death, even though such stories often become fodder for daily newspapers or websites.[3] However, most of us have experienced incivility in our everyday lives. We've probably become frustrated, annoyed, and/or angry when a driver "flips us the bird," a coworker interrupts us in mid-sentence, or a stranger on a cell phone talks loudly about a blistering rash. In such situations, we may typically conclude that the uncivil behavior is a reflection of a rude or selfish person.

Try to recall someone you might describe as offensive. What would you think and how would you feel if this person invaded your personal space,

3

shouted at you, or called you a name? Would your interpretation change if you knew that s/he was born in a different country or a different region in the United States? Would you consider someone ill-mannered if you knew that s/he was a member of the opposite sex and/or much younger than you? Would you be more or less apt to describe someone as "rude" if s/he were a friend or family member rather than a stranger or acquaintance? Would your interpretation of this person's behavior change if s/he were a friend or family member rather than a stranger or acquaintance? Would you consider someone ill-mannered if you knew that s/he was much younger than you and born and raised in a different part of the country, or perhaps in a different country altogether?

In other words, does someone's cultural background, ethnicity, regional background, gender, or age influence the communication of incivility and the interpretation of uncivil behavior? Do our workplace, social media, and our family influence our perceptions of everyday incivility? Alternatively, is civility just a matter of common sense?

## PURPOSE OF UNDERSTANDING EVERYDAY INCIVILITY

*Understanding Everyday Incivility* is not a book about manners or etiquette. It won't teach you the do's and don'ts of polite behavior, nor will it provide you with a set of rules to help you respond to or avoid uncivil communication. While *Understanding Everyday Incivility* does include strategies to contend with uncivil behavior and promote civil communication, the goal of *Understanding Everyday Incivility* is to increase your understanding of what is considered civil and uncivil—and why. It is my hope that this increased understanding will help "keep a conversation going" (or allow a conversation to begin), whether we are communicating in the workplace, online, or at home. This goal is surely worthy of merit. Benet Davetian, author of *Civility: A Cultural History*, writes that he is "not at all sure that we can become a truly civil society unless we develop an in-depth understanding of civility, *as well as* incivility."[4]

You may wonder why *Understanding Everyday Incivility* doesn't include a chapter about incivility in politics. Just as uncivil language, road rage, and cyber incivility occur on an everyday basis, political incivility may also be perceived as occurring "every day" thanks to the proliferation of social media and twenty-four-hours-a-day television news channels.

One reason that political incivility is not included in this book is because we can refuse to access Facebook posts, tweets, and news programs that feature uncivil political communication. However, we may not be able to avoid uncivil communication from someone with whom we share public transportation, a line at the grocery store, or a meeting at our workplace. A second reason is that unlike everyday incivility, political incivility tends to be strategic and is often used intentionally. Politicians may feel so strongly about an issue that denigrating an opponent to rally supporters is considered a worthy political strategy to promote the greater good.[5] Strategic political incivility is also used to communicate sincerity and to mark a high-stakes disagreement.[6]

Similarly, politicians may view their opinions about various issues as being of greater importance than civil communication, therefore providing rationale for uncivil behavior.[7] Thus, when Representative Joe Wilson shouted "You lie!" at President Obama during his 2009 State of the Union address to the House of Representatives, Wilson strategically communicated that he believed strongly and sincerely that Obama lied to the public, and that his moral outrage justified the outburst. Wilson may have also considered that his outburst had the potential to strengthen his stance among conservative Republicans, and indeed, Wilson was "vindicated" after the incident by thousands of bloggers and website commentators.[8]

On the other hand, as noted in the preface, the uncivil rhetoric that characterized the 2016 presidential election found its way into various contexts that people often visit on an everyday basis. Although mirroring the incivility in national politics, it is at the local level where uncivil communication is experienced and where it will be investigated in *Understanding Everyday Incivility*. In addition, the "strategic behavior," "mark of sincerity," and "greater good" rationale are rarely, if ever, used to justify the behavior of people who talk on their cell phones during a film, use crude language in public, or post a disparaging comment on a social media site. "In fact, much of what we perceive as everyday incivility may occur without much thought beforehand and may even be accidental."[9] Therefore, uncivil behavior in politics is not included in the discussion of incivility that occurs every day.

## THE IMPORTANCE OF UNDERSTANDING EVERYDAY INCIVILITY

Two groups of protesters came together on opposite sides of a Dallas intersection and began to shout at each other. On one side were the Black Lives Matter protesters who raised their fists and chanted "Too black, too strong," all the while being watched by Dallas police and SWAT teams. On the other side were counterprotesters who waved American and Texas flags, in addition to black-and-blue flags meant to honor police officers. What could have resulted in a bloody confrontation instead illustrated, as one protester described it, "how walls get torn down."

Approximately one hour after the competing protests began, leaders of the two groups came together with the help of Jeff Hall, a twenty-seven-year veteran police officer, who brokered the peace. The protesters held each other's hands, bowed their heads in prayer, and welcomed the police officers who joined the prayer circle. Britny Morrison, who organized the Black Lives Matter protest, said, "We are not against each other; we are all on the same page. Black Lives Matter does not mean all lives don't matter." Protester Ty Hardaway added, "We need that dialogue so we can get understanding. The police need to explain to us their mentality, then, whether we like it or not, or disagree, we need to be receptive to listen. Then they need to listen to our side." Counterprotester Joseph Offut claimed, "Today we mark history; today we're going to show the rest of the country how we came together." Officer Hall concluded, "I've seen a lot of protests, but I've never seen them come together like that. Makes me feel great to see people with such differences come together and work it out."[10]

The example of the Black Lives Matter protesters, the counterprotesters, and the police enables us to understand how civil behavior can encourage constructive communication and foster a civil society. Furthermore, understanding everyday incivility is also important because the lack of civil communication contributes to what is perceived as a national "crisis of civility." Actions such as being cut off in traffic, contending with obscenity-laced music blaring from open car windows, and dealing with the sounds of texting during a film or theater performance can result in serious consequences which may affect our psychological, emotional, and physical health.

## The Crisis of Civility

The crisis of civility is evident in public opinion polls which illustrate that people believe uncivil behavior is a national problem which has worsened over the past twenty years.[11] For many years, Powell Tate, a division of Weber Shandwick, a global public relations firm, has partnered with KRC Research in conducting annual civility polls. The 2010 *Civility in America: A Nationwide Study* survey discovered that 72 percent of respondents believe that civility has worsened during the past few years, especially in terms of traffic on highways and among the American public in general.

In addition, 39 percent of those surveyed blame incivility as the reason they have "tuned out" of social networking sites by defriending or blocking someone online; refusing to visit an online site; and by dropping out of a fan club or online community.[12] *The Civility in America 2011* survey revealed that more than 70 percent of the respondents consider pop culture, the media, government/political campaigns, and the music industry to be centers of incivility. The same survey found that 43 percent of respondents experience incivility at work and believe that the workplace is becoming more uncivil compared to a few years ago.[13]

In 2012, the Weber Shandwick civility poll focused primarily on politics because it was an election year. Nonetheless, the survey found that personal experience with cyberbullying doubled from 9 percent to 18 percent compared to the previous year's poll. The survey also revealed that 74 percent of the respondents believe that civility training should be taught in schools and universities.[14] *Civility in America 2013* shows that 95 percent of respondents believe that a civility problem exists in America, and 70 percent believe that incivility has risen to a crisis level.[15]

The *Civility in America 2014* poll shows that Americans continue to believe that we have a major civility problem; that civility has declined over the past few years; and that civility will most likely worsen in the future.[16] Although the latest installments of *Civility in America* were not available at the time of publication, Weber Shandwick press releases highlight the survey results. In particular, more than 95 percent of respondents perceive that civility continues to be a national problem, and 70 percent believe that incivility in America has risen to crisis levels (an increase from 64 percent in 2014).[17] Similarly, 79 percent of Americans describe the 2016 presidential election as uncivil and agree that "uncivil comments by political leaders encourage greater incivility in society."[18]

In all, these polls illustrate that "public incivility now defines the national character as much as independence, perseverance, and prosperity."[19] Each *Civility in America* survey:

> reiterates the unfortunate fact that incivility is ubiquitous; no area of American society is untouched. Eroding civility is harmful to our country's future and takes a toll on how we interact with the people and institutions around us. The belief that America has a civility problem and that civility will get worse has not waned since the survey's inception. In fact, it has become our "new normal."[20]

The "new normal" notwithstanding, civil communication enables people with conflicting viewpoints to live peacefully and different groups to get along.[21] However, there are times when incivility may be warranted. Would women have won the vote and African Americans gained civil rights without civil disobedience *and* uncivil (violent) behavior in the twentieth century? On the other hand, the use of civil communication is characterized as a way for disagreeing parties to come together "that turns individual interest into group interest, enabling people to move across barriers of difference into common cause."[22]

Jim Leach, former chairman of the National Endowment for the Humanities, writes that "[Civility] is crucially relevant at every level of community where people rub up against each other. And when disparate communities come together—often with no prior contact or mutual understanding—civility is imperative."[23] While civil communication may be considered imperative, uncivil communication is perceived as commonplace in today's world.[24] Although complaints about incivility have occurred across cultures and throughout history, "what makes our age distinctive is not the presence of such a complaint about the demise of an interpersonally civic society, but rather the intensity and form of the anxiety. A 'crisis' of civility has been identified with greater virulence and enthusiasm than ever before."[25]

## The Negative Outcomes Associated with Everyday Incivility

*What Would You Do?*, which premiered in 2008, is a reality television show that uses hidden cameras to film how ordinary people react to uncivil behavior in various situations.[26] Unknown to bystanders, the people expressing the uncivil communication are actors. *What Would You Do?* features situations such as:

- Parents who berate their white daughter and her black fiancé in a restaurant after they announce their engagement.[27]
- Teenage "mean girls" in a cafe who laugh loudly about their cyberbullying posts on Facebook. The teens also ask cafe patrons to say "Janis, you're really ugly" while being filmed via a cell-phone app. The patrons learn that the video will be posted on YouTube.[28]
- A mom at a grocery store who fills her shopping cart with junk food and another woman who berates the mom's choices in front of her daughter.[29]

The focus of *What Would You Do?* centers on whether bystanders walk away from the uncivil situations or whether they become involved. The bystanders who intervened in the situations described above made comments such as "You have no right to pass any judgment on anybody else or say such hurtful words," and "This is inappropriate in a public place, and you should keep your mouth shut."[30] *What Would You Do?* typically interviews bystanders after each situation plays out, and in the instances above, their responses were accompanied by nervous laughter, tears, and/or anger. The bystanders' reactions illustrate that everyday incivilities, even when they involve people other than ourselves, are important enough to elicit strong opinions and extreme emotions. In other words, we perceive everyday incivility as significant and worthy of concern.

The *What Would You Do?* hypothetical situations mirror real-world everyday incivility, such as when children are disruptive in restaurants and movie theaters; when drivers tailgate us when we drive at the posted speed limit (or higher); when coworkers with specialized knowledge don't come to our aid when needed; and when people throw trash everywhere but the trash can.[31] Cell phones also contribute to the growing concern of uncivil behavior, as what once were private conversations are now heard in public spaces.[32] These and other examples of uncivil behavior are associated with negative outcomes. For example, uncivil communication can negatively impact our self-esteem, cause emotional and psychological harm, and indicate a lack of concern for others. Overall, incivility is described as causing more pain than any other failing.[33] Therefore, "civility cries for clarification and study."[34]

## Everyday Incivility, Beliefs, and Values

Consider the topics addressed by advice columnists during a single day in 2015:[35]

- Jeanne Phillips ("Dear Abby")—What to do about a brother-in-law who makes disparaging remarks about his sister-in-law's political party and uses profane language to express his political opinions.
- Carolyn Hax—Whether the current wife (married forty years) should attend the funeral of her husband's first wife. The husband left the first wife for the current wife; the first wife's daughter will attend the funeral.
- Judith Martin ("Miss Manners")—How to handle patrons who share an orchestra box and whisper throughout a concert.

Our concern and reactions to everyday incivility illustrates our individual beliefs and values. In the examples above, the sister writes that her brother-in-law's comments make her "blood boil" (she values her political beliefs and believes the use of profanity in political discussions is wrong). The current wife wants to attend the first wife's funeral but doesn't want to upset her stepdaughter (she values her stepdaughter's feelings). And the concert-goer wants to know if she should say something to the whispering patrons in her orchestra box during the concert or wait until the intermission (she believes there's an appropriate time and place to discuss rude behavior).[36]

These examples illustrate that our beliefs and values are revealed by our reactions to perceived uncivil behavior. The examples also illustrate that the anger, distress, and frustration that result from everyday incivility is so (potentially) upsetting that we seek the advice of others to contend with uncivil situations. Consider that when we ponder our decisions or engage in reflection, such as the advice-seekers in the examples above, most of us question right and wrong as it relates to our everyday interactions. Therefore, the study and understanding of *everyday* civility is important. While we can imagine how we might handle situations that involve life-or-death decision-making, it is our everyday thinking and behavior that illustrate to ourselves and others our values, morals, and character.[37]

## EVERYDAY INCIVILITY AND COMMUNICATION

Attending a baseball game is a tradition in many families, and even considered by some as an integral part of childhood. Writing in the mid-1950s, social critic and philosopher Jacques Barzun claimed that, "Whoever wants to know the heart and mind of America had better learn baseball." Almost twenty-five years later, Barzun asserted, "Fundamentally, things haven't changed. Baseball still reflects our society; it's just that society has changed." The change that Barzun referred to is the idea that baseball once illustrated the unification of America and the teamwork involved in the game. He additionally stated that "the contentions in baseball parallel the enormous unrest in our society. . . . [A]long with the diminishing appreciation for the rich qualities of baseball, there has developed diminished appreciation for the rich qualities of American life."[38]

If he were alive today, Barzun might conclude that the incivility rampant in modern society is also reflected in the game of baseball. For example, during a Philadelphia Phillies hometown game, former Phillies player Jonathan Papelbon gave up four runs in the ninth inning and the Phillies lost to the Miami Marlins with a 5–4 score. The Phillies fans booed loudly as Papelbon left the field, and in response, he faced the booing crowd and grabbed his crotch. At this point, umpire Joe West threw Papelbon out of the game.[39] One commentator wrote that West "shamed Papelbon, who richly deserved it, and stood for sportsmanship, civility, and basic gentility of the sport. There were families and kids in the crowd: the pitcher's lewd gesture showed disrespect for baseball's traditions, his team, and the people who pay his substantial salary. This is how a culture, a business, and a sport enforces its values."[40]

People explain civility and incivility in a variety of ways. For example, a psychologist is likely to consider personality characteristics, emotions, self-esteem, and achievement to explain uncivil behavior.[41] Regarding Jonathan Papelbon, a psychologist might describe his behavior in terms of low impulse control and personality characteristics such as egotism and narcissism. On the other hand, a sociologist who explores human society might associate uncivil behavior with poverty, criminal behavior, norms, and space competition.[42] This means that a sociologist might describe Papelbon's behavior in regard to deviance, social status, and/or the social norms which guide behavior. Finally, anthropologists who study the cultural development of human beings might explain Papelbon's behavior in terms of cultural values and communication systems. Therefore, an anthropologist might explain Papelbon's incivility by focusing on his rejection of values associated with the game of baseball. *Understanding Everyday Incivility* does not ignore these psychological, sociological, and anthropological perspectives, but the primary focus is on communication—that is, verbal and nonverbal messages that influence the creation of meaning.

## Communication and the Creation of Meaning

When people communicate with each other, both verbally and nonverbally, words and behaviors are interpreted according to just about all that influences us in life, such as "beliefs, personalities, attitudes, power relationships, and social and economic structures."[43] For example, suppose Chris sees Kerry standing alone at a nightclub. Kerry is looking down with her/his arms crossed on her/his chest. Chris decides not to approach Kerry because her/his nonverbal behavior is interpreted as "wanting to be left alone." Perhaps Chris thinks that s/he will stumble during the introduction (the influence of a *belief*) and that her/his introverted *personality* inhibits making new acquaintances. Maybe Chris holds a defeatist *attitude* about most interpersonal challenges, and further considers that her/his low-paying job will cause Kerry to reject the opportunity to develop a relationship (the influence of *economics*).

On the other hand, Dana is not dissuaded by Kerry's nonverbal communication. Dana, also influenced by beliefs, personalities, attitudes, etc., interprets the nonverbal behavior as indicative of loneliness. And, in fact, as Dana approaches Kerry, Kerry mutters, "I wish someone would talk to me." After hearing this comment, Dana engages Kerry in interaction. This illustration shows that both verbal and nonverbal messages affect the creation of meaning and that meaning is determined by people's interpretations (which, in turn, are influenced by beliefs, personalities, attitudes, etc.) rather than the words and/or behaviors themselves.[44]

In sum, the communication perspective centers on the subjective interpretations of the meaning of messages. These meanings are formed by the psychological, sociological, and anthropological influences on the interpretation and communication of uncivil behavior.

## Communication Competence

Destiny Herndon-DeLaRosa, a self-described good daughter and student, became pregnant at age sixteen. She was "ridiculed and mocked, teased and judged" to the point where school administrators offered her the option of transferring. Although she was humiliated and the subject of gossip, Herndon-DeLaRosa remained at her high school, decided to keep her baby, and is now a stay-at-home mom. She recalls feeling "terrified, alone, and desperate," and has subsequently dedicated her life to ensuring that pregnant single women are aware of all options available to them and their unborn child. Herndon-DeLaRosa asks that we don't judge those who are pro-life and those who are pro-choice by the extremists in their camps. Instead, Herndon-

DeLaRosa advocates "education, assistance," and "well-thought-out decisions" rather than "shouting at frightened women . . . hate-filled debates, or holding up signs containing graphic images at organized protests."[45]

In addition to promoting civil communication about the topic of abortion, Herndon-DeLaRosa supports communication that is "competent." Communication scholars Brian H. Spitzberg and William R. Cupach characterize communication competence as communication which is perceived as both effective and appropriate in an interpersonal context.[46] "Effectiveness" refers to achieving our goals, and "appropriateness" refers to conforming to the expectations or norms associated with a particular situation. Norms, sometimes called "communication rules," tell us what we should or shouldn't say or do in certain situations. We can tell that we haven't conformed to a norm when we receive a negative sanction.[47] A dirty look, a poke in the ribs, unexpected laughter, and even a verbal admonition (e.g., "That type of language is unacceptable!") are examples of negative sanctions. In the example described above, Destiny Herndon-DeLaRosa encourages effective communication based on well-thought-out decisions, and appropriate communication void of hateful words and graphic images.

To further illustrate effectiveness and appropriateness, consider the situation that involved Chris, Kerry, and Dana. Although Chris doesn't break a norm or communication rule by failing to interact with Kerry (appropriateness), Chris isn't effective because s/he doesn't meet the goal of conversing with Kerry. In another scenario, let's suppose that Chris actually walks up to Kerry and with downcast eyes and a barely audible voice, nervously stammers, "Umm . . . er . . . if you're not too busy, do you think we can get to know each other and maybe go out together? Well . . . ahh . . . I understand if you're too busy and want to talk to someone else right now."

Once again, Chris is appropriate, but if rejected by Kerry (and it's likely that a rejection will occur at this point), Chris is not effective. Now let's suppose Dana strides up to Kerry and begins talking so loudly and quickly that heads turn to stare and Kerry can only manage to say, "Uh, yes," and "Hmmm." Although Dana is effective—that is, s/he meets the goal of conversing with Kerry—Dana is not appropriate, and receives negative sanctions (stares) from others not involved in the conversation. It's also likely that the "effective" portion of this situation—specifically, engaging in conversation with Kerry—will be short-lived.

These scenarios reveal that *both* effectiveness and appropriateness are necessary to be perceived as a competent communicator. Furthermore, Spitzberg and Cupach's Communication Competence model illustrates that we perceive behavior as uncivil when we break norms that tell us what is and isn't considered appropriate.

It's important to note that the perception of communication competence and the perception of civility or incivility are, indeed, perceptions. In this book, *perception* and *interpretation* are used synonymously since both concern "sense-making." The perception process typically occurs in three stages. First, we attend to certain stimuli in the environment, such as noticing a little boy in a blue uniform playing with boys who don't wear blue uniforms. Second, we arrange or classify the stimuli in terms of various organizational clusters, such as appearance, social role, group membership, etc. In this example, we may categorize the boy in the blue uniform as belonging to a Cub Scout troop. Third, we interpret the stimuli, which involves the creation of meaning. Based on our past experience with Cub Scouts, the meaning we create for the little boy is "This child is a good kid." Our perception of reality also affects whether we consider an action "hurtful or not, civil or uncivil," and implies that "two people experiencing the same reality could have different reactions to it."[48]

In terms of communication competence, Spitzberg and Cupach write that the "crucial feature" in the impression of communication competence is the perceptual process.[49] Perception is a fundamental criterion of appropriateness, since behavior is interpreted as inappropriate when we perceive that norms or rules are violated.[50] When this occurs, we interpret the behavior as uncivil.[51] This also means that in regard to everyday incivility, two or more people can interpret the same behavior differently because the interpretations are based on competing norms.

It's important to emphasize that the perception of appropriateness and incivility is based on norms which change according to the situation or context. This means that the perception of incivility is contextual, and behavior that is considered appropriate in one situation may be considered inappropriate in another.

## THE IMPORTANCE OF CONTEXT AND NORMS

Have you ever told a humorous story and instead of responding with laughter, your listeners merely looked puzzled? You may have reacted by saying, "I guess you had to be there." This response illustrates the importance of the "context," which is a synonym for "situation." The contexts in which we communicate influence which particular norms guide what we say, how we say it, and when and where we say it, if at all.

### Context

In 2005, the Northwestern University women's lacrosse team, the National Collegiate Athletic Association (NCAA) champions, met President George W. Bush at the White House. Prior to the women's lacrosse team visit, pundits argued that poor grooming and attention to dress contribute to the increase in uncivil behavior.[52] Even President Bush mandated a dignified

White House in which he forbade jeans and required men to wear neckties in the Oval Office. Nevertheless, a number of the lacrosse players wore flip-flops to meet the president (the casual type of footwear that leaves toes uncovered). The flip-flop-wearing members of the lacrosse team were described as demonstrating "that respect for even the nation's most sacrosanct institutions is waning."[53]

However, one of the players said that her $16.00 rhinestone-covered flip-flops were not meant for the beach. Others agreed, and said that the women wore dresses, had neat hairstyles, and looked clean-cut. Ellen Goldstein, a spokesperson from the New York Fashion Institute of Technology, stated that wearing flip-flops to the White House can be compared to the flappers of the 1920s who scandalized their elders by wearing short dresses and cutting their hair. Miniskirts and go-go boots in the 1960s and Madonna-inspired lingerie wear in the 1980s are similar examples of young people rejecting the norms of their parents and creating new ways to express themselves through clothing. So the flip-flop-wearing members of the Northwestern University women's lacrosse team may have engaged in behaviors that weren't meant to be uncivil. Additionally, those born between 1981 and 1997, often labeled "Millennials," grew up in an era when parents wore blue jeans and people dressed more informally than in the past. While their elders once dressed up to ride on airplanes and attend houses of worship, members of the Millennial generation embrace informality and hold the norm, "Come as you are." Goldstein summed up the generational difference by stating, "It's a fine line. If it were you or me or any of the rest of the public who were meeting the president—it's inappropriate. But there was nobody there in torn clothes and ratty T-shirts."[54]

This illustration demonstrates that competing norms—i.e., the expectation that calls for formal attire vs. the expectation that calls for freedom of expression—can influence the perception of uncivil behavior. Additionally, the interpretation of civility changes according to the context, as well as over time. The context may refer to environment or physical location as well as people's historical and psychological backgrounds which they bring to an interaction.[55] The historical context includes our past history with a person or topic, and the psychological field of experience includes values, beliefs, and attitudes.[56] These factors influence our perceptions of a situation and how we communicate with others. We may consider the formality or informality or the intimacy or non-intimacy of a situation to determine which norms for appropriate communication we should follow. In the example of the lacrosse team at the White House, the context or physical location and the perception of formality most likely resulted in the criticism directed at the women who wore flip-flops. However, the women's background, which includes certain beliefs and attitudes about appropriate clothing, influenced them to believe that wearing flip-flops to the White House is appropriate.

In all, it's important to remember the situational nature associated with the interpretation of incivility. Perhaps it's possible for a "baseline" version of civility, which may include respect for others and their ideas, restraint in our use of language, and responsibility to the community. However, it is the people involved in conversation, the topic, and the context in which the communication takes place, that influences "the precise meaning, degree, and fittingness of civility"[57] Etiquette books aside, there are no fixed rules or standards that guarantee that communication will be interpreted as civil, because the communication and interpretation of incivility are affected by situational factors. In addition, in every situation there will be competing and oppositional needs that will influence the communication and interpretation of behavior that can be considered civil or uncivil.

## Norms

Recall that norms, which are shared rules for appropriate behavior, guide our interactions with others. Common norms concern what is considered polite and impolite. For example, children in Western cultures are taught that it's impolite to stare, point at strangers, and/or comment on their physical appearance. When children don't conform to a norm, such as when they point at strangers, a negative sanction may be take the form of parental criticism or even punishment.[58] Additional norms shared in Western cultures relate to behavior which is and isn't considered appropriate. For instance, norms teach us that we should:[59]

- return a greeting;
- knock on someone's office door before entering;
- listen to a speaker; and
- apologize if we arrive late for an appointment.

The communication-competence model illustrates that behavior that fails to conform to norms for appropriate behavior is considered uncivil. For example, we will most likely be perceived as uncivil if we:[60]

- put our finger in our nose in public;
- abruptly hang up on someone;
- clip our fingernails during an interview; or
- dress in jeans and a T-shirt for a formal occasion.

Oftentimes norms are associated with a specific context. For example, those who thought that the members of the Northwestern University lacrosse team disregarded a norm requiring conservative attire at the White House perceived the players to be dressed inappropriately. The perceived formality of an occasion also influences our verbal communication. Suppose you find yourself being introduced to important clients at a business meeting. In this case, a norm stressing formality may influence you to say, "Pleased to meet you." On the other hand, you may find yourself being introduced to a few people who know the host of a casual party. In this case, a norm stressing informality may influence you to say, "Hey, how ya doin'?"[61] Additional examples of the influence of contexts on norms include when and where it is acceptable to swear (in a bar, but not while visiting a child's elementary class), and whether it's appropriate to stereotype a group of people (only if you belong to that group of people).[62] Additionally, "looking for a [missing] cell phone [at the movies] might be rude to some. Not helping look for it might be rude to others."[63] The point is that what we perceive as civil or uncivil behavior is affected by where and when the behavior takes place and how we interpret the behavior.

## Changing Norms

Perceptions of incivility are not only influenced by contexts and by established norms, but are also influenced by changing norms. Modern life is characterized by continual change; knowledge, lifestyles, technology, and values continually evolve.[64] These changes affect the norms we follow which guide our behavior. This means that what we perceive as civil and uncivil has changed, particularly during the past one hundred years. Specifically:[65]

- Men no longer lift their hats to women.
- Women no longer have to keep their arms and legs covered in public.
- Swearing has become more socially acceptable, both in private and in public.
- The occasions when men are expected to wear ties are far fewer.
- People have more freedom to grow their hair long, shave their heads, dye their hair green, display tattoos, ornament themselves with nose rings or lip studs, and so on, without making themselves social outcasts.
- Booing, hissing, and catcalling at theatrical performances is no longer acceptable.
- Visiting someone at her/his house without phoning beforehand is now frowned upon in many communities.

Because we are living in an era of rapid change, confusion about norms influences the interpretation of civil and uncivil communication. Current norms "are unstable, and there is consequently some confusion about what they are and what abiding by them signifies . . . [O]ne person's confusion leads to another person's taking offense."[66] This is especially true when we consider the influence of technology on the interpretation of civil and uncivil communication.

## Technology and Norm-Shifting

When Kansas teenager Emma Sullivan visited her state capitol on a field trip, she wasn't impressed with what Governor Brownback had to say. She tweeted her opinion to her 60 followers, writing, "Just made mean comments at gov brownback and told him he sucked, in person #heblowsalot." Despite the fact that Sullivan had not met Governor Brownback nor spoken with him personally, within days Sullivan had amassed more than 12,000 followers and created a public conflict that led to a public apology—although not the one originally demanded.[67]

How did one tweet become a public issue? The tweet, Sullivan said, was part of a conversation she and a friend were having about what they would say to Brownback were they to actually meet him, and was intended for her audience of friends. However, Brownback's office monitors both Twitter and Facebook for comments about the governor. Staff members perceived the tweet to be offensive and informed the organizers of the field trip, who in turn contacted Sullivan's high school. She was called into the principal's office and instructed to write a letter of apology to the governor. Sullivan refused, citing her freedom of speech, and her parents supported her decision.

Eventually, the governor issued a statement of apology to Sullivan, stating that "My staff overreacted to this tweet, and for that I apologize. Freedom of speech is among our most treasured freedoms."[68] While Sullivan would have liked a more-personal apology, others were disappointed that she got off so easily. As one writer put it, "If you were my daughter, you'd be writing that letter apologizing to Kansas Gov Sam Brownback for the smart-alecky, potty-mouthed tweet you wrote after meeting with him on a school field trip. Also, that smartphone? The one you posed with, proudly displaying the tweet. . . . Turned off until you learn to use it responsibly."[69]

Did Emma Sullivan violate a norm for appropriate behavior when she tweeted about Governor Brownback to her sixty followers? Did Sullivan's high school principal break a norm when he demanded that she write an apology to the governor? And rather than receiving an apology, did Governor Brownback violate a norm when he issued an apology to Sullivan? This example illustrates that modern technology is causing rapid cultural and societal transformations. In general, technological developments have historically generated confusion and anxiety, and sometimes, as in the case of Emma Sullivan and Governor Brownback, it's difficult to say whether a norm is violated and/or whether particular behavior is uncivil. In fact, confusion over what the rules are, when they apply, and to whom, are inevitable in a period of rapid cultural change. And with the coming of e-mail, cell phones, BlackBerrys, iPods, the Internet, Google, Facebook, and so on, the rate of change in the ways we interact has become positively bewildering at times. Such confusion naturally leads to more instances of people violating, or being perceived to violate, social conventions. This creates the impression that civility is on the decline, but the impression may be misleading. [70]

Because individuals in modern society are unsure of the norms for civil behavior, we may mistakenly believe that another person is deliberately disregarding a norm and is being offensive on purpose. However, it may be the case that the person who perceives an uncivil act or the person who exhibits the uncivil act is unaware of a norm, and the changing expectations regarding what constitutes appropriate behavior. For instance, those who are not enthusiastic social-networkers may perceive others who talk loudly on cell phones or text during presentations as being uncivil or rude. However, it may be that the cell-phone users are unaware of an older norm that instructs us to speak softly about personal problems in a public space.

Additionally, people who aren't engaged in new technology may not be aware of the changing definition of privacy held by young people who speak on their cell numerous times a day. Moreover, those who text others during a presentation may not be aware of an old norm that instructs us to pay strict attention to a speaker. On the other hand, others who don't text may not be aware of changing norms that instruct us that multitasking is fine, no matter what the context.

Overall, we are witnessing societal change that includes the reshaping of norms and expectations to make sense of the modern world. "Norm-shifting" can occur in a short period of time, and behavior that was once thought of as undoubtedly uncivil can be thought of as unmistakably civil (and vice versa). [71] We need not conclude that we're experiencing a crisis in civility because men are less likely to open doors for women, or young people are less likely to give up their seat on a bus for an adult. It may be that norms have changed, there's less consensus about the clarity and meaning of norms, and "appropriate" behavior may have become less formal. In other words, although we may be willing to respect norms for appropriate behavior, there is no longer consensus about what the norms actually are. [72]

## REVISITING THE "CRISIS" OF CIVILITY

In describing this era of societal change, sociologists Nicole Billante and Peter Saunders write that changes in norms and in subsequent behavior don't necessarily signal a decline of civility. They suggest that any conclusion about whether levels of incivility are increasing or decreasing depends on the examples we choose to illustrate incivility and how we measure them. In fact, we can always find evidence for a "civility hypothesis," whether or not the evidence suggests a decline, increase, or a steady state of uncivil behavior.[73]

To return to the examples at the beginning of this chapter, it's likely that the driver who "flips you the bird" is deliberately being uncivil and breaking a norm to make a point. However, the coworker who interrupts you in mid-sentence may not be selfishly attempting to control a conversation; he may be following a norm associated with his gender, and is actually respecting you and your ability to interrupt in return. Similarly, the rude stranger loudly discussing her rash on a cell phone may be following a norm related to the Millennial Generation's meaning of "privacy." Overall:

> Social interaction between men and women and between young people and their elders has always been central to social rules of behavior. So it is natural that with major changes in the norms governing these relations we are noticing major changes in public behavior. The question, however, is whether the changes in behavior signify a decline in respect. . . . What some commentators have viewed as a civility crisis may in fact be due to this transition.[74]

Although we may *perceive* a crisis in civility in modern society, every age has included those who suggest that uncivil behavior symbolizes the deterioration of their era.[75] For example, consider the following quote about young people: "[T]hey have bad manners, contempt for authority; they show disrespect for elders and love chatter in place of exercise." Although the origin of this quote is in dispute, it is often attributed to Socrates.[76] In addition, some of us yearn for a long-ago "golden age" during which people were overwhelmingly civil to each other. However, there never was a "golden age of civility."[77] Therefore, although we may perceive a modern-day "crisis" in civility, the real problem is that norms are in flux, and thanks to modern technology, we are bombarded daily with examples of uncivil communication. In all, what has influenced our perception of a civility crisis that differs from generations past is "the clarity of the norms and the level of consensus about what they mean."[78]

## ORGANIZATION OF *UNDERSTANDING EVERYDAY INCIVILITY*

*Understanding Everyday Incivility* is divided into two parts. Part I, "Understanding Everyday Incivility," is comprised of five chapters. You've just read chapter 1, "Introduction to Everyday Incivility." Chapter 2, "Characterizing Everyday Incivility," demonstrates that the ability to define and find examples of incivility is often more difficult and complex than expected. Although manners are explored in this chapter, civility is characterized as possessing three characteristics: respect, restraint, and responsibility. Civil communication is also described as ethical.

Chapter 3, "Influences on Everyday Incivility," describes how our culture(s), the region in which we live, our ethnic group(s), gender, and generation influence how and why we perceive behaviors as (un)civil. Our communication style also influences the perception of everyday incivility. Chapter 3 includes an example of a student who shouted "Shut up, you water buffalo!" to a group of black sorority members. The women interpreted the student's comment as a racial slur; however, the student, born and raised in Israel, used the English translation of the Hebrew word *behema* to refer to thoughtless or rowdy people. This example illustrates that what is interpreted as (un)civil by one culture or ethnic group may not be considered (un)civil by another.

Chapter 4, "The Good, the Bad, and the Virtue of Civility," describes the positive and negative outcomes associated with both civil and uncivil communication. While it is easy to consider the negative consequences of incivility as well as the positive consequences of civil communication, uncivil behavior can also produce positive results. The positive results of uncivil communication include strengthening the resolve of an intended target and diffusing anger and stress. Uncivil behavior can also be used strategically to attract attention. In addition, negative consequences of civil communication include being ignored by those in power when asking for change, and limiting freedom of expression because of the fear of offending others. This chapter includes a discussion about whether or not civility is a virtue and why we can't rely on common sense as the basis for civility. Therefore, "conversational civility," which aims to "keep a conversation going," is suggested as a way to reduce routine cynicism and provide us with the hope that we can work together to solve problems.

Chapter 5, "Power and Everyday Incivility," demonstrates that we can't identify the more powerful from the less powerful by studying communication alone. This is because linguistic devices, such as interruptions and indirect communication, communicate power in some situations but not in others. Chapter 5 also emphasizes that those in power typically set the standards for what is civil and what is not. This is evidenced in the influence of privilege on what is considered appropriate behavior, and in the examples of mansplaining, microaggressions, and political correctness. This chapter reveals that the relationship between civility and power is not only contextual, but complicated.

Part II, "Everyday Incivility in Contexts," is comprised of four chapters. The contexts in which readers may have everyday encounters include the workplace, at home, and online.

Chapter 6, "Everyday Incivility at Work," begins with the example of an Internet service subscriber who recorded a conversation with a customer service representative while attempting to cancel his service. The customer service representative communicated in an aggressive manner and insisted the subscriber provide him with the reason for canceling. Although this may be an unusual example of incivility on the job, the consequences of everyday workplace incivility are harmful to superiors, subordinates, and customers. Causes of workplace incivility are discussed in this chapter, along with the benefits of civil communication on the job. The chapter concludes with a description of how employees can cope with workplace incivility and how we can foster civility in work environments.

Chapter 7, "Everyday Incivility Online," uses the example of Justine Sacco, who tweeted uncivil comments about people and their cultures during a flight to Cape Town, South Africa, to illustrate cyber incivility. Although Sacco meant her comments to be read only by her followers, they were retweeted during her flight and drew tens of thousands of angry tweets in response. Sacco's tweets (and her subsequent public shaming) is just one type of cyber incivility. Others include flaming, trolling, doxing, swatting, sexting, and "calling out." This chapter also includes a discussion of cell-phone incivility and presents the causes of and suggestions for contending with online incivility.

Chapter 8, "Everyday Incivility at Home," explains that perceptions of incivility within the family often occur not because of what is said but because of how it is said, along with the hidden meanings behind words that are unexpressed. In addition, the chapter covers the influence of family members' relational histories on interpretations of incivility. Disconfirming communication is described as a type of everyday incivility at home, and we may incorrectly label family communication as "uncivil" because norms differ among families. At times, incivility in the family is so covert and subtle that we may not know exactly why we feel uneasy. *Metacommunication*, or "communication about communication," is presented as a way to address incivility in the family.

*Understanding Everyday Incivility* ends with chapter 9, "Promoting Everyday Civility." This chapter focuses on how we can encourage civil communication in regard to physical spaces; legislation and politics; education (both K–12 and higher education); workplace interventions; community-based initiatives; and self-help. The chapter ends by reviewing conversational civility and suggesting that although we cannot force others to change their behavior, we have the ability to change ourselves. We are reminded that one person can positively change a potentially uncivil conversation to a civil one, and can inspire others to do the same.

## SUMMARY AND CONCLUSION

Most Americans believe that we currently suffer from "crisis of civility." The crisis of civility is evident in public opinion polls that reveal that people believe uncivil behavior is a national problem which has worsened over the past twenty years. It's important to understand uncivil communication because it can negatively impact our self-esteem, cause emotional and psychological harm, and indicate a lack of concern for others. Similarly, the anger, distress, and frustration that result from everyday incivility is so (potentially) upsetting that we seek the advice of others to contend with uncivil situations.

Competent communication is perceived as both effective and appropriate in an interpersonal context. *Effectiveness* refers to achieving our goals, and *appropriateness* refers to conforming to the expectations or norms associated with a particular situation. *Norms*, sometimes called "communication rules," tell us what we should or shouldn't say or do in certain situations. The communication-competence model illustrates that we interpret behavior as uncivil when we break norms that tell us what is and isn't considered appropriate. It's important to note that the perception of incivility is contextual, and behavior that is considered appropriate in one situation may be considered inappropriate in another.

Perceptions of incivility are not only influenced by contexts and by established norms, but are also influenced by changing norms. Modern technology is causing rapid cultural and societal transformations which can make it difficult to know about and adhere to newly created norms. Additionally, although we may be willing to respect norms for appropriate behavior, there is no longer consensus about what the norms actually are. Therefore, although we may perceive a modern-day "crisis" in civility, the real problem is that norms are in flux, and thanks to modern technology, we are bombarded daily with examples of uncivil communication.

Finally, there may be cynics (or "realists," depending on your point of view) who believe that the goal of understanding everyday incivility is a waste of time. They may claim that "understanding" civil and uncivil behavior won't change the way people communicate with each other. They may also contend, and perhaps rightly so, that those in power will always create the standards for what is considered civil and what is not. However, even with these limitations, the *possibility* of improving the human condition makes it worthwhile to study everyday incivility. Communication scholars Ronald C. Arnett and Pat Arneson, authors of *Dialogic Civility in a Cynical Age*, express this idea well when they write that "accepting the reality of limits does not lessen the conviction that making the world a better place is an important human project."[79]

Lady Dorothy Nevill (1825–1915), a British author, horticulturist, and friend of noted authors, artists, and politicians, said that "the real art of conversation is not only to say the right thing in the right place, but to leave unsaid the wrong thing at the tempting moment."[80] It is my hope that *Understanding Everyday Incivility* will help readers to realize that saying the "right thing" in the right place is a perception based on the highly subjective meaning of a comment, and that saying the "wrong thing" at a tempting moment may not be wrong or uncivil after all.

**Box 1-1**
   **Strategies for Change:**
   **Understanding Everyday Incivility**

- We should attempt to understand everyday incivility to "keep a conversation going" (or allow a conversation to begin), whether we are communicating at the workplace, online, or at home.
- We should also increase our understanding of what is considered civil and uncivil because we can't become a truly civil society unless we develop an in-depth understanding of both.
- We should learn about civility because civil communication enables people with conflicting viewpoints to live peacefully and different groups to get along. On the other hand, incivility is described as causing more pain than any other failing; therefore, "civility cries [out] for clarification and study."

## Chapter Two

# Characterizing Everyday Incivility

*We have lost all sense of decorum, that voluntary commitment to behavior that combines a willingness to consider others first . . . and maintain a level of self-restraint.*
—Washington Post *politics and culture columnist Kathleen Parker*[1]

In 1964, the Supreme Court reviewed an obscenity case, *Jacobellis v. Ohio*, which concerned a theater manager who showed a French film titled *Les Amants* ("The Lovers"). In his written opinion, Justice Potter Stewart specified that he would not attempt to define pornography or material described as "pornographic." However, referring to pornography, he commented, "I know it when I see it."[2] In a sense, the same holds true for the definitions and examples of civility and incivility. Law professor Barak Orbach claims that the words *civility* and *incivility* mean what people perceive them to mean. He further asserts that the I Know It When I See It rule applies to civility and incivility because these concepts can't be properly defined.[3]

Others similarly argue that uncivil behavior can be difficult to recognize and therefore we may *not* know it when we see it.[4] Even scholars who study civility and incivility write that consistent definitions of civility are nonexistent.[5] Researchers rarely explain *why* their definitions and examples represent incivility, and lists of uncivil behaviors are chaotic and arbitrary.[6] Furthermore, there is disagreement about particular definitions, such as whether civil communication entails tolerance of opposing views (and the opportunity to persuade those who hold views that conflict with our own), or whether civil communication supports and celebrates opposing views without trying to change them.[7] Not only do people disagree about what is and isn't civil communication, but the same behavior may be considered civil in certain situations and uncivil in others.[8]

This chapter provides a comprehensive review of the definitions of incivility and the similarities across the various characterizations of civility are identified and explained. This chapter also illustrates ways we can communicate respect, restraint, and responsibility in our verbal and nonverbal behavior.

## CHARACTERIZATION OF EVERYDAY INCIVILITY

Senator Kirsten Gillibrand (D-NY) was involved in two interactions in which she perceived she was the target of uncivil communication. While working out at the congressional gym, a male colleague said, "Good thing you're working out, because you wouldn't want to get porky!"[9] On a different occasion, a male colleague squeezed her stomach and said, "Don't lose too much weight now. I like my girls chubby."[10] Gillibrand and others described these comments as "bad manners, rude, demeaning," and "inappropriate." They were also cited as examples of "sexual harassment," and the congressmen who made them were labeled "clueless."[11] However, although *LA Times* reporter Robin Abcarian called the remarks "insensitive," she said that Gillibrand's colleagues "were acting completely normal," and they were not "harassers." Abcarian also labeled the "insult" as "ordinary," and wrote that Gillibrand was overreacting to "offhand" remarks.[12]

This example illustrates that there are numerous synonyms and adjectives used to describe incivility, but most often these words are left undefined. Nonetheless, "intent" and "intensity" are often cited when distinguishing uncivil behavior from civil behavior.

### Intent and Intensity

In her model of workplace incivility, Beverly Davenport Sypher, a communications professor at Purdue University, lists uncivil behaviors that range from being indirect, verbal, and passive to those that are active, direct, and aggressive. In order of intensity and intentionality, these behaviors include: ignoring, not listening, interrupting, exclusion, profanity, rudeness, name-calling, humiliating, desk rage, bullying, verbal aggressions, verbal harassment, verbal abuse, and physical violence.[13] Moreover, developmental and educational psychologist Zopito A. Marini claims that it is easy to cross the line between civility and incivility.[14] He suggests that incivility can be illustrated on a continuum "that runs from annoying to disruptive to dangerous comportment."[15]

"Intentional incivility" is characterized by demeaning and cruel comments that aim to deliberately hurt someone's feelings (e.g., saying "Why are you so stupid?"). "Unintentional incivility" includes responses that may be thoughtless but aren't designed to hurt others (e.g., saying "That's so retarded!" without knowing that a conversation partner has a sibling who is mentally challenged).[16] In their study of clinical nursing teachers and their students, Cindy Hunt and Zopito Marini distinguish incivility from bullying and make use of intensity to distinguish between direct and indirect uncivil communication. Direct incivility occurs when an instigator and target are physically present and the instigator makes no effort to conceal the uncivil act. Indirect incivility occurs when a target is typically absent and the uncivil behavior is covert, such as spreading rumors.[17]

Nurse educator Cynthia Clark also uses intensity to illustrate that uncivil behavior can range from that which is disruptive to that which is threatening. She separates uncivil communication from low-risk and disruptive behaviors that are considered distracting, annoying, and irritating to high-risk and threatening behaviors that are considered aggressive and potentially violent. Specifically, moving from low-risk to high-risk, these behaviors include eye-rolling, sarcastic comments, bullying, taunting, racial/ethnic slurs, intimidation, physical violence, and tragedy.[18]

Finally, communication researchers Rod L. Troester and Cathy Sargent Mester use intensity to distinguish civil behaviors from uncivil behaviors. Although they admit that there is disagreement about which observable behaviors constitute incivility, they identify the following behaviors as examples: ignoring others; gossip, arrogance or condescension; yelling, harassment, or intimidation; deliberate damage of others' reputations; and violence against persons.[19]

The lack of definitional clarity and the failure to note differences among the words used to characterize uncivil behavior are illustrated in the examples provided by Sypher, Clark, and Troester and Mester. Sypher locates "bullying, verbal aggression, verbal harassment," and "verbal abuse" as high-intentionality and high-intensity behaviors, but doesn't characterize or specify the distinctions among these types of uncivil acts. She also fails to define "rudeness." Interestingly, the words "ignoring, not listening, interrupting," and "exclusion," close to the low-intensity / intentionality endpoint of her continuum, can be used to characterize "rudeness," located almost midpoint on her continuum.[20] Furthermore, Clark doesn't define and fails to distinguish "bullying" from "taunting" and "intimidation" from "physical violence."[21] And while Troester and Mester label the words used in their continuum as "behavioral manifestations," they don't define or describe behaviors such as "harassment" and "intimidation."[22]

## Intent and Incivility

Psychologists concur that "human beings are notoriously inaccurate at assessing intentionality."[23] Specifically, an "intentionality bias" influences us to interpret all behavior as intentional.[24] A person who violates a norm that directs appropriate behavior is typically thought of as uncivil, whether or not he or she intentionally behaves in an uncivil manner. We can overcome the habit of viewing all behavior as intentional by making a deliberate attempt to find alternative explanations. However, even if we do interpret uncivil communication as unintentional, "responsibility is still assigned when the outcome is considered to have been preventable by the agent."[25]

For example, perhaps you've waited in line at a grocery store and two lines over is a person on a cell phone, speaking loudly enough for you to hear. Your immediate reaction may be to think that the person and her/his behavior are uncivil. But because the people in front of you have large purchases, you have time to think of other explanations for the behavior. Your final thought is that even if the person on the cell phone isn't being intentionally uncivil, *s/he should know that you don't need to shout into a cell phone to be heard* (in other words, the speaker could have and should have prevented the uncivil behavior). In all, "whether intentional or unintentional, or low risk or high risk, uncivil behaviors can have harmful and lasting effects."[26] Therefore, the use of intent to classify types of uncivil communication is problematic.

## Intensity and Incivility

In addition to using intent as a way to categorize uncivil communication, definitions of incivility often list behaviors in regard to intensity, directness, or threat. However, the use of intensity as a way to categorize uncivil acts is problematic. Specifically, those who study incivility often don't clarify why some communication behaviors are considered more intense than others. For example, Sypher doesn't explain why "profanity" is characterized as less intense than "rudeness." Troester and Mester don't explain why "using respectful terms of address" is considered to be more civil than "open-minded listening." Similarly, Clark doesn't specify why "bullying" and "taunting" are less intense than "racial/ethnic slurs" and "intimidation."

The use of intensity to categorize uncivil behaviors has caused some researchers to believe that low-intensity forms of uncivil communication are less harmful and less in need of critical study than high-intensity forms of civil communication.[27] Additionally, the communication behaviors identified as low-intensity and high-intensity forms of incivility may not matter to the recipient of uncivil acts.

A specific example of a low-intensity uncivil behavior is social rejection. Examples of social rejection include being excluded from lunch with co-workers, not being invited to a party, and being ignored by others.[28] However, "repeated instances of disregard, exclusion, interrupted talk, and insults are not less troublesome and no less likely to escalate and lead to feelings of isolation, anxiety, and lowered self-esteem than more intense and intentional forms of name-calling, profanity, put-downs, and other more verbally aggressive displays considered deviant, unjust, and harassing."[29] Therefore, similar to using "intent" as a way to organize uncivil behaviors, categorizing uncivil behaviors in terms of intensity is problematic.

## CATEGORIES OF EVERYDAY CIVILITY

In 2014, after a hostage siege in Sydney, Australia, that left the hostage-taker and two others dead, Muslims in Sydney were fearful of revenge attacks. In this period of anti-Muslim sentiment during which it was reported that people were spitting on women who wore traditional Islamic clothing, Sydney resident Rachael Jacobs sat near a woman on a train who silently removed her *hijab*. Jacobs ran after the women at the train station and said, "Put it back on. I'll walk with you." The woman began to cry and hugged Jacobs. Jacobs described the situation on a Twitter post that was retweeted by a radio producer and reporter. A hashtag, #ill-ridewithyou, was formed in support of the effort, and the majority of Twitter posts which occurred throughout Australia and throughout the world focused on the compassion and goodwill that resulted from the violence.[30]

Do you think the "I'll ride with you" example illustrates civil behavior? If so, is it because Jacobs respected the Muslim woman? Is it because her offer of help was restrained and appropriate? Is it because Jacobs, the radio producer, and thousands of people worldwide felt responsible for Islamic members of society? Just as there is disagreement regarding the definition of incivility and what constitutes uncivil communication, the way we categorize civility is unclear. Scholars in the areas of philosophy, communication, linguistics, political science, and sociology organize civility into various "types" or categories that illustrate behaviors. Specifically, there are single categories, dual characterizations, and tri-part definitions of everyday civility.

### Single Categories

Single-category descriptions of civility typically emphasize one or more characteristics associated with behavior. Rather than argue for two or three "types" of civility (e.g., a type of civility used in politics and a type of civility used in everyday interaction), a single category or definition is used to describe what is considered civil or uncivil. For example, a few single-category definitions center on manners and politeness.[31] Others emphasize the need to get along with others.[32] A number of single-category descriptions concentrate on respecting others.[33] Still others stress concern for others and the common good.[34] Additionally, in accordance with the "appropriateness" component of the Communication Competence model, some single-category definitions focus on adherence to norms or rules that guide interaction.[35]

## Dual Categories

Social theorist Edward Shils and philosopher Cheshire Calhoun contend that there are two types of civility. Shils argues that civility as "good manners" applies to both private and public life. Good manners function to communicate respect and to minimize insult, and they enable people with diverse beliefs to work together. However, good manners alone don't create a "civil society"—that is, one in which "civility regulates conduct between individuals and between individuals and the state."[36] According to Shils, the civility of a civil society is both an attitude and a form of behavior. In this manner, civility entails an appreciation of institutions such as religion, education, and politics, and it involves concern and responsibility for the good of society. Civility as a feature of civil society also regards all citizens, including opponents, as worthy of respect.[37]

Cheshire Calhoun writes that political philosophers interpret civility as the defining characteristic of the good citizen. "Political civility" concerns citizens who live in a pluralistic society who tolerate others and their views, even if they disagree. However, in order to practice self-restraint and to communicate tolerance, citizens must use rational dialogue in an effort to reach compromise. Therefore, "polite civility" entails not only restraining speech but also listening to others. Polite civility also recognizes a differing viewpoint as one that is worthy and on which people may disagree.[38] Political and polite civility emanate from "tolerance, considerateness, mutual respect, and a sense of justice."[39]

## Tri-Part Categories

Sociologists Nicole Billante and Peter Saunders claim that civility is typically applied in two ways. One concerns being a good citizen in a liberal democracy and possessing the ability to compromise so that people can get along. This type of civility, labeled "political civility," also includes listening to and being tolerant of others' viewpoints. "Social civility" relates to norms that are guides for appropriate behavior. Although this type of civility often is associated with good manners, social civility actually involves three components: respect for others; consideration for people we know and those we don't know; and self-regulation (i.e., restraining self-interest to maintain harmonious relations with members of the society in which we live).[40] However, Billante and Saunders write that civility should be understood in terms of three elements that are consistent across most characterizations of civility:

- respect for others;
- a moral quality (such as feeling responsible for strangers via the Good Samaritan ethic, and "a generalized empathy which we feel we owe to all who share society with us"); and
- sacrifice, which concerns self-regulation and prioritizing harmonious relations with others rather than pursuing what would be one's own immediate self-interest.[41]

Similarly, developmental psychologist Marilyn Price-Mitchell writes that the psychological elements of civility include self-control (restraint), respect, and "putting the interests of the common good above self-interests [responsibility for the community]." Mitchell claims that civility requires we treat others with decency no matter how we differ.[42]

Overall, there is no one true definition for "civility" and "incivility," and the existing definitions and categories aren't consistent.[43] The previously mentioned definitions and categories of civility are summarized in Table 2.1, "Definitions of Civility." The various definitions of civil communication center on one or more of the following components: manners/politeness (i.e., adhering to norms that guide appropriate behavior); respect for others; restraint; and responsibility to others and for the community. Manners/politeness, respect, restraint, and responsibility are related and often intersect, and it's sometimes difficult to categorize an uncivil act based on just one of these concepts. In addition, these characterizations are evident in our verbal communication (i.e., the words we speak) and nonverbal communication (tone of voice, gestures, movement, eye contact, etc.).

## COMPONENTS OF EVERYDAY CIVILITY

In June 2010, Armando Galarraga was about to celebrate the first perfect game in the history of the Detroit Tigers. However, umpire Jim Joyce called Cleveland's Jason Donald "safe" at first base, which meant Galarraga did not pitch a perfect game. Joyce freely admitted that he had made a mistake. "It was the biggest call of my career [and] . . . I just cost that kid a perfect game."[44] Although upset, Galarraga refrained from using harsh words or condemning Joyce after the call was made. In addition, Joyce personally apologized to Galarraga and hugged him after the game. They shook hands the following day, and a tearful Joyce gave Galarraga a pat on the shoulders. Galarraga commented, "There's no doubt he feels bad and terrible. I have a lot of respect for the man. It takes a lot to say you're sorry and to say in interviews that he made a mistake."[45]

This example illustrates both verbal communication (Joyce's apology and Galarraga's praise of Joyce) and nonverbal communication (Joyce hugging

**Table 2.1.   Civil Communication—Definitions and Categories**

| Single Categories | Manners/ Politeness | Respect | Restraint | Responsibility to Community |
|---|---|---|---|---|
| Weeks (2014) | X | | | |
| Smith, Phillips & King (2012) | X | | | |
| Davetian (2009) | X | | | |
| Laverty (2012) | X | | | |
| Orbach (2012) | X | | | |
| Arnett, Harden Fritz & Bell (2009) | X | | | |
| Troester & Mester (2007) | | X | | |
| Billante & Saunders (2002) | | X | | |
| Williamson (2012) | | X | | |
| Arnett (2001) | | X | | |
| Ferris & Peck (2002) | X | | | X |
| Shils (1992) | | | | X |
| **Dual Characterizations** | **Manners/ Politeness** | **Respect** | **Restraint** | **Responsibility to Community** |
| Shils (1992) | X | X | X | X |
| Calhoun (2002) | | X | X | X |
| Patton (2004) | | | | X |
| Rood (2014) | | X | | |
| **Tri-part Definitions** | **Manners/ Politeness** | **Respect** | **Restraint** | **Responsibility to Community** |
| Billante & Saunders (2002) | | X | X | X |
| Price-Mitchell (2015) | | X | X | X |

Galarraga, their handshake, Joyce's tears and the pat on the shoulder that he gave to Galarraga). It also illustrates respect, restraint, and responsibility. Both Galarraga and Joyce were respectful because they acknowledged each other's thoughts and feelings. Galarraga and Joyce showed restraint when they refrained from name-calling and exchanging insults, and they realized that their comments had the potential to affect their "community"; in particular, other baseball players, umpires, fans, and just about anyone knowledgeable about the incident. In sum, both Armando Galarraga and Jim Joyce exemplified civil communication. Manners, respect, restraint, and responsibility can be characterized in many ways; just as there are various definitions for the terms *civility* and *incivility*, there are also a variety of characterizations for each of the four components of civility.

## Manners

On a beautiful spring day in South Carolina, a twenty-year-old man sat down with a friend at a fast-food restaurant. The man burped out loud, which prompted a patron to ask if he was going to say "Excuse me." The man replied in the negative, and the patron picked up a chair and hit the man on his elbow. The patron then grabbed the man by the throat and tried to head-butt him. Afterwards, an employee convinced the patron to leave the restaurant.[46] While reactions to "rude" behavior aren't typically this violent, people who fail to exhibit good manners are often perceived as rude and uncivil.

Our culture teaches us that manners in the form of rituals are considered polite.[47] For example, an "introduction" ritual considered appropriate and mannerly involves saying "Hello," stating your name (verbal communication), and shaking the other person's hand (nonverbal communication). Such rituals vary by culture; for instance, one culture may consider it polite to shake hands, while another may consider it polite to bow when meeting and/or greeting someone. Similarly, one culture may consider it polite to kiss someone lightly on each cheek when saying good-bye, while another may consider it polite to place our palms together in front of our chest and say "*Namaste.*"

In addition, just as manners vary in terms of culture, manners constantly change and evolve. Manners may "deteriorate" in one context (e.g., language used in public) but improve in another (e.g., comments posted on an online forum).[48] No matter the form of verbal or nonverbal communication, manners can express respect, deference, and amiability, and they can also restrict the expression of offensive comments and decrease friction in a diverse society.[49] Similarly, if people in conversation disagree with a controversial topic under discussion, the use of good manners can help to facilitate the interaction.[50]

Although good manners can facilitate communication, manners can also function to keep people "in their place." Manners of this type are without moral significance and include those which may signify social class; for example, the "correct" way to hold a fork or drink a glass of brandy. Class-based manners function to bond members of a particular class and are used to determine who is and who is not a member of the particular class.[51] George Bernard Shaw's *Pygmalion* illustrates the class distinctions of Edwardian England which are demonstrated by the use of manners. Linguist Henry

Higgins teaches Eliza Doolittle, a member of the lower class, to perform the accent and manners of the upper class. Upon meeting the Eynsford Hill family, Eliza displays upper-class manners when she asks, "How do you do?" (verbal communication) and gracefully sits down (nonverbal communication). However, Eliza's topic of conversation and speech patterns almost give away her lower-class background:[52]

**Eliza:** They all thought she was dead; but my father, he kept ladling gin down her throat till she came to so sudden that she bit the bowl off the spoon.

**Mrs. Eynsford Hill:** Dear me!

**Eliza:** What call would a woman with that strength in her have to die of influenza? What become of her new straw hat that should have come to me? Somebody pinched it; and what I say is, them as pinched it done her in.

**Mrs. Eynsfofd Hill:** What does *doing her in* mean?

**Higgins:** Oh, that's the new small talk. To do a person in means to kill them.

This example not only illustrates that manners are related to socioeconomic class, but also that manners are artificial and aren't inherently good or bad. This idea becomes especially clear when the Eynsford Hill family truly believes that Eliza's conversational topics and way of speaking represent the newest form of small talk. Literary critic Mark Caldwell summarizes this idea when he writes: "[E]very instance where manners are morally momentous counterbalances another where they're trivial—situations where wrongness is plainly a matter not of ethics but taste, and where miscalculations signal only that one hasn't mastered the ways of whatever class or clique one wants to join."[53]

When based solely on manners, civil communication may be perceived as superficial and inconsequential. Civility as "good manners" is said to gloss over symptoms of deeper problems, such as inequality and injustice. However, good manners are a way to communicate that we care about a conversation partner and how she or he may perceive us. Good manners are not merely superficial, because they "do the everyday busywork of goodness."[54] Similarly, there may be a connection between subtle forms of disrespect (such as bad manners) and costs to humanity. For example, people who are denied the respect associated with good manners may begin to feel dehumanized and degraded, and the rejection of "superficial" forms of civility may reflect concealed disdain or malevolence that can erupt into outward displays of prejudice and bigotry.[55] Good manners are the way we communicate our belief in the dignity of others and that a conversation partner is of value.[56] However, civility isn't just about manners.[57] It also involves the communication of respect.

## Respect

Larry Martin is a white, male, semiretired construction worker and Tea Party member who disdains "big government"; specifically, the Affordable Care Act, which consists of health-care insurance reforms. Linda Bell is a black, female, stay-at-home mother and Democrat who campaigned for President Obama. During a street demonstration outside of a town hall meeting about national health care, advocates and Tea Party members exchanged angry words. Martin spoke to Bell, and according to Martin, "she responded in a calm, respectful way."[58]

When Bell noticed the message on Martin's shirt—"Texas Right-Wing Extremist"—she touched his shirt, saying she didn't believe he was an extremist. A newspaper photographer snapped a photo which was printed in the next day's edition of the *Dallas Morning News*. Bell phoned Martin and said she was upset because the photo made their exchange appear confrontational rather than respectful.

The next day Martin and Bell had breakfast together, the first of many get-togethers that later included their spouses. Martin says that his connection with Bell reminds us that "You're not going to change anybody's mind by yelling them down. Just stop and have a conversation with them."[59] Reporter James Ragland, who shared lunch with the Martins and the Bells, wrote that their gathering "was more than a lesson in civility. It was a humbling lesson in humanity."[60]

It is also a lesson in respect.

Although definitions of *civility* vary, most people agree that civil behavior should be respectful.[61] For example, social theorist Edward Shils maintains that "civility is basically respect for the dignity and the desire for dignity of other persons. . . . [C]ivility treats others as, at least, equal in dignity, never as inferior in dignity."[62] However, not all characterizations of respect include the idea of "dignity"; in fact, others contend that dignity, a birthright that includes value and worth, differs from respect, which is earned.[63] Nonetheless, respect is considered a baseline for civility. Philosopher Cheshire Calhoun asserts that a function of civility is to communicate respect, and law professor Stephen Carter claims that civility is an attitude of respect toward others.[64] Furthermore, philosopher and educational theorist Megan Laverty suggests that civility allows us to respectfully contend with comments to which we may take offense or those we may misunderstand, and this creates the possibility of further interaction.[65]

There are numerous definitions of respect and various ways we can verbally and nonverbally communicate respect to others. Pier M. Forni, director of the Civility Initiative and author of *Choosing Civility: The Twenty-Five Rules of Considerate Conduct*, writes that respect is based on empathy; that is, the "ability to identify with others."[66] Philosopher Emrys Westacott characterizes respect in terms of an "open-minded attitude, setting aside prejudices, [and] not making one's mind up too quickly but being willing to consider a claim on its own terms."[67] He suggests that one type of respect concerns tolerance for others' beliefs; however, not all beliefs merit respect. According to Westacott, withholding respect from certain beliefs is a component of critical thinking. We can also have respect for an ability, which can refer to esteem (e.g., "I respect your artistic creativity"), deference (e.g., "I respect your right to believe in what you think is right"), and the recognition and acceptance of something such as a cultural tradition on which we'll not impose on our values (e.g., "I respect your choice to wear a *hijab*").[68]

However, the type of respect that people most commonly expect and discuss is respect for others. Respect for others can take two forms: one to which all people are entitled based on their humanity, and one that people claim because of their particular qualities and experiences. We can communicate the first type of respect for others by using good manners (i.e., saying "please" and "thank you") and by exercising control, such as refraining from humiliating others. In sum, "respect for persons by virtue of their humanity is expressed through the way we treat them."[69]

Forni writes about respect for others in conversations, respect for others' time, respect for others' space and self-respect. He contends that respect for others in conversation means being open to the words that conversation partners use to address us. According to Forni, respect in conversations is based on the ability to consider that we may be wrong and the ability to admit that we may not know an answer. Respect for others' time entails punctuality, waiting to take our turn, and placing reasonable time demands on our friends. We nonverbally communicate respect for others' space by leaving enough room between ourselves and our conversation partners so they won't feel intimated or uncomfortable. Self-respect is indicated when we establish boundaries and by being sensitive to our own needs. We demonstrate self-respect by being assertive rather than aggressive or submissive when we communicate.[70]

One way that we can communicate respect, whether it's respect for beliefs, attitudes, or for people in general, is by listening. Michael Josephson, founder and president of the Josephson Institute of Ethics, states that while respect "is demonstrated by being courteous [and] by [being] civil . . . an important but often neglected aspect of respectfulness is listening to what others say."[71] Unfortunately, confrontational listening often occurs when we believe that people who hold views that differ from our own aren't entitled to respect. Confrontational listening is based on the certainty that a conversation partner is "wrong," and therefore not worthy of our respect. This type of listening occurs when we listen only for flaws in an "opponent's" argument so we can plan our refutation.

On the other hand, civil listening is respectful because it is based on equality and suggests that what a conversation partner has to say is worthwhile. However, civil listening isn't easy because it calls for us to experience a conversation partner's world as our own. Civil listening is also time-consuming, necessitates that we listen to beliefs and opinions with which we don't agree, and requires us to be open to the possibility that our own beliefs and opinions may be wrong. However, if we wish to have others listen civilly to us and give us a chance to get them to share our viewpoints, then we must listen civilly to others and give them an opportunity to convert us to their way of thinking.[72]

In addition to civil listening, we can demonstrate respect when we communicate formally. Perhaps you've heard the saying, "Familiarity breeds contempt." We can "flip" this saying to "Formality fosters respect." Formality that is respectful "is not a distant and stilted one; it is not the kind that makes one feel that there is a barrier between self and other that will not be removed."[73] "Civil and relaxed formality" is serious in intent, but at the same time, has a light touch. For example, if a professor calls students by their last names (e.g., "Ms. Smith" or "Mr. Jones") to foster respect, the instructor can demonstrate civil and relaxed formality if s/he calls a student by her/his first name based on a student's request.[74] Similarly, while first names are likely to be used among friends, first names are now being used by strangers. However, this may be perceived as a form of disrespect because "the use of a stranger's first name requires an invitation. It is a form of social intimacy, not entitlement. Using a more formal manner in addressing those we have just met is more than common courtesy—it is a sign of respect."[75] Overall, the use of formality allows us to maintain a certain amount of distance from others while allowing for the possibility of rapport.[76]

Some researchers assert that the symbolism associated with respectful communication behavior is more important than the outcome of that behavior.[77] For example, even though we may offer our seat on a crowded bus to an elderly person, her/his refusal doesn't deny the fact that the offer is respectful. Additionally, "whether we are following a set of rules just for appearances' sake, or following the rules from a sense of sincere dedication to their validity, or committing specific civil behaviors, all that we have done that others have labeled 'civility' is based in a perceived or actual attitude of respect for others."[78] However, others claim that if civility is associated with the open exchange between people, then it must go beyond the purview of respect.[79] According to several researchers, civility must also entail "restraint."

## Restraint

On June 16, 2014, the LA Kings won the Stanley Cup, the highest award in professional hockey. Los Angeles mayor Eric Garcetti, who celebrated the win at a rally on live television, wore a Kings jersey and held up an empty bottle of beer. Garcetti announced, "They say never, ever be pictured with a drink in your hand and never swear. But this is a big f****** day."[80] The sold-out crowd roared and the players applauded. Luc Robitaille, Hockey Hall of Fame member, spoke after Garcetti. Looking at the mayor and giving him a thumbs-up, Robitaille said, "Well, we told our players not to curse; thanks."[81]

Some hockey fans who didn't attend the rally also made positive remarks about Garcetti and his use of the "F-bomb." One Kings fan said that Garcetti's appearance reduced the "snobby and stuck-up" reputation of Los Angeles; another said, "It makes me have much more respect for him."[82] However, not everyone was pleased with Garcetti's use of a televised obscenity. Fox Sports West broadcast the rally and interrupted the coverage to apologize for the bad language.[83] Similarly, some of the posts on Garcetti's Facebook page denounced him as a "wannabe hipster," a jerk, and a bad influence on children.[84] Former sports announcer Vince DeLisi labeled Garcetti's language as "immature and classless."[85]

Even those not associated with hockey or sports weighed in on Garcetti's use of the F-bomb. For example, a legal ethicist wrote that if Garcetti "thinks that a hockey game victory provides a sufficient pass to issue officially sanctioned vulgarity to America, what chance do parents and teachers have when they try to instill manners—that is, routine respect for those we interact with—into their young charges?"[86] Garcetti, known for a disciplined campaign style, did not offer a public apology for his use of the F-bomb. Political scientist Jaime Regalado suggested that Garcetti's use of an obscenity was planned to draw media attention. Regalado explained that Garcetti has been criticized for not seeking out the media and refraining from making bold statements. According to sportswriters Zahniser, Reyes, and Branson-Potts, "[Garcetti] made a bold statement."[87]

Seeking media attention without regard for those who may possibly be offended places personal needs and wants above the needs and wants of others. However, restraint calls for us to "sacrifice" or "hold back" for the good of our larger community, and to foster harmonious relationships with strangers.[88] Forni defines restraint as "an infusion of thinking and thoughtfulness into everything we do."[89] Political theorist and philosopher Mark Kingwell characterizes restraint as being sensitive to context and goals.[90] In this manner, Kingwell is illustrating the Communication Competence model, which posits that effectiveness (meeting one's goals) and appropriateness (communication based on norms that reflect the context or situation) are required to be perceived as a competent communicator. Moreover, his notion of restraint is similar to "tact" in that it involves knowing that we need not say all we want to say.[91]

Communication scholar Janie Harden Fritz's idea of restraint is comparable to Kingwell's in that restraint is conceptualized as verbal editing or filtering that selects what is appropriate in content and style for a specific person, purpose, and context.[92] "Verbal editing" and "filtering" doesn't mean that we restrict self-expression; instead, it means we understand that not everything we want to express may be worthy of expression. Even passionate disagreement and criticism fall within the boundaries of civility if they are based on restraint. While some may argue that practicing restraint could cause us to stifle our self-expression, self-restraint actually illustrates that we can choose to express a particular part of ourselves rather than others. In other words, restraint itself is a form of self-expression. With this in mind, we can define self-expression as a "happy medium between self-effacement and self-indulgence."[93]

Some scholars suggest that today's "vocabulary of the self" is devoid of restraint and accountability, and reflects an overemphasis on individualism as a societal value. Words such as "self-assertion, self-realization, self-approval, and self-acceptance" are favored more than words such as "self-denial, self-discipline, self-reproach," and "self-sacrifice."[94] This vocabulary implies that "the old ethic of self-discipline has given way to a new ethic of self-esteem and self-expression. This has endangered the practice of traditional civility."[95] Psychologist Roy Baumeister, lead author of *Losing Control: How and Why People Fail at Self-Regulation*, claims that the failure to regulate the self is the major social pathology of the modern era.[96] Baumeister disparages the focus on self-esteem that is emphasized in modern families and taught in some schools, and contends that we should shift our focus from "self-esteem" to "self-control" and "self-discipline," in order to truly benefit self and society.[97]

Lack of self-control is also blamed on the perception that we have minimal, if any, obligations to others. Therefore, we confuse desires with "rights," and turn to the US Constitution to protect offensive speech and behavior. Although the First Amendment protects a variety of our rights, our cultural and social norms should provide us with the discipline to exercise these rights with respect for others and the larger community we are a part of. This means that although uncivil communication may reflect constitutionally protected rights, it doesn't mean that it's "right" to say whatever we want without regard for others.[98]

We can demonstrate restraint by keeping our temper and by being respectful to those with whom we disagree.[99] Research reveals that people who are less likely to express anger inappropriately are perceived as civil.[100] Studies also illustrate that people with low levels of self-control tend to engage in uncivil behavior, such as neglecting to say "Thank you," and that we tend to describe such individuals as "disagreeable" and "rude."[101] We can also illustrate self-control by refraining from making idle complaints and by giving and accepting constructive criticism.[102] Additionally, rather than blurting out anything that comes to mind, we can practice restraint by asking ourselves questions, such as "Do I really want to do this?," "Is anybody going to be hurt by this?," and "Will I like having done this?"[103] Calhoun reminds us that considering other's feelings "depends primarily on acts of concealment,"[104] specifically:

> In social life, there are unending opportunities to find other people boring, disagreeable, repulsive, stupid, sleazy, inept, bigoted, lousy at selecting gifts, bad cooks, infuriatingly slow drivers, disappointing dates, bad philosophers, and so on. The civil person typically conceals these unflattering appraisals, since conveying them may easily suggest that one does not take others' feelings or the fact that they may have different standards to be worth taking into consideration or tolerating.[105]

Considering others' feelings is also associated with another component of civility: responsibility.

## Responsibility

Attorney Jack Marshall presents seminars about business, government, and leadership ethics. In June of 2014, Marshall presented a seminar to over four hundred people, mostly attorneys. During one exercise, Marshall segmented the crowd and asked them to vote on various topics by raising handheld numbered ballots. The groups he formed included family law attorneys, government attorneys, mothers, men, women, and people sitting in certain sections of the room. One of the cases Marshall discussed involved a transsexual person, and he suggested that the transsexuals in the audience vote about the case. No one raised their hand and the group laughed. The next week, Marshall received a note from one of the participants:

> You asked the transsexuals to vote and said you were sure they were some attending . . . which produced laughter. Were I a transsexual, I would have felt ostracized and deeply offended. These are people with congenital/hormonal conditions that clash with our social constructs of gender identity. But most importantly, they are people. You are, of course, statistically right to guess that in a group of lawyers that size, probably there were not many—probably not any. That does not make it OK to perpetuate their ostracism. This is not about political correctness; it is about acknowledging shared humanity.[106]

Marshall responded to the note by writing that he didn't understand why she took offense at this comment. He countered by saying that he advocates transsexual rights and that it is valid to assume there are transsexuals in the legal profession. He also replied that he doubted whether members of the audience considered or knew why they erupted in laughter. Marshall argued that asking transsexuals to vote doesn't impugn their "shared humanity." He also claimed that his critic couldn't be sure how a transsexual member of the audience would feel because neither she nor other members were transsexuals. Marshall wrote that "we should all stop apologizing for offending a few people with legitimate, non-malicious discourse. The kind of sensitivity being demanded makes spontaneous utterances a minefield. I can't live, think, speak, and work that way, and no one should have to."[107]

Most readers agreed with this viewpoint after Marshall posted the story on this blog. Other readers suggested that Marshall may have been insensitive. One reader wrote that asking for a public vote was like asking people who passed for white prior to the civil rights era to self-identify. Another reader commented that the incident was similar to asking gay people to "out" themselves during the 1960s or 1970s. Yet another responded that without tenure or job security, self-identifying transsexual members of the audience might find their job security in jeopardy.[108]

Speakers are taught to adapt to their audience in terms of a topic and how best to communicate the subject matter. Even if our "audience" is comprised of one conversation partner, responsible speakers should use verbal communication that relates to the topic, that the audience will perceive as inoffensive, and that the audience will understand.[109] It is unclear whether Marshall adapted to his audience. And whether or not you agree with Marshall or the sentiments expressed in the workshop participant's note and in some of the blog posts, this situation concerns responsibility. *Responsibility* refers to our concern for and obligation to the community.[110] This idea is evidenced in the Latin *civitas*, or "city," from which the word "civility" derives. The historical meaning associated with civility is to be a good citizen.[111]

One way we can practice our citizenship is by voting and engaging in volunteer work.[112] Another way we can be responsible is by being aware that our communication has consequences; that is, it can positively or negatively affect others.[113] Both examples of responsibility imply that we understand and honor our obligation to the community. However, understanding and honoring the "social covenant" or common good sometimes appears to be lost in our modern information age. Because many people view traditional values as restrictive, especially those that limit individual freedom of choice, some believe that we can do as we like without any obligation to others and society.[114]

To assess how people think and behave toward their community and society, sociologist Corey L. M. Keyes used a three-part categorization of "social civility" to assess the level of responsibility held by US citizens. Social civility was defined as "social responsibility" (sense of duty to society), "social concern" (concern for others), and "social involvement" (the extent of volunteer activities). Keyes found that survey respondents reported a high level of civic and filial/interpersonal social responsibility. Additionally, 40 percent of the respondents volunteered in hospitals, schools, charities, or for political groups over a six-month period. Interestingly, the degree of social concern for others was lower than social concern for one's own life.

Keyes concluded that historical comparisons which suggest that today's US citizens have little or no social civility are unwarranted. However, Keyes's research didn't study the extent to which we hold shared values.[115] While Americans may have a high degree of social civility, a lack of common values makes it difficult to engage with others and creates feelings of alienation and isolation. Compounding the situation is the fact that many communities are comprised of diverse and transient populations which make it difficult to get to know others.[116] In fact, "a big part of our incivility crisis stems from the sad fact that we do not know each other or even want to try; and, not knowing each other, we seem to think that how we treat each other does not matter."[117] Similarly, the social trend of "cocooning" (staying at home rather than going out) is at least partially due to people bringing private behavior and a disregard for others into public places.[118] Unfortunately,

> [i]n hiding behind our own walls, we lose community, that reminder that one is answerable to something larger than one's self. . . . The idea that there is something called the common good and that we all owe something to it seems to have passed away unnoticed somewhere in the last generation. We should be troubled by what we have embraced in its stead. A culture where nobody owes anybody anything.[119]

## Ethics

We have read that civility can encompass manners, respect, restraint, and responsibility. Some researchers and philosophers also believe that civility belongs in the realm of ethics.[120] Consider the example of a World War II concentration camp guard who says, "Excuse me, sir; could you please step into the gas chamber?" This horrific example illustrates politeness ("Excuse me"), respect ("sir"), restraint (refraining from name-calling), and responsibility (to the Nazi community). However, this is not considered to be an illustration of civil behavior because it is unethical.[121] "Broadly understood, ethics is concerned with how we should live our lives. It focuses on questions about what is right or wrong, fair or unfair, caring or uncaring, good or bad, responsible or irresponsible, and the like."[122] We will learn more about civility and its relationship to ethics, virtues, values, and morals in chapter 4, but for now, the knowledge that civil communication must be ethical is evidenced in the characterization of civility that will be used in this text; that is, "[C]ivility is based on respect, restraint, responsibility, and ethical choices that enable us to initiate and maintain communication with others and to adapt appropriately to a given situation."

## SUMMARY AND CONCLUSION

To review, there are numerous synonyms and adjectives used to describe incivility, but most often these words are left undefined. In addition, the words used to define incivility are typically not distinguished from each other and are used without reference as to why they define uncivil behavior. Scholars in the areas of philosophy, communication, linguistics, political science, and sociology organize civility into various "types" or categories that illustrate verbal and nonverbal behaviors. The various characterizations of civil communication center on one or more of the following components: manners/politeness; respect; restraint; responsibility; and ethics/morals/virtues. Manners/politeness, respect, restraint, and responsibility are related and often intersect, and it's sometimes difficult to categorize an act as uncivil based on just one of these concepts.

Good manners constantly change and evolve, and they may be related to socioeconomic class. There are numerous definitions of respect and various ways we can verbally and nonverbally communicate respect to others. Respect is characterized as an open-minded attitude, tolerance for others' beliefs, and the acceptance of actions upon which we will not impose our values. Respect is also communicated by listening well to others and using a "relaxed formality" in an appropriate situation. Restraint can be characterized as verbal editing or filtering that selects what is appropriate in content and style and for a specific person, purpose, and context. While some may argue that practicing restraint causes us to stifle our self-expression, self-restraint actually illustrates the choice to express a particular part of ourselves rather than others. In other words, restraint itself is a form of self-expression. Responsibility refers to our concern for and obligation to the community. One way we can be responsible is by being aware that our communication has consequences; that is, it can positively or negatively affect others.

**Box 2-1**
   **Strategies for Change: Communicating Civility**

## MANNERS:

- Demonstrate rituals, such as those for introductions, greetings, and good-byes, which are considered appropriate for the culture in which you live (e.g., shake hands, bow, kiss, etc.).

## RESPECT:

- Set aside prejudices and keep an open-minded attitude and willingness to consider various beliefs and attitudes (but be mindful that not all beliefs deserve respect).
- Use good manners (e.g., saying "please" and "thank you").
- Refrain from humiliating others.
- Be open to the words that conversation partners use to address you.
- Consider that you may be wrong and admit that you may not know an answer to a question.
- Be punctual, wait to take your turn in a conversation, and place reasonable time demands on your friends.
- Leave enough physical space between you and your conversation partners so they won't feel intimidated or uncomfortable.
- Establish boundaries for yourself and be sensitive to your own needs.
- Communicate assertively rather than aggressively or submissively.
- Listen well to others and attempt to experience a conversation partner's world as your own.
- Communicate "relaxed formality" (e.g., use a stranger's last name until you receive an invitation to use their first name).

## RESTRAINT:

- Think about others' potential reactions before making an utterance.
- "Hold back" for the good of the larger community and to foster harmonious relationships with others.
- Be sensitive to the context and goals of the conversation.
- Be tactful; know that you need not say all that you may want to say.
- Engage in verbal editing or filtering that selects what is appropriate in content and style for a specific person, purpose, and context.

- Manage your temper; be respectful of those with whom you disagree; give and receive constructive criticism.
- Consider others' feelings.

## RESPONSIBILITY:

- Adapt your communication to your "audience"; use communication that relates to the topic, that the audience will perceive as inoffensive, and that the audience will understand.
- Demonstrate good citizenship.
- Be aware that your communication has consequences; that is, it can positively or negatively affect others.

## Chapter Three

# Influences on Everyday Incivility

*I'm more than middle-aged, but I do get on buses, and young people give me a seat. Men never do. But younger people do, even a young woman will do it. I think it's just a sign of respect.*
—*A focus group participant discussing "minor acts of incivility"*[1]

American Donal Carbaugh experienced a number of puzzling exchanges with British conversation partners when he lived in Oxford, England. An interaction typically began with pleasantries, after which Carbaugh was asked why he was visiting Oxford. When Carbaugh responded with, "I'm visiting Linacre College," the British questioner typically asked if he was a student. In one particular conversation, Carbaugh answered this question by laughing and saying, "In a broad sense, yes, but I've come to join two research teams." The British conversation partner subsequently asked an additional question, "Are you a member of the college?," to which Carbaugh replied, "I'm here at the invitation of Professor Harre." The British conversation partner responded to this information with a pause and asked a few more questions about what Carbaugh studied, before the interaction ended with "a rather frustrated, conversation-stopping, and less-than-satisfying, 'Oh, yes, uh-huh.'"[2]

Although asking a professor if he is a student may be considered uncivil by some, Carbaugh responded good-naturedly and the conversation continued. But Carbaugh concluded that this exchange "was less than fully satisfying," and eventually realized that different cultural orientations contributed to the often frustrating interactions. Specifically, when asked if he was a student, the British questioner was attempting to identify or position Carbaugh into the Oxford University hierarchy. Upon receiving somewhat ambiguous information, the questioner followed up by trying to discover more information about Carbaugh (hence, the question about being a member of

47

the college). The subsequent pause indicated that the response didn't satisfy the questioner, and he asked a few more about the topic of Carbaugh's studies before the conversation ended.

Carbaugh eventually concluded that his responses to such questions, in addition to the questions themselves, are "culturally loaded" in that they identify one's rank in the Oxford hierarchy of positions and prestige, concepts that are important and prevalent in Oxford. Reflecting on these conversations, Carbaugh realized that he wasn't providing information that his English conversation partners would be "relieved to hear," such as the fact that he was elected by college members to be a Visiting Senior Member of Linacre College. This information would have allowed his British conversation partners to place Carbaugh in a social hierarchy in one of the graduate colleges familiar to them and respond accordingly. Carbaugh concluded, "This kind of identification, or reference—as a position within a social hierarchy—is less valued in some American scenes in which I had been socialized, because it foregrounds issues of social class, social differentiation, and stratification. Rather than these themes, I had been taught to prefer that one's personal interests and experiences be expressed, while minimizing social differences."[3]

Although there's no indication that the British questioners perceived Carbaugh to be uncivil, what do you think might influence perceptions of civility if the situation were reversed—that is, if an American had asked an English conversation partner a number of "getting-to-know-you" questions and the answers were based on status and prestige? Consider the US value of "equality," which includes the idea that "all (wo)men are created equal." Even though this ideal is often violated in terms of the treatment of marginalized groups, most Americans hold a fundamental belief that all citizens are of equal value. US citizens typically admire high-status people who can be described as "down-to-earth" and who avoid "putting on airs."[4] Similarly, Americans compliment those who are wealthy and hold a high-status position with comments such as, "He's just a regular guy" and "She doesn't lord it over you." This means that respected high-status individuals in the United States "promote a feeling of equality, the preferred social mode among Americans."[5]

Let's return to how an American might perceive a British conversation partner who, during a getting-to-know-you interaction, talks about his/her status, prestige, rank, social position. The American might describe the British conversation partner as "stuck-up, a braggart, conceited, snobby," and "uncivil."

This example illustrates that what is interpreted as uncivil by one culture may not be considered uncivil by another. Consider the differences in civility practices among French, US, and English citizens:

- France: Never ask to use your hosts' washroom while dining at their house even though the dinner may last six hours.
- America and England: Make sure your washroom is clean and pleasingly arranged for your guests.
- France: Never address someone you have just met by their first name(s).
- America: Establish intimacy right away in the name of friendliness.
- England: Establish a cautious friendliness without invading privacy.
- France and England: Do not pry into someone's profession when you first meet them.
- America: Ask what the other does for a living very early on to show interest in their life.
- France: It is all right for a man and wife to argue in public.
- America and England: Desist from revealing marital conflict when in the company of anyone, sometimes even one's closest friends.
- France: It is necessary to teach children the rules of behavior by criticizing them whenever necessary.
- America: It is necessary to teach children by setting an example that does not demean their self-esteem.
- England: It is necessary to teach children discipline and rational behavior by teaching them emotional restraint.[6]

Our encounters with everyday incivility can be explained by the "appropriateness" component of the Communication Competence model. Recall that what is considered appropriate is based on norms, which are rules for behavior. When we violate a norm, we may be perceived as disrespectful, exhibiting unrestrained behavior, and not caring for the welfare of others in our community. The appropriateness component of the Communication Competence model is situation-specific; that is, not only does the physical environment impact what is perceived as appropriate, but the social environment also influences the degree to which we perceive behavior as appropriate. The social environment includes our culture, gender, and generation; all three influence whether communication is interpreted as civil or uncivil. Therefore, to avoid miscommunication and the perception that others are uncivil based on their "inappropriate" behavior, it's important to understand how culture and co-cultures, such as those based on geography, ethnic groups, gender, and generation, influence communication and the perception of incivility.

## CULTURE AND COMMUNICATION STYLE

A young man wandered into a tiny nondescript restaurant late at night in Chiang Mai, a rather dicey city in Thailand. He was the only patron in the restaurant and ate his dinner in silence. After he finished his meal, the young man realized that he didn't have any money in his pockets. However, for safety reasons, he had stashed some money in his shoe. When the elderly female cook asked the young man to pay for his meal, he took off his shoe so he could settle the bill. The woman immediately began to scream at the shocked and uncomprehending patron. She pointed to a picture of the Thai king hanging on a wall and then pointed to his shoes. The young man finally realized that "since the feet are considered filthy in Thai culture, I had committed a terrible faux pas by putting an image of the sacred Thai King [printed on the currency] under my feet. I tried to explain there was American money in there too, so I had insulted the USA as well, but she wasn't having any of it."[7]

Although most of us haven't experienced a situation like this one, it's very possible that we'll have contact with a person from a culture who doesn't share the beliefs, values, and norms associated with the culture into which we were born. This is especially likely because technological advances have made communication with citizens of other countries quick and easy. However, understanding others' cultural backgrounds will enable us to understand how and why they behave in particular ways.[8]

## Culture

The word *culture* refers to the "shared assumptions, values, and beliefs of a group of people which result in characteristic behaviors."[9] We learn about cultural beliefs and values through communication, observation, and sources such as art, folklore, and history. This process is essentially subconscious and enables us to behave in familiar situations without having to stop and think about how to act. Because we internalize culture, we believe that the way we think and behave are "natural" and/or "normal." In fact, "culture is so basic, learned at such a tender age, and so taken-for-granted, that it is often confused with human nature itself."[10] Since culture creates and maintains our perception of reality, the potential for miscommunication and the perception of incivility should be expected.[11] We often mistakenly believe that rather than cultural factors, individual personality characteristics such as rudeness and incivility influence behavior.[12]

Anthropologist Edward T. Hall wrote that culture is like an iceberg in that some aspects of culture, such as behaviors, are visible, while other aspects are invisible, such as beliefs and values. The beneath-the-water part of the iceberg, which is sometimes labeled "internal culture" or "unconscious culture," is what influences cultural behavior.[13] For example, we've already read about the US cultural value of equality. Additional beneath-the-water American values are freedom and individualism. Concerning individualism, Americans live in an age of idolatry of the Self. We have persuaded ourselves that first and foremost we live to realize our own Selves for our own good. Having made the Self the central concern and value in our lives, we should not be surprised if self-centered behaviors have become more prevalent than altruistic ones. We shouldn't be surprised if civility has suffered. [14]

Consider the responses that people may offer when challenged about their uncivil behavior, whether it's talking too loudly on a cell phone, interrupting face-to-face conversation to multitask on other projects, or blocking the ability to lean a seat back on a crowded airplane:

"It's a free country!"

"I can do and say what I want!"

"Mind your own business!"

These responses reflect the American "beneath-the-water" values of freedom and individualism, and can explain why Americans may be perceived as communicating in an uncivil manner. US citizens typically believe that everyone has individual identities and contend that their different preferences, styles, and interests should be recognized by others. [15] When asked about their culture, Americans often say that they have no culture, because they think that everyone is an individual who is free from the cultural assumptions that are imposed on them. In fact, the right to express oneself is considered a guiding tenet of American culture. [16] Although we have a right to wear offensive phrases on our T-shirts and blast four-letter obscenities from car speakers, such actions are considered uncivil because they are not based on respect, restraint, and responsibility.

Perceptions of incivility also result when we judge people from other cultures on the basis of our own cultural beliefs and values. [17] For example, Americans find it difficult to fully understand that people from "collectivist cultures" may not perceive themselves as distinct from others. Collectivist cultures, such as those in Asia, focus more on the group (e.g., the family, village, or organization) than the individual. Members of cultures that are primarily collectivist are more concerned with the opinions of group members and maintaining harmonious relations than members of individualist cultures.

Japan is considered a highly collectivist culture in which the internal beneath-the-water cultural values of hierarchy, harmony, and formality are evidenced in eye contact. Because prolonged eye contact is considered disrespectful and uncivil in Japan, Japanese children are taught to look at a person's throat or avert their eyes during a conversation to signal humility and formality. [18] Westerners may be unaware that these two norms explain why Japanese children may not look teachers directly in the eyes. This may cause a teacher from the West to interpret an Asian child's lack of eye contact according to Western beliefs and values—as a sign of rudeness and disrespect. In other words, a Western teacher may perceive a child's behavior as uncivil, while in truth, the child is communicating respect and civility according to Japanese behavioral norms based on beneath-the-water beliefs and values.

The example of a Japanese student and a Western teacher illustrates that perceptions of incivility often occur because we are unaware of the beliefs and values associated with another culture. Similarly, we judge others' behavior based on the beliefs and values associated with our own culture. This example also illustrates that although the concept of civility is cross-cultural, what is considered civil communication can differ according to the beliefs, attitudes, values, and norms associated with the culture in which we live.

Nonetheless, all cultures teach us which verbal and nonverbal behaviors are civil and uncivil and when it is appropriate and inappropriate to communicate verbally and/or display nonverbal behaviors. "In other words, culture provides the rules for playing the game of life [and] the rules will differ from culture to culture."[19] Understanding the different "rules for life" based on others' cultural beliefs and values will also enable us to understand their communication style.[20]

## Communication Style

Sociolinguist Deborah Tannen studies how various groups of people communicate and what influences their communication patterns. Tannen believes that the perception of what is civil or uncivil is determined by the social groups to which we belong. She contends that conversational styles are learned as we grow up and that we tend to denigrate those who communicate differently than we do. Tannen explains that "In countries all over the world, there are speakers from some geographic regions who speak more slowly than those from others. And in every one of those countries . . . , people from the slower-speaking regions are stereotyped as stupid, and those from the faster-speaking regions are stereotyped as too aggressive."[21] Tannen stresses in her lectures, articles, and books that differences in the way we communicate are just that—*differences*—and that any one style is neither better nor worse than another. However, she consistently finds that people resist this idea:

> A friend, for example, tried to explain to a European that when Americans ask personal questions of new acquaintances, they are trying to show interest and establish rapport. The European thought he knew what was really going on and kept repeating, "The point is, Americans are rude." Similarly, I had a student from Texas who sent her mother a tape of an interview in which I explained about conversational style. Her mother didn't like it at all; she wrote to her daughter, "The one thing that was never brought out [was that] not speaking out or interrupting is not so much culture as it is manners."[22]

Similarly, during a radio talk show, Tannen explained how members of some co-cultures talk at the same time as others—not to interrupt, but to show enthusiasm for the topic and the conversation. However, the host resisted Tannen's explanation, asserting, "It's just not polite." Tannen began to explain how politeness is culturally relative, but the host interrupted her (ironically) and affirmed that such behavior isn't polite, period.[23]

Tannen's attempts to explain that what is considered uncivil by some and not by others is based on communication style. Communication style, sometimes referred to as conversation style, involves both verbal and nonverbal communication. Our culture provides us with an implicit set of rules or norms that govern our communication style, which may include:

- When to talk and when to be silent
- The preferred amount of talk and silence
- What is appropriate to talk about
- The degree of familiarity with which conversational partners speak
- How fast we should speak (pacing)
- How long we should wait after another person speaks to communicate our thoughts (pausing)
- What is the appropriate intonation (pitch, loudness, rhythm)
- How direct should we be[24]

The elements of conversational style are automatic, arbitrary, and perceived to be universal.[25] Therefore, we tend to focus on undesirable personality characteristics when people violate a conversational norm which is considered appropriate in our culture. In other words, we fail to realize that conversational style varies in terms of culture and co-cultures, which include geographical regions, ethnicity, gender, and generation. In truth, no style is better than or worse than another. The act of conversational turn-taking illustrates a conversational norm that many believe is universal. Researchers suggest that we evaluate others based on how turns are allocated and how smoothly the turn exchanges are accomplished. "Effective turn-taking may elicit the perception that you and your partner really 'hit it off well' or that your partner is a very competent communicator; ineffective turn-taking may prompt evaluations of 'rude' (too many interruptions), 'dominating' (not enough turn-yielding), or 'frustrating' (unable to make an important point)."[26] Not all cultures follow the same turn-taking norms, and, as a result, competent and civil communication in one culture may be perceived as incompetent and uncivil in another.

Note that communication style, although influenced by personality, is not a personality type. Because communication style is contextual—that is, influenced by the situation—you can make use of various styles as you deem appropriate.[27] For example, you may use a particular style when communicating with a good friend (e.g., loud volume, rapid speed, the use of "short-cuts" or indirect communication, etc.) and a different style when communicating with someone you've just met (e.g., moderate volume, moderate speed, more-complete descriptions and direct communication to facilitate understanding, etc.). Overall, we can't say that *all* members of a culture or co-culture use the same communication style. Such a blanket generalization ignores the influence of individual personality and contextual factors, such as physical setting, someone's role, sexual orientation, and spiritual/religious background.[28]

## NATIONAL CULTURES

Jeffrey Walsh works with multinational companies and helps to solve intercultural communication problems. He once worked with an American team leader who described his Japanese counterpart as "weak, incompetent, and completely disinterested" because he failed to speak up at meetings. Members of the Japanese team were characterized as constantly questioning data and "nit-picking everything." The Japanese team perceived the situation differently. The Japanese team leader was revered by the team members, as he had taught and supported them, and promoted their careers. The Japanese team members suggested that the American team leader was given a weak team because "he must always present things himself [and] can't rely on his team for support." The Japanese team members therefore didn't believe the data that the American team members had sent to them.[29] Mr. Walsh concluded that:

> Both sides were interpreting the other's behavior strictly in terms of their own corporate and national cultural assumptions. Where the Japanese executive was demonstrating confidence and support for his team, the Americans saw passivity and disinterest. In trying to correct that perceived problem, the American executive unintentionally convinced the Japanese that the American team members were not up to the task at hand—anything that did not come from the American executive himself could not be trusted.[30]

This example illustrates that beliefs, values, and norms associated with national cultures influence perceptions of behavior. For example, Americans tend to value talk while the Japanese tend to value silence. Not knowing nation-based cultural beliefs, values, and norms may cause us to perceive incorrectly that culturally appropriate behavior (such as a team leader who says nothing in meetings) is actually inappropriate and uncivil. But we can't say that *all* Americans value talk and all Japanese value silence. It's important to note that culture is not a "strictly national phenomenon" and that any behavior may be influenced by situational factors such as a person's background and personality. We should always remember that generalizations based on nationality may cause us to stereotype and disregard individual differences. Therefore, we should consider cultural variations as "guidelines" rather than "rules" and recall that ethnic background and geography, gender, and generation will influence the extent to which national cultural norms affect behavior. Nonetheless, "the inhabitants of any country possess certain core beliefs and assumptions of reality which will manifest themselves in their behavior."[31]

## Verbal Communication

Eden Jacobowitz was an eighteen-year-old-freshman at Penn State University who was trying to study in his dorm room around midnight. However, members of a black sorority celebrated Founder's Day by singing, shouting, and stomping noisily outside of his residence hall. Jacobowitz shouted "Please be quiet!," but the women continued to party. Jacobowitz then leaned out of the window and yelled, "Shut up, you water buffalo! If you're looking for a party, there's a zoo a mile from here." The sorority women interpreted "water buffalo" as a racial slur and said that additional racial insults were shouted from the residence hall windows, although they couldn't say specifically whether Jacobowitz had yelled them. Nonetheless, Jacobowitz was accused of violating Penn State's racial harassment policy.

Jacobowitz said that his comment had nothing to do with skin color; instead, it was a response to the noise that the partyers were making. As the sorority women stomped their feet, they seemed to make a "woo, woo" type of noise, which caused Jacobowitz to think of "water buffalo." Jacobowitz, who is an orthodox Jew, explained that the Hebrew word *behema*, translated into English, means, "water buffalo." He explained that no one finds the term offensive among the Jewish community. *Behema* is not a racial slur and is merely a mild insult at best; it refers to a thoughtless or rowdy person and often is used affectionately among Jews who speak Hebrew. After two interviews with Jacobowitz, a university official found that there was "reasonable" evidence that Jacobowitz had violated Penn's racial harassment policy. However, a subsequent hearing with students and faculty exonerated him and Penn State dropped the charges against Jacobowitz.[32]

The "water buffalo" incident illustrates that verbal communication considered appropriate and civil in one culture may be considered inappropriate and uncivil in another. It also illustrates that it is important to have some knowledge of verbal cultural differences so that misinterpretations can be avoided, or at least minimized. For example, consider the phrase "You shouldn't have." Many Americans use this response when someone goes to considerable effort on behalf of others. "You shouldn't have" is supposed to communicate the recognition of the amount of time and energy expended on behalf of an individual and demonstrates that the relationship between the two is important. The person who utters "You shouldn't have" wants to communicate that the other's well-being is more important than the trouble s/he has gone through to help and/or please another individual.

However, an American most likely doesn't realize that saying "You shouldn't have" may be considered an uncivil response in the French culture. The comment is described as almost "cruel" because it can be interpreted as minimizing the time and effort spent trying to please someone, and the phrase may imply that the speaker is ungrateful and/or unaware of the effort expended to carry out a request or to benefit a person. Even a comment that is considered highly complimentary in the United States may be perceived as rude and uncivil in France. For example, telling a woman "You look like a million bucks!" is viewed as a compliment in the United States because "money is beautiful." However, this compliment may be perceived as uncivil in France because the French culture does not prize money as highly as the American culture. In fact, the "compliment" may actually be interpreted as an insult that suggests the recipient is being compared to a prostitute. [33]

The meaning of words translated from one culture to another is just one illustration of how we may mistakenly assume someone is exhibiting uncivil behavior. Furthermore, the way certain words are used in one culture may not be the way they are used in another; this may be an additional cause of misinterpretation and the perception of incivility. For example, it's easier to communicate respect in Spanish and other languages than it is in English. English speakers don't distinguish between the word "you" used in an informal context and "you" used in a formal context. In German, the words *du* and *Sie* signify informal and formal situations, as do the Spanish words *tu* and *usted*. The formal *Sie* and *usted* communicate respect as well as formality and acknowledge a social hierarchy.

However, the use of the word "you" in English reflects US values such as equality and informality; that is, the English "you" doesn't recognize the status of a conversation partner and/or the formality of a situation. However, "in other languages, the deliberate use of non-formal ways of speaking in more formal contexts can be insulting to another person." [34] Languages such as Chinese, Japanese, and Hindi have particular words for family members. Words for "older brother" or "younger sister" remind speakers to show respect and recognize the status of family members; they also remind the entire family of the norms that guide appropriate behavior associated with their roles within the family.

Conversely, the individualist cultures in which people speak English do not have specific words to replace "you" when talking to family members. Moreover, English is the only language that capitalizes "I" in writing, and unlike the formal *Sie* in German, does not capitalize "you." In fact, many languages have different words for "I" based on a relationship with others.

"There are more than twelve words for 'I' in Vietnamese, more than ten in Chinese, and more than a hundred in Japanese."[35] It may be very easy for native speakers of Vietnamese, Chinese, and Japanese to mistakenly perceive Americans as disrespectful because English emphasizes the individual and deemphasizes the recognition and status of conversation partners.

## Nonverbal Communication

In 1996, the opening of Parliament in Bangladesh included unexpected fury toward shipping minister A. S. M. Abdur Rab. The reason? Mr. Rab gave the widely known "thumbs-up" gesture to nonverbally communicate "All right!" or "Good going!" However, this gesture is considered an insult in Bangladesh, and a deputy leader of the opposition party announced, "This is a dishonor not only to Parliament but to the nation." Although the "thumbs-up" gesture is a friendly way to communicate nonverbally, in Bangladesh, as well as in Australia and in Islamic countries, the gesture is the same as an upraised middle finger.[36]

The thumbs-up example illustrates that in addition to verbal communication, culture has an impact on nonverbal communication and the rules that guide its display. Display rules govern when and under which circumstances nonverbal behaviors are considered appropriate. For example, people from Mediterranean cultures are likely to believe that intense displays of emotion are appropriate, whereas Americans of northern European background tend to believe that people should display neutral or calm emotions in public.[37] Furthermore, cultures differ in terms of meanings that are attributed to nonverbal communication. Specifically, interpretations of nonverbal communication are based on whether the behavior is considered to be random (i.e., it has no meaning whatsoever), idiosyncratic (i.e., when only partners understand the relational meaning), or shared (i.e., when people collectively understand that a shrug of the shoulders means "I don't understand").[38]

Because repertoires, display rules, and interpretations of nonverbal communication differ cross-culturally, misperceptions about the civility of such behaviors are common. Nonverbal display rules are usually learned via observation and experience, and remain out of our awareness unless our expectations are violated. This means that members of a specific culture typically use their own display rules to judge the civility of nonverbal behavior associated with other cultures. Negative judgments of others' personalities, attitudes, and intelligence often result when members of one culture use their own rules to interpret and evaluate the nonverbal communication of people from other cultures.[39] In other words, judging another's nonverbal behavior based on our own nonverbal cultural rules may cause us to make misinterpretations about civility. Misinterpretations about civil communication based on differing national norms are evidenced in how people conceive of and use gestures, interpersonal space, and vocal qualities.

## Gestures

In addition to the thumbs-up gesture, other gestures have different meanings across cultures. For example, the "A-OK" gesture (when the thumb touches the tip of the pointer finger, making a circle) has a different meaning in Venezuela than it does in the United States (it is the equivalent of an "Up yours" gesture made by lifting only the middle finger). In addition, in China, Italy, and Colombia, "Good-bye" is communicated by moving the palm and fingers back and forth toward the body; however, this gesture means "Come here" in the United States. Overall, gestures vary in terms of meaning, extensiveness, and intensity across national cultures.

Compared to Africans, southern Europeans, and Mexicans, northern Europeans and northeast Asians are more restrained in their use of gestures. This may cause Italians, Egyptians, and Greeks to describe Americans and northern Europeans as unexpressive. This may also cause Americans to label the nonverbal behavior of people from the Mediterranean as undignified and overly emotional.[40] In other words, the behavior is thought to be inappropriate and uncivil. Similarly, while it is considered appropriate to point at others and objects under certain circumstances in the United States, the same does not hold true for nations in the Middle East. In particular, pointing at someone in Saudi Arabia is perceived as impolite and offensive. Furthermore, left-handed people are at a disadvantage in Saudi Arabia, as the left hand is considered "dirty" and used only for personal hygiene. Finally, pointing the soles of your shoes at a Saudi, such as when you cross your legs, communicates disrespect and is an insult.[41]

## Interpersonal Space

Interpersonal space, often labeled *proxemics*, refers to the distances between people in conversation. How far away or how close we sit or stand next to a conversation partner depends on what a particular culture teaches us. In general, people from cold climates prefer more space between themselves and others than do people from warm climates. Specifically, people from the United Kingdom and English Canada consider a large interpersonal distance as appropriate, while people from southern Europe and French Canada consider close interpersonal distances as appropriate. Not knowing cultural preferences regarding interpersonal distances can cause us to interpret behavior perceived as civil in one culture as uncivil based on our own cultural norms for appropriate behavior. Specifically, "it is common for Americans to perceive Mexicans as rude and Arabs as pushy because they maintain close personal-space boundaries and expect and employ closer interpersonal distances than do Americans. Conversely, Arabs and Mexicans may perceive Americans as aloof and unfriendly because of cultural differences in proxemic behavior."[42]

## Vocal Qualities

Voice qualities describe how something is said and includes speed, loudness, pitch, rhythm, accent, and articulation. These qualities are often referred to as *paralanguage*. We tend to stereotype based on vocal qualities and negatively evaluate people whose vocal qualities differ from our own. For example, Chinese speakers may often sound nasal to speakers of English, while English speakers sound guttural and harsh to speakers of French. Moreover, Europeans tend to interpret the volume at which Americans speak as aggressive and uncivil, while Americans may perceive the low volume used by many in the United Kingdom as signifying that they are secretive.[43]

In addition to stereotypes based on vocal qualities such as nasality and volume, we also tend to interpret communication as uncivil in terms of pitch and speed. *Pitch* concerns the degree of highness or lowness of sound or tone, and *inflection* refers to variations in pitch. For example, speakers of "American English" use pitch at the end of sentences to suggest questions, comments, and demands. A medium falling tone at the end of a question is considered appropriate, inviting, and even friendly to American English speakers. However, too sharp a drop in pitch is perceived as indicating a demand or brush-off.

It's important to note that the use of pitch at the end of sentences to indicate the type of comment being communicated (that is, question versus demand) isn't shared by all cultures. In Chinese, for example, pitch may change within words, but it does not change systematically at the end of sentences. "When English is spoken with Chinese inflection, sentences lack the rise and fall in pitch that Americans expect in friendly conversation. To the American ear, this flat speech sounds brusque, imperious, or angry. Similarly, Americans may respond to British speakers of English as condescending, Germans as rude, and Latins as excitable."[44] Being aware that nonnative speakers of any language may use variations in pitch and inflection based on their native language can prevent us from misinterpreting others and their communication as rude and disrespectful.

## Communication Style

Kirsti, an eighteen-year-old Finnish exchange student, met Mary, an American student, when she first arrived in the United States. Two weeks later, Kirsti saw Mary while in town and they began a conversation. Mary asked Kirsti how she was doing and if she was enjoying her stay in the United States. After Kirsti responded affirmatively to both questions, Mary said, "It's a beautiful day outside, isn't it?" Kirsti once again responded in the affirmative and they spoke for a short time afterwards.

The next day, Kirsti saw Mary across the street and moved toward her, smiling and waving. Mary smiled and waved in response but continued to walk quickly to her car. These two exchanges influenced Kirsti to view Americans as friendly, but at the same time, superficial.[45]

We can explain Kirsti's negative evaluation of Americans by considering how Finns and Americans perceive conversation. In particular, after an initial conversation that includes small talk, a communication relationship has developed between a Finn and a conversation partner. This relationship includes the norm that requires a conversation partner to talk again, even briefly, when s/he meets the other partner at another time. This social obligation reaffirms the connection that is established in the initial encounter and suggests that initial conversations for Finns carry more relational significance than for Americans. In the example of Kirsti and Mary, Mary violated a Finnish norm about conversations by continuing to her car and not stopping to speak with Kirsti.

Moreover, Finns adhere to additional conversational rules, such as "one should not state what is obvious" and "one should say something worthy of everyone's attention." However, Mary violated these rules in her conversation with Kirsti by saying, "It's a beautiful day outside." In reaction to such a statement, Finns might think that stating the obvious is "silly." Therefore, Kirsti perceived Mary to be superficial, if not uncivil.[46]

The use of silence also causes misinterpretations and the attribution of incivility. In particular, it may be that the stereotype of the "rude" Frenchman or -woman comes from the way the French view silence. The French will typically engage in eye contact, smile, and converse with someone they know; however, in the absence of any relationship, the French will remain silent. Raymonde Carroll, author of *Cultural Misunderstandings: The French-American Experience*, writes that "this is why in the elevator, in the street, on the bus, and in practically every place where the other is almost totally foreign to my daily life, where the context does not call for ties to be formed or else lends itself to misunderstandings, 'people don't talk to each other readily in France.' "[47]

In fact, French visitors to the United States are surprised by the eye contact, smiles, and the friendly brief exchanges that occur among strangers. In France, one need not smile at strangers because smiles are reserved for those with whom we have a relationship. Unfortunately, it is "in public places that Americans in France for the first time have the experience, at times amusing, but often unpleasant and even painful, of cultural misunderstanding. They feel rejected, disapproved of, criticized, or scorned without understanding the reason for this 'hostility,' " and they can draw one of only two conclusions: " 'the French hate Americans,' [or] 'the French are cold (hostile, unpleasant/arrogant, despicable).' "[48]

In general, Americans can't stand more than a few seconds of silence. However, in Finland, silence is an important part of communication, and is not uncomfortable.[49] In fact, "silence, for Finns, reflects thoughtfulness, appropriate consideration, and intelligence."[50] Similarly, Asian countries and South African cultures emphasize silence, unspoken meanings, and saying as little as possible. In fact, cultures influenced by Confucian and Buddhist beliefs and values actually prefer communication without using language.[51] For instance, what is the meaning of silence in response to the question, "Will you marry me?" In Western cultures, the lack of a verbal response would most likely be interpreted as uncertainty. However, in Japan, the lack of a verbal response would be interpreted as acceptance.[52]

## REGIONAL AND ETHNIC CO-CULTURES

How would you feel if a street name included a disparaging word about your ethnic group? This is the question that Sandra Tanamachi answered when she fought to change the name of "Jap Road" in rural Fannett, Texas. Ms. Tanamachi maintained that the street name was derogatory and demeaning to Japanese Americans. However, Earl Callahan, who has lived on Jap Road most of his life, said that he feels like a part of his heritage is being destroyed. Mr. Callahan asserted that he and his neighbors who live on Jap Road are against the use of racial and ethnic slurs. He also maintained that there's a difference between calling a road "Jap" and calling a person a "Jap."

The word *Jap* became a slur during and after World War II when it was used to demean the Japanese and Japanese Americans. On July 28, 1986, Congressional Resolution 290 was passed, which states that the word *Jap* is racially offensive and prohibits the word for use on any federally owned building or land. But Mr. Callahan and others don't perceive "Jap Road" as being offensive. Local historians point out that the Yoshio Mayumi family, who owned a farm in the area, named the road. Mr. Callahan's family bought the Mayumi farm in 1924, and the street sign has evoked fond memories of the Mayumi family for Mr. Callahan. He suggested that the word *Jap* isn't a problem and that the true issue is the feelings behind the word. "If we lived in a society where everyone and everything is equal, and where there is an atmosphere of forgiveness, then words can't hurt you," he contends. Other citizens of Fannett have said that the blame rests on the overblown need to be politically correct and that it will be impossible to make the "J-word" disappear.

Although Jap Road at one time may have been used to honor a Japanese family, the Japanese Americans who fought to rename the road suggest that it holds a much different meaning for people who live outside of Fannett. Ms. Tanamachi said that if the name of the road doesn't change, it will remind her grandchildren of a time during which Japanese Americans were hated in the USA. Mr. Callahan counters that he and others are only trying to preserve the Japanese heritage in the area, and now there's a possibility that it will be eradicated with a name change that has no ties to the Mayumi family. "Years from now, my grandchildren may not even know that there was once a Japanese family who lived there," he said. [53]

The situation involving Jap Road shows that members of the same national culture may perceive a situation differently because of the influence of the co-cultures(s) to which they belong. A co-culture is a group within a larger dominant culture that has its own values and beliefs which sometimes may be at odds with the dominant culture. Co-cultures are based on ethnicity, geography, race, class, region, sexual orientation, gender, class, ability, and age. [54] The various co-cultures to which we belong influence our communication style and our interpretations of uncivil behavior.

## Communication Style

Identifying behavioral norms associated with co-cultures within the United States can help us to recognize potential sources of misinterpretation. However, one problem associated with studies about co-cultures and communication style is that the European-American communication style is often considered the standard communication against which all others are compared. It's important to note that all communication styles have merit and that the European-American style is considered the "standard" because those who make use of this style typically hold the economic and political power in American culture.

This also means that what is considered civil or uncivil is determined by the co-culture(s) which are powerful. In addition, many Americans are members of and identify with more than one co-culture, and their communication style illustrates various features associated with a number of co-cultures. Furthermore, members of co-cultures don't exhibit all of the features associated with a particular communication style, all of the time. Therefore, keep these ideas in mind when considering the description of communication styles associated with co-cultures so that we don't stereotype and assume they are rigid descriptions of how people communicate in every situation.

### Regional Distinctions

In the United States, negative impressions result from the differences in communication styles associated with Northerners, Southerners, Easterners, and Westerners. For example, people who live in New York tend to value talk. New Yorkers typically like to talk to strangers to communicate friendliness, such as when standing in line or sharing an elevator. Most non–New Yorkers will pretend not to hear a conversation between two strangers, but many New Yorkers think it's okay to add a comment if it's relevant. Although the New Yorkers may think they're demonstrating friendliness, non–New Yorkers may perceive that New Yorkers are nosey and "butt in" on conversations. New Yorkers also possess a particular style of asking questions. "Machine-gun questions" are meant to show a high degree of interest, and are characterized by a fast, clipped form that can be uttered in the middle of a sentence or at the same time as someone ends a sentence. This "high-involvement style" is meant to show interest and enthusiasm for a conversation partner and/or topic. If someone makes a good point or tells a good story, the New Yorker may show appreciation by reacting quickly and loudly.

However, people who use a "high-considerateness style," such as Californians and Midwesterners, believe that a speaker should complete a sentence before a conversation partner takes a turn. The high-considerateness style includes holding one's vocal volume in check and leaving long pauses so that others in conversation can speak. High-considerateness communicators want to make sure that others will listen to what they have to say. This can cause a person who uses the high-considerateness style to believe that the high-involvement speaker interrupts to take over a conversation rather than overlaps to show enthusiasm for a conversation. A high-considerateness speaker may also perceive a high-involvement speaker as pushy, aggressive, and uncivil. On the other hand, a person who uses the high-involvement style may perceive that a high-considerateness speaker isn't interested in the topic of conversation, doesn't appreciate the conversation, and doesn't participate enough to keep the conversation going.

Although these communication styles and others are relative, culturally variable, and learned, it can be difficult to admit that different ways of speaking are equally valid. Similarly, it may be difficult to accept that rather than personality characteristics (such as being labeled "rude" or "impolite"), uncivil communication results from differing perceptions of what is considered an appropriate communication style.[55]

## Ethnic Distinctions

Differences in communication style are also associated with particular ethnic groups. It bears repeating that what is considered civil or uncivil is determined by the cultures and co-culture(s) which are powerful, and that all communication styles are worthy of merit. Remember that descriptions of ethnic communication styles are based on tendencies and will vary in terms of speakers (gender, socioeconomic status), topics, situations, etc. Therefore, we shouldn't assume that these descriptions are without exception. We also shouldn't assume that people are speaking in an uncivil manner when their communication style differs from ours.

In general, the European-American communication style is the style against which all other ethnic co-cultural styles are compared. People who use the European-American communication style tend to be direct and explicit. European Americans typically assume that the spoken word is of primary importance and that nonverbal communication is secondary and serves to modify the meaning of words. Furthermore, Americans of European ancestry tend to be informal and address everyone in the same way (such as using first names easily and early in relationships). European Americans also may dislike people who "talk too much," preferring a form of interaction in which speakers take frequent turns after only a few sentences are spoken.[56] In fact, the European-American style of turn-taking has been likened to a game of table tennis during which "your head goes back and forth and back and forth so fast it almost makes your neck hurt."[57] Finally, European Americans tend to be uncomfortable with silence, and may fill a pause in conversation if it lasts for more than a few seconds.[58]

Compared to the European-American communication style, the African-American communication style is sometimes described as more creative. African-American speech may exhibit a rhythmic quality similar to African languages in that some syllables are accented stronger, accented differently, and held longer than the speech of communication styles associated with other co-cultures.[59] African Americans and European Americans may also employ different rules for conversational turn-taking. European Americans typically take turns that last as long as the number of points require. This requires conversation partners to wait their turn until all the points have been made. On the other hand, African Americans may take a turn whenever it's possible to do so, such as after at least one point is made. This occurs to establish the value or truth of each point before new points can be discussed.

In addition, the Asian-American communication style typically illustrates sensitivity toward others. This style includes prolonged silence, indirect communication, and tact, and often recognizes status and authority.[60] In fact, "Asian Americans may prefer silence to spoken language in situations where interpersonal disagreement is evident." Compared to the European-American communication style, the communication style associated with Asian Americans tends to be restrained, indirect, and respectful.

Compared to the European-American communication style, the Latinx communication style tends to be more expressive and eloquent. This style emphasizes learning about and getting along with others rather than a task-related focus.[61]

Members of co-cultures that value a succinct communication style may judge the communication style of Latinxs as being "flowery" or "overly dramatic." The Latinx communication style tends to be courteous and agreeable and illustrates that a speaker enjoys socializing with others. Unfortunately, this tendency may cause frustration among individuals who want to get down to business. Latinxs also value respect and in general will refrain from arguing or disagreeing in public. Similar to other co-cultures, Latinxs may use English and Spanish to communicate their identities and cultures.

## GENDER CO-CULTURES

The Rosetta spacecraft, which landed on a comet 310 million miles from Earth, collected scientific data and sent images from the surface of the comet. Dr. Matt Taylor, one of the scientists responsible for the mission, was interviewed on live television about the mission and his involvement in the project. Rather than focus on Dr. Taylor's comments, reactions to the interview centered on his clothing. Specifically, Dr. Taylor wore a Hawaiian-style shirt that pictured Heavy Metal comic-book images of large-busted women who carried guns and appeared in various stages of undress. Unexpectedly, a number of women criticized his choice of clothing as crude and uncivil. Astrophysicist Katie Mack asserted, "I don't care what scientists wear. But a shirt featuring women in lingerie isn't appropriate for a broadcast if you care about women in science." Journalist S. E. Smith of *XOJane* wrote, "The fact that a scientist of any gender, but especially a man, would think it's a good idea to wear a shirt covered in naked women while representing a major space agency and a significant research project is appalling; and clearly, he had no idea that he was engaging in exactly the kind of causal sexism that drive women away from STEM [referring to the male-dominated fields of science, technology, engineering, and math]."[62] The backlash against his shirt was so furious that during another televised interview about the mission, Taylor choked back tears while apologizing and said, "I made a big mistake and I offended many people, and I am very sorry about this."[63]

While some may argue that Taylor didn't intend to send a message that belittled women, the perception of and participation in uncivil communication often depends on our gender. Although many people use the terms interchangeably, *gender* and *sex* are not the same thing. While *sex* is based on anatomy, endocrinology, and neurology, *gender* refers to the influence of the environment and socially constructed meaning.

*Agonism*, a ritualistic form of insult and nonliteral fighting, illustrates how gender affects the perception of and engagement in "uncivil" communication. Agonism occurs among those who enjoy fighting for its own sake and who perceive trading insults as a form of a game. Agonistic exchanges occur when communicators try to top each other with clever insults in a war of words. Although it's not unheard of for women to participate in such rituals, typically men engage in agonism more than women. This type of behavior, which includes put-downs and one-upping, may be perceived as uncivil by women. However, men who engage in agonism may perceive such exchanges as exciting and enjoyable, and therefore civil.[64] This suggests that we may not realize that men and women follow different norms for appropriate communication and have different perceptions of appropriate conversational style.[65]

Even if we engage in repeated interaction with someone of a different gender, we may not understand how gender influences our communication or the interpretation of our partner's comments. In fact, repeated interaction reinforces perceptions of stubborn, uncooperative, and uncivil behavior on the part of our conversation partner.[66] Sociolinguistic research about gender and communication reveals that boys and men tend to perceive communication as a means to an end. Boys are taught that talk is used to achieve instrumental goals, such as negotiating power and position on a status hierarchy, to assert identities, to solve problems, and to argue points of view. Conversation is viewed as a way to demonstrate knowledge and superiority and as a method to gain respect. On the other hand, girls are taught that communication functions to build and maintain harmonious relationships that take priority over instrumental goals; communication is perceived as a way to foster intimacy and is the crux of relationships.

The instrumental-based conversation style of men and the intimacy-based conversation style of women are equally valid; neither style is better or worse than the other. However, these gender-based views of communication influence perceptions of incivility.

## Troubles Talk

Consider the following conversation:

**She:** My coworker Anne is such a pain.

**He:** What did she do this time?

**She:** She keeps coming to my workspace and telling me about her love life.

**He:** Well, just tell her that you have work to do; tell her to go away.

**She:** I don't need you to tell me what to do!

In general, when women talk about their problems, their underlying message is a request for acknowledgment and validation. Therefore, women engage in "troubles talk" as a way to connect with others and to demonstrate empathy and concern. One way that women communicate their understanding of a situation is by disclosing a similar situation of their own. So, if a woman tells a female conversation partner about the trouble she's having with a coworker, the conversation partner will engage in troubles talk if she says something like, "I know what you mean. I know someone like that in my office."

Because women see conversation as a way to establish connections, they become frustrated and perceive men to be uncivil when they respond to their problems with advice and instructions rather than providing empathy and understanding. On the other hand, men may become frustrated because communication is used to solve problems and it doesn't make sense to tell someone about a problem without discussing ways to solve it. Similarly, men may perceive that women "complain for the sake of complaining" when they don't converse about how to solve their problems.

Just as women may become angry when men attempt to solve their problems rather than communicate empathy and understanding, men may become angry and perceive women to be uncivil when they attempt to comfort them with a similar disclosure of their own. For example:

**He:** I'm really tired. I didn't sleep well last night.

**She:** I didn't sleep well either. I never do.

**He:** Why are you trying to belittle me?

**She:** I'm not! I'm just trying to show that I understand![67]

A man may perceive that a woman is attempting to put herself in a one-up position and minimize his problem if she communicates that she's experienced a similar problem.[68] Since men typically view communication as a way to assert status and dominance, a woman's attempt to create understanding and intimacy may be instead perceived as a way to prove that her problem is greater, worse, or more significant than his. This idea is illustrated in the conversation above.

Of course, not all men perceive communication as a way to achieve instrumental goals and not all women perceive communication as functioning primarily to establish and maintain relationships. However, such views of communication can influence women and men to perceive the same situation differently.[69]

## Listening and Asking Questions

Similar to troubles talk, different views of what it means to listen can influence the perception of incivility. In a study of approximately 4,500 women, 77 percent of the respondents reported that they thought of men as "uncivil" listeners in general; 69 percent said that men are uncivil listeners because they fail to ask questions about their partner's opinions or activities; and 41 percent thought men exhibit nonverbal cues that indicate they don't listen when women speak.[70] Women's perceptions of uncivil listening may be due to differences in communication style. For example, compared to men, women tend to ask more questions and communicate more "prompts," such as "uh-huh" and "mmmm," to indicate they are listening. Furthermore, while women use "yeah" to indicate that they are paying attention and to encourage a speaker to continue, men tend to use "yeah" only when they agree with what a speaker says. The result is that women perceive men as really not listening to them when they speak.[71]

Men and women may also perceive communication to be uncivil because of their different ways of asking questions (or because they don't ask questions when questions may be called for). For example, since men typically view communication as a way to establish dominance and assert authority, they may not ask for help in a problematic situation. This means that for some men, a lengthy search for a product is a better alternative than asking a salesperson about its location in a store. This occurs because the self-sufficient image that is important to many men may be diminished when a question is perceived as an admission of ignorance.[72] On the other hand, since many women view communication as a way to connect with others, asking for help is a way to establish a sense of community, even if an exchange lasts for only a minute or two. This may result in a woman perceiving a man to be stubborn and uncivil if he refuses to ask for help in circumstances where assistance from others could solve a problem.

A few caveats are in order when it comes to the relationship between gender and perceptions of incivility. For example, research reveals that there are more similarities than there are differences regarding how gender affects communication (and interpretations of civility), and that an overemphasis on differences doesn't paint a realistic picture of gender and communication.[73] In addition, our language patterns don't typically follow one particular gender style to the exclusion of the other. We can choose whether to communicate verbally in a manner that reflects a masculine style, a feminine style, or a style that reflects aspects of both.

## GENERATIONAL CO-CULTURES

"Mic," a New York website, is designed to be a leading news source for members of the Millennial generation. Mic was developed by Millennials and hires Millennial workers. CEO Chris Altchek, who is twenty-eight years old, has created a company climate that's described as "playful" and "aggressive." Free snacks are available in the kitchen; a number of employees ride hoverboards to get from one location to another; NERF dart guns are used to relieve stress; and some workers use a megaphone for spur-of-the moment announcements. Even the lead designer's dog, Dino, a white Maltese terrier, is allowed to roam from desk to desk. Altchek stated that he's "proud of the freewheeling office culture." Specifically, he noted that "It helps us to have everyone speak out, and [the] best ideas rise to the top. . . . What that can feel like or sound like is rudeness. But I'd rather have a lot of people speaking their minds than a very controlled environment."[74]

Whether you perceive speaking one's mind to be an example of incivility or an example of how the best ideas can rise to the top may be a function of the generation to which you belong. Generations are sometimes compared to people because they each have personalities and because each is affected by events that occur within their time frame.[75] Additionally, generations are shaped by common beliefs, attitudes, values, and behaviors. However, caution should be used when describing generations according to events and characteristics. There will always be "exceptions to the rule" and individual differences negate the sweeping statements used to describe generations. But it is still possible to characterize generations in terms of the biological impact of aging, unique historical occurrences, and "period effects," such as the scientific and technical breakthroughs of the time.[76] For example, although there is disagreement about the characteristics used to describe the Millennial generation, the one agreed-upon generalization is that Millennials have grown up with personal computers, the Internet, and cell phones; they've lived all of their lives immersed in technology.[77]

### Millennials and Generation Z

The Millennial generation includes individuals born between the mid-1980s and 2004.[78] They are lauded as being optimistic, engaged, authentic, creative, and caring.[79] However, they are also criticized by Baby Boomers and Gen Xers as being self-entitled, narcissistic, unmotivated, and disrespectful.[80] The way we perceive Millennials depends on the beliefs, values, and behaviors associated with our generation, and the knowledge of the events that continue to influence members of the Millennial generation. For example, Gen Xer parents, who may have grown up as "latchkey kids" or in day care, tend to be very involved in their children's lives. Parents of Millennials often chose to raise their children to be strong and to communicate their opinions to others. Parents of Millennials also enrolled their children in team sports, tech camps, after-school programs, and/or other activities, encouraging them to work closely with members of their particular groups or teams.

Similar to Millennials, members of Generation Z (born after 1995) are immersed in technology. Members of "Gen Z," sometimes labeled "digital natives," "the Net Generation," and the "iGeneration," are growing up in a world of smartphones and social media, and digital connectivity distinguishes them from other generations.[81] "Connectivity permeates their lives—from friendships to relationships, news entertainment, shopping—and has transformed how they interact."[82] They are described as being better at multitasking than Millennials because they can shift easily between work-oriented tasks and non-work related activities, even with multiple background distractions. Compared to Millennials, members of Gen Z are characterized as more entrepreneurial, expect instant access to information, and will become more global in their thinking and interactions with others.[83]

Judging members of a particular generation in terms of norms associated with a different generation will influence the perception of civility. For example, Millennials typically communicate in a direct manner which can be perceived as "impolite" by some Gen Xers and Baby Boomers.[84] Furthermore, Millennials may often expect to play a key role in teams at school and in the workforce, and are therefore perceived as "challenging" or "threatening" by instructors and supervisors/coworkers from previous generations. Members of earlier generations may also view Millennials as "brash, entitled, uncivil," and needing to earn an important place on a team by proving themselves over time.[85] Similarly, the limited amount of research about Gen Z reveals that today's teenagers are particularly sensitive about feeling disrespected. Members of Gen Z tend to be esteemed more than members of other generations because much of their interaction occurs online. Young people online are respected because they are perceived as knowledgeable and as equals; they are also treated respectfully because users don't know how old they are.[86] This can create a problem during face-to-face interactions, such as when they're asked for proof that they're old enough to watch an R-rated movie or when they perceive they're required to complete "meaningless" work in their high school and college classes.

## Changing Norms

In addition to the influence of Gen Xer parents, changing norms affect Millennials' behavior and the general perception of them as uncivil. For example, a survey of approximately six thousand Millennials demonstrated that this generation adheres to norms that differ from those associated with Gen X and the Baby Boomer generations. Specifically, their lifelong immersion in technology and participation in groups influence Millennials to be in touch with their friends no matter where they may be physically present, whether they're in a store, at work, in a bathroom, or walking down a street.[87] The same holds true for members of Gen Z. Furthermore, Millennial online self-disclosure behavior suggests that norms are changing regarding what is considered appropriate information to share with others. A USC Annenberg Center for the Digital Future study found that compared to Gen Xers, Millennials tend to share more information about themselves with online businesses and are willing to allow access to their personal data if they get something in return.[88] Millennials are replacing a need for privacy with a need for a networked society in which it is advantageous to share details on social media. It's predicted that "when this generation comes to power in government and corporate settings, social norms [about disclosure and privacy] will be more formally adjusted . . . and a new 'netiquette' will also emerge."[89] Similar to Millennials, members of Gen Z are "significantly less concerned than other generations about their privacy when using technologies native to them, such as mobile payment apps and social media."[90] This means that older people will continue to be surprised at what they consider to be the widespread disclosure of personal information by members of younger generations.[91]

## Technology

Because technology defines Millennials and members of Gen Z, it makes sense that perceptions of incivility center on how Millennials and members of Gen Z use technology. For example, a number of Americans believe that the use of a cell phone while eating, attending a meeting, or in a classroom is inappropriate, and therefore uncivil. In particular, one survey found that 62 percent of respondents perceived the mere presence of a cell phone on a table during a meal as uncivil. Additionally, 76 percent of respondents believed that texting during a meal is uncivil, as is e-mailing (79 percent) and using the Internet (80 percent). Furthermore, 84 percent of respondents perceived that talking on one's cell during a meal is uncivil.

However, Millennial survey respondents were more accepting of technology use, whether it occurs at home, in the workplace, or in a classroom. Specifically, 56 percent of Millennial respondents believed it is appropriate to place a mobile device on the table while eating, compared to 31 percent of respondents who were thirty and older. Similarly, 50 percent of Millennial respondents perceived texting during a meal as appropriate behavior, while 15 percent of older respondents perceived texting while eating as uncivil.[92] For the highly networked Millennial generation, the use of technology at the table is similar to the use of technology anywhere else; it is an appropriate way for users to be connected with others. Similarly, members of Gen Z believe that it is appropriate to use their cell phone while eating dinner with their family or on a dinner date.[93] However, for older generations, the use of technology at the table breaks a norm of appropriateness and therefore is considered rude and uncivil.

Moreover, Baby Boomers and Gen Xers may perceive Millennials to be uncivil based on e-mails that members of this generation send to others. Millennials are used to the immediate responses they receive when texting, and they expect instant responses from everyone in their world.[94] Some Millennial college students assume that their professors are available 24/7 and barrage them daily with e-mails.[95] Professors also complain that Millennial-student e-mails are inappropriate because they often lack salutations (or use a professor's first name in the salutation), include slang, computer shorthand (such as "R U" rather than "are you"), and overly casual writing.[96]

In addition, in a study about professionalism on college campuses, faculty nationwide indicated a 71 percent increase in inappropriate student e-mails, characterized by poor grammar, spelling, and language, over a five-year period.[97] While some professors may perceive that Millennial students are deliberately uncivil and disrespectful in their e-mails, the probable cause is that Millennials may be unaware of the norms associated with professional e-mails. Millennials are used to the norms of brevity and informality that characterize texting and instant-messaging. Similarly, they don't recognize that sending a stream of overly informal e-mails to their professors negatively affects instructors' perceptions of students. Professors tend to view e-mails as closer to letters rather than text messages, which means that a clear subject line, a formal salutation, standard punctuation, spelling, and grammar, etc., are expected.[98] Rather than perceiving Millennials' use of e-mail as rude and uncivil, professors should consider that norms associated with this generation are different from their own. Instead of responding to problematic e-mails with frustration or sarcasm, instructors might view their response as an attempt to educate their students regarding what is and isn't an appropriate professional e-mail.

## SUMMARY AND CONCLUSION

In summary, what is considered uncivil by one culture or co-culture may not be considered uncivil by another. To avoid miscommunication and the perception that others are uncivil based on their "inappropriate" behavior, it's important to understand how culture and co-cultures such as those based on geography, ethnic groups, gender, and generation, influence communication and the perception of incivility. Our culture provides us with beliefs, values, and norms that influence what is considered appropriate behavior. Perceptions of incivility occur when we judge people from other cultures on the basis of our own cultural beliefs, values, and norms. Culture also affects our communication style, which concerns both verbal (the spoken word) and nonverbal communication. When someone's communication style differs from our own, we often perceive that person as rude and uncivil. However, others' cultural norms and communication style are neither better nor worse than our own culture and communication style. Similarly, negative judgments of others' personalities, attitudes, and intelligence often result when members of one culture use their own rules to interpret and evaluate the nonverbal communication of persons of other cultures.

In addition to our national culture, regional and ethnic co-cultures, gender co-cultures, and generational co-cultures influence our behavior and how we perceive the behavior of others. A co-culture is a group within a larger dominant culture that has its own values and beliefs which sometimes may be at odds with the dominant culture. Ethnic and regional co-cultures influence verbal communication, nonverbal communication, and communication style, as do gender co-cultures and generational co-cultures. Overall, it's important to remember that generalizations about culture and co-cultures describe behavioral tendencies rather than unchanging characterizations about beliefs, values, norms, and behaviors. It's also important to recognize that our negative impressions of others and their behavior should be tempered with the knowledge that we are all influenced by norms which often differ.

**Box 3-1**
**Strategies for Change: Influences on Everyday Incivility**

- When labeling someone or someone's behavior as uncivil, remember that norms affect what is considered appropriate and that people from diverse cultures may *not* be behaving in an uncivil manner; rather, they may be following norms that differ from our own.
- If you characterize others as uncivil based on their communication style—that is, how they use verbal and nonverbal communication— pause for a moment and consider that differences in communication style are just that: differences.
- When conversing with someone from a different culture, remember that compliments in one culture may be perceived as insults in another (and vice versa). Similarly, misinterpretations about civil communication based on differing national norms are evidenced in how people use gestures, interpersonal space, and vocal qualities. We

should therefore keep an open mind when conversing with diverse others. Rather than perceiving them as uncivil, acknowledge that nationally based cultural norms may be influencing their behavior.

- Instead of focusing on someone's negative personality characteristics if s/he communicates differently than you, consider that behaviors understood as civil for Americans vary in terms of the many co-cultures that exist within the United States. For example, ethnic and regional co-cultures may have different norms concerning eye contact, touch, pronunciation, interruptions, conversational turn-taking, etc.
- Men and women have their own norms for appropriate communication and different ideas about appropriate conversational style. Because women see conversation as a way to establish connections, they may become frustrated and perceive men to be uncivil when they respond to their problems with advice and instructions rather than providing empathy and understanding. On the other hand, men may become frustrated because for them, communication is used to solve problems, and it doesn't make sense to tell someone about a problem without discussing ways to solve it. Men and women should note that responding to problems with empathy and responding to problems with advice both illustrate the communication of civility.
- Norms for appropriate behavior associated with Millennials and members of Gen Z may differ from norms associated with Baby Boomers and Gen Xers. Millennials are replacing a need for privacy with a need for a networked society, and should not be judged as uncivil for sharing what older generations consider private information.

*Chapter Four*

# The Good, the Bad, and
# the Virtue of Civility

*We obeyed the general acceptance of what society expected of us. Today*
*society has changed so much . . . I like good manners . . . they like their*
*freedom; they like to do things their way.*
—An elderly focus group participant commenting on how norms of politeness
*and good behavior have frayed during her lifetime* [1]

Charlo Greene, a KTVA television reporter in Alaska, had a secret. After a
newscast about the Alaska Cannabis Club and the push to decriminalize
marijuana, Greene identified herself as the owner of the club and stated,
"Everything you've heard is why I, the actual owner of the Alaska Cannabis
Club, will be dedicating all my energy toward fighting for freedom and for
fairness, which begins with legalizing marijuana in Alaska." She then ended
her report by saying "[expletive deleted], I quit."

KTVA apologized for Green's "inappropriate language" and fired her.
Taylor Bickford, spokesperson for the Campaign to Regulate Marijuana like
Alcohol, stated, "I hope her language, which clearly was not appropriate for
television, doesn't distract from the importance of her message." Greene
countered that her parting words hadn't harmed her cause and said, "Are we
talking about it, or not, because of what I did? Period." Soon thereafter,
Green set up a "public figure" Facebook page and obtained approximately
30,000 "likes" in less than twenty-four hours. [2] In addition, a video of her
newscast was posted on YouTube and received over 8.8 million hits a few
days after the broadcast. [3]

We may never know for sure whether Greene's use of profanity or her
arguments for the legalization of marijuana caused people to talk about the
issue. However, her on-air use of profanity and her subsequent termination

caught the attention of the Associated Press. Stories about Greene's departure appeared in outlets such as the *Huffington Post*, the *New York Daily News*, and *US Weekly* magazine. Would she have received such media coverage if she had said good-bye to her viewers in a civil manner? Probably not. Failing to capture attention is just one of the possible outcomes that can result from communicating civilly. On the other hand, we've learned that manners can express respect, restrict the expression of offensive comments, and facilitate conversations about controversial topics.[4] And although we know that uncivil behavior can result in negative outcomes, it may come as a surprise that positive outcomes can result from uncivil communication.

## THE BENEFITS AND COSTS OF INCIVILITY

Highland Park High School (HPHS) is located in a wealthy city in the Dallas–Fort Worth area in Texas. The award-winning high school is known for its academic rigor, outstanding athletic program, and affluent white students. The high school also became infamous in 2005 for a dress-up tradition during homecoming week called "Thug Day." Media reports described eighteen seniors who wore baggy jeans, bandanas, fake gold teeth, and Afro wigs to portray maids, rappers, gardeners, and gang members. Although not officially sanctioned by HPHS, Thug Day had been held since Homecoming Week 2002. School district officials said they canceled Thug Day after the 2005 event because it disrupted the learning environment; however, some wondered why officials waited until Thug Day received media attention to cancel it.

The *Dallas Morning News* characterized Thug Day as offensive and racist, resulting from the racial isolation that exists in cities such as Highland Park.[5] Nevertheless, the HPHS senior class president refuted the charge of racism when she explained that "We had a 'Country Club Day' last year, and I don't see any difference between dressing up in country-club style and dressing up thug . . . We weren't being racist. It's a Highland Park tradition."[6]

Others suggested that while the students didn't intend to be racist, they were nonetheless insensitive and disrespectful. Newspaper columnist Jacquielynn Floyd wrote that Thug Day "was less about racism than it was about rudeness. It was deliberately ill-bred behavior, the empty-headed mockery of people who got dealt a lower hand in life's arbitrary card game."[7] The columnist further contended that the students embarrassed their neighbors, adults, and fellow students. Floyd also asserted that the students stereotyped themselves as elitist and vulgar, and the residents of Highland Park "as rich, greedy, selfish airheads."[8]

## Costs Associated with Uncivil Communication

The students who celebrated Thug Day failed to demonstrate respect, restraint, and responsibility. As a consequence, they received national attention and negative press for their uncivil behavior. Although we'll most likely not encounter a situation similar to Thug Day, the costs associated with everyday incivility are many and varied. Studies reveal that the consequences of uncivil behavior include increased health problems due to anxiety; lost productivity at work; accidents caused by aggressive driving; personal injury caused by sidewalk rage, parking-lot rage, and air-travel rage; damage caused by acts of violence; and damage to the human spirit.[9] Even subtle forms of incivility are harmful in that they communicate that targets of uncivil behavior are neither our equals nor deserving of dignity.[10]

Uncivil communication at work distracts employees from their tasks, increases stress, and negatively affects the climate of an organization. Incivility in the workplace also creates distrust and cynicism. This, in turn, causes employees to lose enthusiasm and motivation for their job.[11] Furthermore, incivility at work causes employees to intentionally lower their productivity, sabotage coworkers' projects, and eventually leave their place of employment.

In terms of higher education, uncivil communication increases student stress and causes students to believe that they don't "fit in."[12] Students who are excluded socially also feel depressed and helpless, and believe that they can't cope with college life.[13] Additionally, incivility in the classroom interferes with student growth and learning.[14]

Regarding social media, while online bullying is often associated with children and teens, 11 percent of middle-aged respondents and 6 percent of senior respondents indicate in the 2013 Digital Future Report, *Surveying the Digital Future*, that they were targets of online harassment.[15] Depending on the frequency, length, and severity of cyber incivility, online bullying and harassment can result in emotional distress, depression, anger, and severe psychosocial and life problems.[16]

## Benefits Associated with Civil Communication

Just as there are costs associated with uncivil behavior, there are benefits associated with civil communication. Rusty Wright illustrates the benefits associated with civility in his personal story about cultivating respect and learning to disagree in a civil manner. Wright attended a university during the late 1960s when the Vietnam War raged and when campus life was impacted by the civil rights movement and the sexual revolution. Wright joined a fraternity comprised of Jews, Christians, and atheists; conservatives and liberals; and scholars and athletes. The mix of students in Wright's fraternity allowed him and his fraternity brothers to learn about and from each other. He also learned how to disagree civilly when a speaker from the group "Campus Crusade for Christ" came to his fraternity house. Although some fraternity members heckled the speaker, the speaker engaged the hecklers in dialogue and demonstrated how to disagree respectfully with others. Wright writes that his experience with diverse fraternity brothers taught him to communicate civilly:

> We lived, worked, studied, and played together and forged friendships that have endured despite time and distance. Many of us still gather for reunions and still enjoy each other's company. That environment was a crucible that helped me develop communication and relationship skills. [17]

Various researchers agree that there are multiple benefits associated with civility. One benefit is that civility communicates equality among people and groups. Political scientist Richard Boyd writes that "We have an obligation to be civil to others out of deference to the respect in which we are not better than they."[18] Civility also facilitates the ability to get along with others. Advances in technology and transportation have made it easier to communicate with others both in our own neighborhoods and halfway around the globe. Therefore, it's important that people of diverse cultural backgrounds be able to work together peacefully and accommodate others.

Boyd argues that "what is necessary for civil life is less some fundamental moral consensus about the rightness or wrongness of abortion, cloning, stem cell research, etc., than a way for different groups to minimize the conflicts and maximize the cooperation that this project of collective life entails."[19] Boyd also provides the method to minimize conflict and maximize cooperation when he asserts that "[civility] allows those with different and conflicting views of the good to live peacefully side by side."[20] Philosopher Cheshire Calhoun agrees when she writes that "civility, particularly toward members of socially disesteemed groups, protects individuals against the emotional exhaustion of having to cope with others' displays of hatred, aversion, and disapproval."[21]

The contention that civil communication is crucial for different people and groups to work together is supported by other researchers. Education scholar Chris Mayo suggests that advocates perceive civility as a way to overcome barriers of difference and to create a sense of commonality.[22] Similarly, sociologists Nicole Billante and Peter Saunders contend that civility facilitates social cooperation and interaction among individuals,[23] and philosopher Megan Laverty claims that civility prevents the expression of intolerant and hurtful remarks.[24] Furthermore, communication scholar Janie Harden Fritz writes that civil communication not only enables us to coordinate our behavior with others, but also allows for the coexistence of individuality and connection.[25]

It's relatively easy to see the connection between uncivil communication and negative outcomes and civil behavior and positive outcomes. However, it may be difficult to recognize the benefits associated with uncivil communication, and even more difficult to identify the costs associated with civil behavior. However, both incivility and civility are related to negative and positive outcomes.

## Benefits Associated with Uncivil Communication

Ryan Anderson is a reporter for the *Daily Signal* who believes that marriage should be between a woman and a man and that redefining marriage will negatively affect society. Anderson argues for traditional marriage in policy papers, in speeches on college campuses, and on television news shows. He believes that "the only way forward in our national debate about marriage is to make the arguments in as reasonable and civil a spirit as possible."[26] Anderson also strives "to treat all people with the dignity and respect they deserve as we carry on this conversation."[27]

However, Josh Barro, a reporter for the *New York Times*, tweeted Anderson to say that some people are not worthy of respect and deserve to be treated uncivilly. Barro then argued that Anderson should be treated uncivilly because of his opinion about same-sex marriage. Anderson responded to Barro by writing that "we should always treat people with respect and dignity—we should honor their basic humanity. We should always engage with civility—even when we sharply disagree with them."[28] He further lamented that people like Barro try to shut down the discussion about marriage by demonizing those who hold opposing viewpoints. Anderson further claimed that this is the first time in recorded history that we can have open and honest communication about same-sex marriage, and we should realize that the conversation is just beginning and needs to continue rather than shut down.

The outcome of the exchange between Anderson and Barro is that Anderson remains steadfast in his commitment to keep marriage between a man and a woman. "What Josh Barro says or does doesn't really affect me. I'm not a victim, and I'll keep doing what I do."[29]

It may be counterintuitive to imagine that positive outcomes can result from everyday uncivil behavior, but the Anderson–Barro conflict illustrates that incivility may strengthen the resolve of an intended target. If you once were the target of uncivil criticism, did you adopt an "I'll show them!" attitude? Maybe you became determined to solve a problem, complete a task, or not change anything at all on the basis of another's uncivil communication. In addition to strengthening one's resolve, uncivil communication in the form of cursing and profanity may actually be associated with positive outcomes. For example, swearing sometimes helps to diffuse stress and anger in certain contexts. In particular, cursing with a group of friends may imply that we are relaxed and feel free to "let off steam." Swearing can also be an effective way to vent aggression and forestall physical violence.[30]

Philosopher Emrys Westacott contends that there are three situations in which incivility, defined as "rudeness," is acceptable and beneficial: in a sudden crisis or emergency (such as abruptly ending a conversation to stop a child from running into a busy street); to promote long-term benefits (such as confronting someone with a difficult truth; e.g., she or he is overly reliant on alcohol); and to make a statement (such as feeling justified to break a behavioral expectation for political purposes).[31]

In terms of the workplace, David Yamada, director of the New Workplace Institute at Suffolk University Law School, suggests that incivility may be an understandable outcome of a disagreement or argument. Yamada writes that researchers who study workplace communication typically agree that incivility is detrimental to positive outcomes.[32] He agrees that when uncivil behaviors go unchecked, they can morph into bullying and create a poor organizational climate. Yamada claims that passive-aggressive behaviors may result if we don't have the emotional release that incivility provides us. However, Yamada asserts that "some expressions of incivility, while not enjoyable or advisable as a general state of affairs, can be part of a process of resolving workplace differences and disputes, at least under the right circumstances."[33]

Even if we reject the idea that uncivil communication can result in positive outcomes in certain situations, we should consider philosopher Edward Shils's caution that "A society in which no one thought of anything but the common good might be extremely boring, spiritually impoverished, and intellectually infertile. Disagreement, individual self-seeking initiatives, saying things which might give offense, breaking away from the cover of collective self-consciousness, are part of the spice of life."[34]

## Costs Associated with Civil Communication

The National Union of Women's Suffrage Societies (NUWSS) was founded in England in 1897 by Millicent Fawcett, who urged that women be granted the right to vote. Fawcett believed that women should engage in peaceful protest and that those who believed in suffrage should be patient and persuade via logical argument.[35] NUWSS members brought petitions to Parliament and distributed literature advocating suffrage.[36] The progress of the suffragettes was slow, and frustrated with the lack of headway made in achieving suffrage, the Women's Social and Political Union (WSPU) was founded in 1903 by Emmeline Pankhurst and her daughters, Christabel and Sylvia. Although Pankhurst and the WSPU suffragettes also wanted women to have the right to vote, they refused to join the NUWSS.[37] Suffragette Dora Montefiore contended that the WSPU "revolted against the inertia and conventionalism which seemed to have fastened upon the NUWSS."[38] The motto of the WSPU was "Deeds, Not Words."[39]

The suffragettes began their campaign for the vote with uncivil communication, such as heckling and interrupting politicians while they presented their speeches. The suffragettes became even more militant as the years passed and their pleas were ignored. They chained themselves to the gate that surrounds Buckingham Palace, vandalized golf courses, and attacked politicians. They also broke windows along Oxford Street, burned down churches, and fire-bombed homes and theaters.[40] In 1908, soon after being released from prison for interrupting a Liberal Party meeting, Christabel Pankhurst made a speech that attracted public attention to suffrage and the WSPU:

> For forty years, this reasonable claim has been laid before Parliament in a quiet and patient manner. Meetings have been held and petitions signed in favor of votes for women, but failure has been the result. The reason of this failure is that women have not been able to bring pressure to bear upon the government, and government moves only in response to pressure. Men got the vote, not by persuading but alarming the legislators. Similar vigorous measure must be adopted by women.[41]

Historians and others continue to debate whether, or how much, the suffragettes' militant tactics influenced the British government to change the voting laws, and whether the violent acts actually helped or hindered their cause.[42] "[T]here is no doubt, however, that the suffragettes raised the profile of the issue of women's votes to that of national consideration."[43]

## Attention, Influence, and Strategy

It is unlikely that the suffragettes would have received such attention if they had continued to use civil behaviors to persuade Parliament to give them the vote. At times it may prove necessary to communicate uncivilly if our goal is to call attention to ourselves and/or a topic. Politicians can claim that they engage in uncivil behavior because they believe that persuading voters to accept their stance on issues is more important than communicating civilly. In a political situation, incivility may be a small cost if the gain—such as being reelected—is the ultimate victory.[44]

When Representative Randy Neugebauer shouted "Baby killer!" when participating in health-care debates during the Obama administration, he was being strategically uncivil. Neugebauer asserted that "the intensity of the American people was represented in my intensity last night . . . I still believe that that Senate bill is a baby-killing bill."[45] And Lubbock County GOP chairman Chris Win asserted that Neugebauer need not fear voter backlash, because his comment reflected the beliefs of his constituents.[46] In terms of everyday incivility, we may be strategically uncivil to:

- make a point (e.g., to let others know we are "not pleased" with their driving skills);
- influence coworkers to quit their jobs;
- communicate our position on a status hierarchy (e.g., the more status we hold, the less we need to behave in a civil manner); and
- to shame others online.

However, we are less likely to use everyday uncivil behavior in a strategic manner compared to its use in the political arena. For example, we may interpret others' behavior as uncivil even when it's unintentional—when people speak too loudly on their cell phones or when they fail to smile and shake hands when being introduced.

## Hypocrisy, Constraint, and Freedom of Expression

Another problematic outcome associated with civil communication concerns the ritualistic quality of civility, which can promote hypocrisy and the potential for deception.[47] Imagine someone described as "charming" who communicates in a civil manner only to ingratiate her/himself with a powerful other. Civil communication also has the potential to preclude close relationships among people and can prevent the discussion of important topics due to the constraints associated with norms of civility.[48] For example, you may decide not to discuss politics and religion during a gathering of friends and acquaintances. Even though such discussions may be stimulating and insightful, you avoid topics that may generate passionate debate. In a similar manner, civil behavior may inhibit creativity and freedom of expression because of the fear of offending others. Billante and Saunders claim that "Excessive civility threatens to squash innovation and fresh thinking . . . One of the complaints about so-called 'political correctness' in intellectual circles, for example, is that it makes it impossible to express opinions or explore evidence which might give offense, even if they might turn out to be true or valid."[49]

## Conformity and Groupthink

In addition, civil communication can be used to enforce conformity. In a group setting, norms of civility may prohibit the correction of errors, amplify misperceptions, and exclude diverse opinions because no one wants to be stigmatized by being considered "uncivil."[50] Furthermore, poor decision-making can occur when group members censure themselves ("restraint") in an effort to appear civil. Norms of civility can also contribute to "groupthink," which occurs when group members fail to weigh alternatives and critically analyze a course of action.

Groupthink is identified as a key factor in the invasion of Iraq during George W. Bush's administration; the collapse of Swissair, a once financially stable company; and the cover-up of the child sexual abuse scandal involving football coach Joe Paterno at Penn State.[51] Civil behavior can also be used as a way to discriminate against others. As you read in chapter 2, the use of good manners can function as status markers that make distinctions between "us" and "them," and exclude certain others from participating in particular interactions and associations.[52] Finally, and perhaps most egregiously, norms of civility can function to keep the social hierarchy in place and confirm the superior status of certain groups. Specifically:

> "Rude" and "uncivil" are labels that have been applied throughout history to discredit the marginal and disempowered. At one time African Americans who tried to behave with dignity or to achieve socially were described as "uppity." The suffragettes were understood too as rude women who did not understand the obligations to polite society. Gandhi was a nuisance to the British. So efforts to eliminate what is considered to be "rude" behavior might be forms of political control.[53]

## THE VIRTUE OF CIVILITY?

Eleven-year-old David Williams's interest in civic affairs prompted his mother to take him to a Dallas City Council meeting to voice his opinion about whether teachers should be allowed to carry weapons at their schools. Williams asked the council members about alternatives to bringing weapons to campus, and as he waited for their response, he noticed some uncivil behaviors. A few council members looked distracted and others walked around the room. Williams asked, "Do you feel it is acceptable for City Council members to be up and walking while their constituents are addressing them?"[54] Council member Dwaine Caraway was the only person who apologized and responded to Williams's question: "It is not so respectful to walk around when visitors are speaking, so I will adhere to that."[55] Caraway later complimented Williams not only for speaking about the subject of school safety, but also for sending a message of "positive criticism that other people can appreciate."[56] Williams's mother also said she was proud of her son because of his "honesty and courage."[57]

Virtues such as honesty and courage are defined as behavior showing "high moral standards" and qualities "considered morally good or desirable in a person."[58] These virtues, along with respect, restraint, and responsibility, can be used to characterize civil communication. However, those who study civility disagree as to whether civility itself is a virtue. Some scholars contend that civility is a moral obligation, moral proposition, and/or moral virtue, while others claim that civility is a minor virtue that doesn't help solve important political problems.[59] Still others contend that civility enables us to *communicate* a virtue or that civility is not associated with virtues at all.

Civility is sometimes described as a value; that is, "a core belief that motivates attitudes and actions."[60] Values are also inherent in morals, which help to define right from wrong and get their authority from religion, government, or society.[61] The Ethics Resource Center lists "respect, self-control," and "responsibility" as examples of values.[62] Furthermore, when we associate civilly with others, the values embodied in the association include liberty, membership, and social dignity.[63]

Complicating the already-complex matter of whether civility is a virtue or value is the question of whether civility has a distinct ethical status. Some argue that knowing and adhering to behavioral norms (the "appropriateness" component of the Communication Competence model) enables societies to function because we expect to be treated with trust, mutual respect, and recognition. But this viewpoint insists that there also must be a moral aspect to civility in order to grant it ethical status; we can't be civil just to get what we want.[64]

Overall, we can combine the definitions of virtue, virtue ethics, values, and morals by saying that they involve "a disposition to respond to everyday situations in ways that both define and contribute to human excellence, protecting and promoting practices and outcomes considered worthwhile for human beings to strive for and attain in the course of a good life."[65] The various ideas regarding civility as a virtue are summarized in Table 4-1, "The Virtue of Civility?"

## Civility Is a Virtue

Many scholars suggest that civility is a virtue. For example, sociologists Billante and Saunders argue that "civility is a universally acknowledged virtue across different political philosophies and ethical priorities."[66] Philosopher Edward Shils contends that "civility is a virtue expressed in action on behalf of the whole society." Shils argues that because civility allows virtues to be cultivated and because it minimizes conflict via self-restraint, it is therefore a virtue.[67] Civility is characterized similarly as a virtue by political science professor Richard Boyd, who writes that civility is a virtue and a moral obligation to others to demonstrate equality and respect.[68]

Others maintain that civility is a value, moral proposition, or a moral virtue. Sociologists Abbott Ferris and Dennis Peck suggest that "civility is recognized universally as a value in all cultures, across time and geopolitical boundaries."[69] Law professor Stephen Carter writes that civility as a moral proposition includes the idea that treating others respectfully is a moral

**Table 4.1. The Virtue of Civility?**

| Author(s) | Ethics/Morals/Virtues |
|---|---|
| Barrett (1991) | A social good and ethical value |
| Billante & Saunders (2002) | A moral quality; a public virtue across different political and ethical priorities |
| Boyd (2006) | A moral obligation we owe others |
| Calabrese (2015) | A lesser virtue than justice |
| Caldwell (1999) | Values on which civility rests differ among people |
| Calhoun (2000) | Not a moral virtue (or a minor one at best); functions to *communicate* moral attitudes; a communicative form of moral conduct |
| Carter (1998) | An ethic for relating to strangers; a moral obligation to treat others respectfully |
| Ferris & Peck (2002) | A value in all cultures, across time and geopolitical boundaries |
| Forni (2002) | Civility belongs in the realm of ethics |
| Harden Fritz (2013) | A communicative virtue, but no agreement of the "good" for human life and conduct |
| Laverty (2012) | Not a virtue, because all conversation partners must agree on what is "civil" |
| Leach (2012) | A virtue (need agreement about what is "civil" and what is "good") |
| Mayo (2002) | Civility is related to power and justice |
| Peck (2002) | Civility is a matter of moral education |
| Price-Mitchell (2012) | The foundational virtue of citizenship |
| Schmidt (2000) | A minor virtue that doesn't help solve important political problems |
| Shiell (2012) | Not always the virtue of being nice; disagreement about when we are morally justified to be uncivil |
| Shils (1997) | A virtue expressed in action on behalf of society |
| Sypher (2004) | A moral concern for and understanding of the other |

duty.[70] According to Carter, we are civil when we follow behavioral rules not because the law demands it, but because we know the virtue of restraining our communication for the community in which we live.[71] Billante and Saunders further claim that civility is a moral virtue because "civility is good in and of itself: 'It is morally better to be civil than uncivil.' Being civil towards others is part of being a good and moral person."[72] Moreover, rhetorician Harold Barrett asserts that "at the heart of rhetorical maturity, civility is a social good—and ethical value—and a rich source of ethos. It is expressed in the symbolic behavior of one with another."[73]

Philosopher Robert Pippin considers the virtue of civility from an American perspective. He suggests that the American "mind your own business" individualist viewpoint and the norms that guide appropriate behavior in American culture don't really matter in regard to the virtue of civility. Pippin claims that even though civility is an ambiguous idea, it is "a form of trust and mutual respect or recognition."[74] The virtue of civility rests on being able to depend on others in fundamental ways, and that civil acts in daily life are based on our attempts to "recognize and help promote each other as free beings."[75] This means that the virtue of civility "involves some sort of appreciation of the dependence of my life on others within some community of dependence, and the enactment . . . [of behavior] appropriate to that dependence."[76]

## Civility Is Not a Virtue

On the other hand, there are those who claim that civility is not a virtue. Philosopher Cheshire Calhoun writes that there are three reasons why philosophers do not include civility as a moral virtue: The first is that civility is too closely related to good manners and is a marker of class distinction. Second, civility, more than any other virtue, is closely associated with following rules of etiquette and civil law. This is problematic when laws are unjust, because civility becomes more related to conformity than morality. Third, civility and incivility are broad concepts, and the scope of their application is unwieldy. Specifically, uncivil behaviors include shoving, shouting, bossiness, breaking appointments, offering unsolicited advice, scratching, proselytizing, intimidating others, rioting, and not obeying laws.[77] Calhoun concludes that civility functions to "*communicate* basic moral attitudes of respect, tolerance, and considerateness."[78]

Philosopher Megan Laverty takes this idea a step further when she explains why civility is not a virtue. Specifically, she argues that civility based in communication and interaction can't be characterized as civil unless all parties involved in conversation characterize the conversation as civil. Since our culture, ethnicity, geographical location, gender, and generation influence the interpretation of civility, it may not be possible for all people engaged in interaction to agree on what is considered civil. In addition, what one considers "good" influences whether we believe civility is a virtue.[79] Harden Fritz admits that "there is no public agreement on the 'good' for human life and conduct," and therefore we can't rely on common sense to guide appropriate behavior. Philosopher Mark Caldwell agrees when he writes that we can't regulate civility, because the value(s) on which civility rest "are always somebody's values, and somebody else, perhaps equally worthy and well-meaning, may hold other, very different ones."[80]

The different beliefs about what is "good" affect our communication behavior, and these beliefs are difficult to change.[81] Furthermore, "this era of disagreement, labeled with the term *postmodernity*, highlights the fact that our confidence in a universal sense of the 'good' is no longer normative, no longer the accepted reality."[82] An example of how dissimilar ideas of the "good" affect the interpretation of civility involves generational differences. Specifically, members of the Baby Boom generation may value the respectful recognition of status and age, which can be evidenced in e-mail salutations that include titles, last names, and formal greetings. "Dear Professor Smith" illustrates this virtue. On the other hand, Millennials typically value equality, communicating this in terms of casual and familiar salutations that avoid titles and include first names. "Hey, John" illustrates this virtue. Consequently, a Baby Boomer may bristle at a Millennial's "disrespectful" e-mail salutation and respond with a request for formal communication in future e-mails. Likewise, the Millennial may resent the Baby Boomer's uncivil display of "superiority and arrogance."

Recall that we base "civility" on respect, restraint, responsibility, and ethical choices that enable us to initiate and maintain communication with others and to adapt appropriately to a given situation. Which specific virtues, values, ethics, and morals should be used to characterize civility? Communication scholars Ronald Arnett and Pat Arneson contend that "a minimal common ground" is needed to guide communication in this "age of diversity and difference."[83] This minimal common ground can be expressed as the need to "keep a conversation going."

## CONVERSATIONAL CIVILITY

The first day of the fall 2014 convention of the American Studies Association (ASA) was unlike those in the past. Day one of the conference included a panel about the ASA's yearlong boycott of Israel. Specifically, the panel discussed the role of political ideology in academics and whether the ASA should engage in political boycotts. However, the panel was portrayed by attendees as promoting "for or against" thinking and for harming the ASA. After trying to remain neutral about the academic boycott, sociology professor Micki McGee said that she refused to give in to the politics of dichotomization. She advised the pro- and anti-boycott members of the ASA to "Step up and have a [expletive deleted] conversation."[84] Beginning a conversation (and keeping it going) is also considered essential for diplomacy, as evidenced by the United Nations 2014 peace talks between both sides in Syria's civil war. After the first week of the talks, the UN cited "as the biggest achievement the fact that the two sides were still speaking."[85]

Recall that in our current era, people have different ideas about what is "good" and about what counts as values and virtues. Virtues such as patience, courage, honesty, tenacity, integrity, etc., compete with each other in terms of which are more important in one person's life and which are more important to a majority of people. For example, suppose you value the virtue of tenacity and you demonstrate its importance in your personal life by working long hours so you can "climb the corporate ladder." However, suppose your relationship partner values family life over tenacity and demonstrates this by asking you to spend more time at home rather than at work. This example illustrates that it's difficult to agree on which virtues are more important than others. Moreover, if you believe that civility is a virtue, you may discover that there are other virtues that are more valuable than civility. One such good may be "equality," and therefore you may behave uncivilly to promote this form of social justice.[86] Since virtues are influenced by culture, time, and place, we should recognize that what we consider to be good may be in flux, and that we must make choices among competing virtues.[87]

So let us return to the question: "Which specific virtues, values, ethics, and morals should be used to characterize civility?" Is it even possible to designate any in the current era during which what is considered good is constantly in a state of flux? Perhaps not. However, the minimal common ground or virtue/good on which we can agree as the basis for civility is the need to keep a conversation going. If we agree that it's important to keep a conversation going in spite of perceived uncivil behaviors and conflicting values, we may be able to reach consensus and solve problems that we otherwise could not. This is the goal of "conversational civility."

## Keep a Conversation Going

Newspaper columnist Matthew Hansen wrote an article about women who are confronted by men they don't know who say, "Why don't you smile?" The article appeared on the front page of the *Omaha World-Herald* and was posted on the paper's Facebook page. The nineteen women he interviewed said that being told to smile by male strangers occurs on a regular basis. The women asserted that "Why don't you smile?" makes them feel like an ornament; moreover, it's sexist (women don't typically walk up to men they don't know and tell them to smile) and it carries a menacing undertone of "Smile, or else."[88] Less than one week after publication, Hansen wrote a column about the replies he received to the "smile" article. Readers posted over four hundred comments in response to the online version of the article, posted three hundred more on the Facebook page, and over one hundred readers sent e-mails with their opinions about men who tell women to smile.

Hansen separated the e-mails into three groups: women who sent "Why don't you smile?" stories of their own; men who had never heard of "smile" stories but became enlightened after talking with their wives, daughters, and female friends; and men who were "infuriated" by the article. Hansen wrote that unlike the first two groups, the e-mails in the last group were "short, had no narrative, told no story, and rarely attempted to explain or describe a point of view." Even worse, "these e-mails weren't written in an attempt to continue a conversation. They were meant to shut that conversation down, the writing equivalent of clamping your hands over your ears and screaming 'NO! NO! NO!' at the top of your lungs."[89]

Hansen ended his most recent article with a plea that we keep a conversation going by listening and responding with an open mind to others whose life experiences differ from our own. In essence, Hansen was asking that we engage in "conversational civility." Conversational civility (labeled "dialogic civility" in scholarly works), during which we attempt to keep a conversation going in the face of disagreement, is crucial in interpersonal relations. Philosopher Mark Kingwell asserts that "we must go on talking together if we are going to succeed in living together. . . . [S]ocial life is, in some sense, a matter of finding our full interests only by talking to one another."[90]

In addition, a number of communication scholars contend that keeping a conversation going is the "good" or virtue that should be the basis of civil communication. In particular, Michael Hyde argues that human existence requires us to keep a conversation going in order to acknowledge others and include them in our lives.[91] Furthermore, Leonard Hawes writes that we have an "ethical responsibility . . . to sustain conversations in which all sides, all positions, and all discourses engage to the extent each is willing."[92] Finally, Julia Wood asserts that "[conversational] civility does not require individuals to alter private attitudes, but it does require them to be motivated by a pragmatic goal to keep the conversation going."[93]

The ability to begin and keep a conversation going is difficult in our current era because of diversity and difference. But it is still imperative to agree on a baseline so that we may continue to interact with others to get along in everyday life. If we want to "keep a conversation going" as the baseline for competent communication (that is, communication that is effective and appropriate), we can make use of the characteristics associated with "conversational civility" to facilitate civil interaction.

## Characterization of Conversational Civility

*Washington Post* columnist George Will wrote that we are seeing a new form of entitlement that gives us the right to live our lives without dealing with any type of unpleasant thought. Will based his contention on the Texas Division of the Sons of Confederate Veterans' (SCV) fight to include a

Confederate flag, a part of the group's logo, on specialty license plates.[94] The Texas Department of Transportation refused to create the plates because an official decided that the logo was controversial. (The Texas Transportation Code allows the disapproval of specialty plates if the design may be considered offensive to any member of the public.) The case was presented in district court and a US Circuit Court of Appeals. The SCV argued that all of the district courts that had reviewed specialty license plate cases considered the words and symbols on the plate "private speech" that was protected by the First Amendment. The case was eventually heard before the US Supreme Court. In a five-to-four decision, the Supreme Court ruled that Texas did not violate the First Amendment by refusing to allow specialty license plates emblazoned with the Confederate Flag.[95]

Will disagreed with the rulings and claimed that the Texas Department of Transportation was infringing on freedom of speech.[96] In response to Will's column, letter-to-the-editor author Mark Fitzpatrick countered that Will ignored "the commonsense view that Confederate flags on government-issued licenses are discredited symbols" and that the flag is a "historically racist symbol." Moreover, a similar symbol such as a swastika or a questionable one, such as a "middle-finger salute," would also be disallowed on license plates. Fitzpatrick concluded that Texas has no law prohibiting the display of a Confederate flag on a bumper sticker or directly on a vehicle, and this means it is the SCV who feel they are entitled.[97]

The views of George Will and Mark Fitzpatrick illustrate the lack of consensus about virtues or what is considered good in the current era. In this case, freedom of expression—along with an emphasis on the self (or group) rather than the other (or other groups)—clashes with the virtue of responsibility to the community. Furthermore, Fitzpatrick's appeal to a "commonsense view" is unrealistic because common sense is based on agreed-upon virtues and common practices. In this era of diversity and difference, common sense exists only among groups of people; there is no overarching agreement about virtues or "goods." This means that there is no agreement about what constitutes *common* sense.[98] Consequently, conversational civility is a way to "reach out to one another using behaviors that are civil" and provide an underlying virtue to which all can agree; that is, to "keep a conversation going in the midst of difference."[99]

Conversational civility fosters mutual respect and understanding based on asking questions and listening. Conversational civility additionally focuses on the relationship between communicators and enables us to recognize that we will have different interpretations of similar experiences. Therefore, communication based in conversational civility may include disagreements and, at the same time, allow for the possibility of learning and change.[100] In particular, conversational civility recognizes "the value of remaining in the tension between standing one's own ground and being profoundly open to the other."[101] In other words, conversational civility allows us to respect our opinions and ideas of what is "good" and, at the same time, respect others' opinions and ideas of what is good.[102] Conversational civility not only entails respect for others and their beliefs about virtues—it also entails a realistic idea about hope.

## Routine Cynicism and Hope

StoryCorps, in conjunction with the American Federation of Teachers and the National Education Association, initiated the Great Thanksgiving Listening project in 2015. In 2016, StoryCorps urged young Americans to use the Thanksgiving holiday to record a conversation with a senior citizen, typically a grandparent, about the recent presidential election and discuss how to "bring people together in a time of division."[103] StoryCorps' founder and president, Dave Isay, asserted that:

> We're living in a moment where the divide is just so massive and the discussions will give people a chance to reflect on what happened in the last two weeks [of the presidential election]. I can't think of anything more important right now than listening to each other and finding a way forward.[104]

All of StoryCorps projects, including the Great Thanksgiving Listening project, are focused on others' feelings rather than winning or losing political debates. Isay says that since 2003 when StoryCorps was founded, all recorded conversations have been civil. Isay further contends that especially in this era of diversity and difference, we need to "start to listen to each other again."[105]

StoryCorps' Great Thanksgiving Listening project provides us with the hope that we can keep a conversation going by listening to others and considering their feelings. *Hope* can be described as the opposite of cynicism, which involves a persistent "What's in it for me?" orientation and involves fault-finding and a constant attitude of negativity.[106] Cynicism is created and sustained in the current era because we cannot agree on the virtues that guide behavior.[107] Sometimes described as "the enemy of civility," cynicism erodes trust in others and can cause us to emphasize our conversation-stifling individual rights to say whatever we want at any time we want.[108] On the other hand, cynicism is also used as a survival tool to protect ourselves from the reality of everyday deception (e.g., "The payment is in the mail") by distrusting and disbelieving what others say.

Instead of using unreflective cynicism as a way to cope in our era of diversity and difference, we can wed cynicism and hope—that is, adopt a perspective that includes knowing the human potential for evil as well as knowing the human potential for good.[109] Conversational civility—which includes a balanced approach to the good and bad that people can do, and provides us with hope for a better future—can decrease the use of routine cynicism as an unreflective survival tool. Moreover, "when hope and cynicism inform and temper each other, one result is the possibility of civil communication that keeps the conversational door open, or at least ajar."[110]

The need for conversational civility was requested by Dallas Independent School District (DISD) trustee Miguel Solis in 2015. In his essay, "Eyes on Improvement," Solis pointed out routine cynicism when he wrote that while on the campaign trail, constituents asked, "Why the school board? That's the last place change occurs."[111] Solis also referred to a confrontation between the DISD superintendent and a DISD trustee in which the trustee showed up unexpectedly at a closed meeting at school that the superintendent was visiting. The trustee refused to leave and the superintendent ordered the police to escort her off campus. Solis wrote that people often stop communicating with each other when they don't get along, and in the case of the superintendent and trustee, neither side apologized.

Solis stated that members of the school board should "cast aside the antiquated approach of cutting ties."[112] In other words, Solis was referring to the need to keep a conversation going, and he emphasized this need by writing that cutting ties in the DISD leadership has led to problems such as "Churn at the top. Taxpayer dollars divvied out to search firms. Students and staff starved of stability. And a perpetuated perception that takes the focus off the great things our district is now accomplishing."[113] Solis offered hope when he wrote that "Your leaders can, must, and will do better. As the New Year begins, I offer a resolution for the leadership of this district: call on the better angels of our nature. Cast aside the antiquated approach of cutting ties."[114]

It's important to note that the need to keep a conversation going and conversational civility are not appropriate for every situation in which we find ourselves. Introductory books about interpersonal communication warn readers that communication won't solve all of our problems; in fact, communication may cause more problems than it may solve. For example, suppose partners in a relationship find themselves in an argument. The argument escalates, and one of the partners warns the other that s/he is getting extremely angry and that they should stop arguing so they both can calm down. The other partner continues shouting, making accusations, etc., and subsequently the first partner explodes with venomous personal attacks. In this instance, "keeping the conversation going" has made a bad situation even worse.

Conversational civility may also be inappropriate in situations involving advocacy and the quest for equal rights. Specifically, similar to the suffragettes, strategic and confrontational communication may be called for when people with little power, such as members of minority groups that have historically been denied a voice, demand recognition and a response from a dominant group.[115] Moreover, conversational civility must "fit" a particular era, because what is considered civil in one historical era may be interpreted as uncivil in another.[116] Therefore, communication and conversational civility should not be considered a cure-all that will lead to positive outcomes in every situation. However, even though communication can cause as many problems as it can solve and conversational civility may be ineffective in certain situations, its use has the potential to improve communication and solve problems.[117]

## SUMMARY AND CONCLUSION

Just as there are costs associated with uncivil communication and benefits associated with civil behavior, there are benefits associated with uncivil communication and costs associated with civil behavior. Specifically, uncivil communication can result in increased health problems, accidents, and personal injury, and can create distrust and cynicism. Civil communication can result in a sense of equality among people and groups and can facilitate the ability to get along with others. On the other hand, uncivil communication can strengthen the resolve of an intended target, be used to "let off steam" and clear the air, and to make a statement that will attract attention. Similarly, civil communication can promote hypocrisy, inhibit freedom of expression because of the fear of offending others, and can be used to enforce conformity.

People disagree as to whether civility is a virtue. Some scholars believe that civility is a virtue because it is expressed as behavior that positively affects society and causes us to restrain our communication to benefit the community in which we live. However, other scholars believe that civility is not a virtue because it is too closely associated with good manners and can be used as a mark of class distinction. Furthermore, civility is not considered a virtue because the values on which civility rests are not universally agreed-upon.

Since a minimal "common ground" is needed to guide communication in this era of diversity and difference, conversational civility, based on respect for others, the topics of discussion, and multiple perspectives (including those with which we disagree), can help to keep a conversation going. Conversational civility also involves a marriage of cynicism and hope—a perspective that includes knowing the human potential for evil as well as the good that humans can do when working together. Although communication can cause as many problems as it can solve and conversational civility may be ineffective in situations that involve a quest for equal rights, it is still possible to improve the human condition by keeping a conversation going.

**Box 4-1**
   **Strategies for Change:**
   **The Good, the Bad, and the Virtue of Civility**

- Assess the topic, listener(s), and the overall situation before deciding to engage in civil or uncivil communication. Uncivil communication isn't always harmful and civil communication isn't always beneficial.
- We can keep a conversation going in the midst of difference by making use of the characteristics associated with conversational civility. These characteristics include listening, asking questions, and considering the relationship between ourselves and our conversation partners.
- Remember that the need to keep a conversation going and conversational civility are not appropriate for every situation in which we find ourselves. Therefore, communication and conversational civility should not be considered a cure-all that will lead to positive outcomes in every situation.

*Chapter Five*

# Power and Everyday Incivility

*Those in power seldom suffer from incivility; instead, they are often perceived as the instigator.*
*—Texas A&M professors Priynaka V. Doshy and Jia Wang* [1]

When Hillary Clinton ran for president in 2008 and again in 2016, she was criticized as shouting too much, communicating in a shrill manner, using a "nagging voice," and "cackling" when she laughed. Republican National Committee chairman Reince Priebus tweeted that Clinton was angry and defensive, failed to smile, and looked uncomfortable during a televised forum.[2] Linguists contend that the underlying message was that Clinton was unfeminine and employed a masculine speaking style. However, a soft-spoken and cooperative speaking style associated with femininity doesn't correlate positively with perceptions of leadership or power.[3] This means that Clinton found herself in a lose-lose situation: She was either perceived as tough and therefore not possessing the characteristics of "a good woman" (e.g., empathy and sincerity), or she was perceived as compassionate and caring and therefore not possessing the characteristics of an effective commander in chief.[4]

Interestingly, after the first televised Clinton vs. Trump debate, some pundits suggested that the interruptions, eye-rolling, and power-based condescension displayed by Trump toward Clinton mirrored what women often experience in their everyday lives.[5] Psychologist Janet Civitelli wrote that women experience similar uncivil and patronizing behavior from men during every workday, and author Tyler King suggested that the debate made visible the subtle and not-so-subtle sexism that women have experienced for centuries.[6]

## THE INFLUENCE OF POWER ON EVERYDAY INCIVILITY

The ability to define what constitutes civil and uncivil behavior belongs to those who are powerful.[7] Regarding the Communication Competence model, this means that what is considered "appropriate" is determined by the people who have, or have access to, political, economic, military, and educational resources. Who do you think holds most of the positions of power in the United States (that is, they have powerful, high-paying jobs; make most of the business and governmental decisions; and have more representation in powerful institutions, such as medicine, law, business, and government)? The answer is "males of European heritage."[8]

At this point, you may be tempted to put down this book to avoid reading about generalizations that blame everything on white males. However, I urge you to keep reading. Recall from chapter 2 that "respect" is considered a baseline for civility. Respect entails being open-minded and not coming to conclusions too quickly. Respect also requires us to listen well, evaluate a claim on its own terms, and to consider that we may be wrong. Additionally, respect is based on empathy, which refers to our ability to identify with others and view the world from their perspective. Although you may not agree with the controversial ideas and suggestions in this chapter, I ask that you keep an open mind and "put yourself in the other person's shoes" when you evaluate the influence of power on everyday incivility.

In terms of everyday incivility, civil communication can be criticized as reflecting and maintaining a power hierarchy, such as when Hillary Clinton and other women are chastised for possessing a "strident" speaking style while men are lauded for possessing the same "assertive" speaking style. We'll read more about *patriarchy*, a term that describes societies in which men hold the positions of power, later in this chapter. For now, we should understand that we can't always tell who possesses power from communication style alone.

### POWERFUL AND POWERLESS COMMUNICATION

Linguistic features used in one conversation, such as giving orders via a direct command or hinting via an indirect statement, are used in some cases by the powerful and in other cases by those who are powerless.[9] Similar to indirect messages, interruptions have different possible meanings and interpretations. In all, power doesn't determine the use of linguistic features and word usage doesn't identify power:

> The same linguistic means can be used for different, even opposite, purposes and can have different, even opposite, effects in different contexts. Thus, a strategy that seems, or is, intended to dominate may in another context or in

the mouth of another speaker be intended or used to establish connection. Similarly, a strategy that seems, or is, intended to create connection in another context or in the mouth of another speaker may be intended or used to establish dominance. [10]

## Indirectness

A university president once asked her secretary to carry out some tasks by saying, "I've just finished drafting this letter. Do you think you can type it right away? I'd like to get it out before lunch. And would you please do me a favor and hold calls while I'm meeting with Mr. Smith?" Mr. Smith, a member of the university's board of trustees, was in the president's office and overhead her talking to her secretary. He later told the president that she had spoken in an inappropriate manner to her secretary, but not because he perceived that she was being uncivil. Mr. Smith explained that the president's indirect speaking style gave him the impression that she felt she couldn't make demands of her secretary. In truth, speaking indirectly is not necessarily a sign of powerlessness and doesn't mean that a speaker lacks confidence. Indirect communication can be used to establish and maintain rapport among individuals. Therefore, the university president may have thought she could best get her way by using indirect communication to reinforce the harmonious relationship with her secretary. In truth, "the ability to get one's demands met without expressing them directly can be a sign of power rather than the lack of it." [11]

The perception and interpretation of direct and indirect communication styles as civil or uncivil is influenced by culture, region, ethnicity, gender, and generation. Additionally, the context or situation and the communication norms of appropriateness that we adhere to influence our perception and interpretation of direct and indirect messages. Consider the following: If a boss fails to use the word *please* when s/he tells a subordinate to "type this letter now and get it out before lunch," will you perceive the demand as civil or uncivil? Listening to someone giving orders in a direct manner may be labeled uncivil by some, yet civil by others. Those who want instructions offered in a "polite" manner may be offended with direct communication that is void of the inclusion of *please* or *thank you*. However, those who don't want others to "hint around" or "beat around the bush" may perceive indirect communication as uncivil and something less than truthful.

The point is that direct and indirect communication are both equally valid ways of getting a point across and/or suggesting a course of action. Similarly, we can't say that powerful people tend to be more direct while less-powerful people tend to be more indirect. This is because we tend to use indirectness in various situations and in various ways. [12] Suppose a commanding officer says to her/his recruits, "It's hot in here" and expects the recruits to know that this means they should open the windows. Is this statement uncivil because it hints at a course of action (that is, the recruits should jump up and open the windows)? Is the statement, or perhaps the commanding officer, uncivil because the direct order, "Open the windows" is not uttered? In this situation, the power differential between the officer and recruits is evidenced in the norm that "the burden of interpretation is on subordinates" in the military.[13] Therefore, it is appropriate and civil in the military culture for a powerful person to make demands in an indirect manner.

National cultures also provide us with norms that we use to judge whether indirect communication is perceived as civil or uncivil. Indirectness is a norm in many cultures; in Japan, there's a word for the highly prized ability to communicate indirectly: *haragei*.[14] Overall, this means that "there is nothing wrong with indirectness as a strategy when it is shared. When it's not shared, however, trouble can result—not from the indirectness, but from the difference in styles."[15]

## Interruptions

A 2015 South by Southwest (SXSW) panel formed to discuss innovation in technology included speakers such as Google executive chairman Eric Schmidt, chief technology officer for the United States, Megan Smith, and Steve Jobs biographer Walter Isaacson. The panel discussion eventually turned to the topic of attracting new talent, especially women and people of color, to foster creativity. After a while, some audience members noticed that Schmidt kept interrupting Megan Smith to present his views about diversity. During the question-and-answer session, a female member of the audience raised her hand and asked, "Given that unconscious bias research tells us that women are interrupted a lot more than men, I'm wondering if you are aware that you have interrupted Megan many more times." The audience then burst into applause. And the woman who raised her hand during the Q-and-A portion of the presentation? It was Judith Williams, the head of Google's global diversity and talent management program.[16]

The ability to stop someone who is speaking so that another can take the floor is commonly associated with power. Research indicates that in general, men interrupt more often than females, and females are the more-interrupted gender.[17] This may occur because, as linguist Adrienne Hancock explains, "interruptions can be used to display or gain dominance" and "a man may be more likely to see conversation as a 'competitive game.'"[18] In fact, the term *manterrupting* has been coined to describe the "unnecessary interruption of a woman by a man."[19]

However, as we read in chapter 3, communication overlaps that occur while someone else is talking are often meant to show enthusiasm and interest rather than to demonstrate power by taking over a conversation. Norms of appropriate communication (along with our culture, regional and ethnic co-cultures, gender, generation, and the context in general) influence whether one interprets two people speaking at the same time as an interruption (that is, an uncivil power move by one conversation partner to direct the conversation) or as an overlap meant to show solidarity and connection.[20] In particular, if we adhere to the norm that talking along with people is a way to demonstrate enthusiasm for the topic and speaker, we utter overlaps to communicate connection and solidarity. On the other hand, if we adhere to the norm that only one person should speak at a time, we interrupt others in a power move to take the floor.[21]

Assumptions about how long we should pause between sentences also influence whether we "interrupt" others. We tend to believe that the length of pauses between sentences, which signals when one person may take the floor to speak, is "natural." However, the appropriate length of pauses between one speaker's turn and another is based on a norm that can vary among cultures, regions, ethnic groups, genders, and generations. An unbalanced conversation occurs when one conversation partner expects a longer pause between turns and the other does not. The conversation partner who waits for the longer pause may find it difficult to get a turn to speak because the conversation partner who is used to shorter pauses will find the "silence" uncomfortable and will jump in to save the interaction. The result may be that the conversation partner who waits for but never gets the longer pause accuses the other of interrupting and dominating the conversation in an uncivil manner. Similarly, the conversation partner who expects shorter pauses accuses the other of rude behavior by remaining silent or withholding talk.[22]

In addition to considering culture, regional and ethnic co-cultures, gender, and generation to interpret whether an overlap is an interruption, or vice versa, we must consider the context or situation (e.g., a casual conversation or a formal interview). We must also consider our conversation partner's usual communication style (e.g., the high-involvement style, which condones overlaps, or the high-considerateness style, which does not) and how both speakers' styles work together.[23] Furthermore, "it takes two to tango" is an idiom that can be used to describe whether an utterance is an overlap or an interruption. Meaning is made and shared by the combination of both conversation partners rather than their words alone. One person must stop speaking while another continues for a linguistic strategy to be labeled an "interruption." Therefore, the claim that men interrupt women more than women interrupt men is based on the behavior of the women who are interrupted as well as the men who do the interrupting. It's plausible to assume that in many situations, men believe that women are of equal status and therefore have the same power they do to compete for the floor.[24]

Although there isn't a definitive solution to the problem of women being interrupted by men, there are several actions that both women and men can take to ensure that women are heard. A woman who believes that unnecessary interruptions are being used as a power move can refuse to acknowledge the interruptions and continue speaking, or she can firmly assert, "Stop interrupting me."[25] Similarly, if we hear a woman being repeatedly interrupted, we can interrupt the interrupter (e.g., "I'd like to hear what she has to say").[26] We can also repeat a woman's idea after she is interrupted and make sure that she receives credit for her ideas.[27] Additionally, men can make a conscious effort to refrain from interrupting women and be aware of when they begin to dominate conversations. Men should also hire more women in positions of power, "so that hearing women speaking—without interruption—becomes normal in their places of business."[28]

## PRIVILEGE, PATRIARCHY, AND EVERYDAY INCIVILITY

Diane Ragsdale, an African-American female, was a Dallas city councilwoman when Dallas police officers shot or wounded twenty-nine civilians. The victims included eighty-one-year-old crime watch volunteer David Horton and seventy-year-old Etta Collins, who called the police when she thought her home was being burglarized. Both Mr. Horton and Ms. Collins were African Americans, as were most of the civilians shot by the police. Councilwoman Ragsdale and others accused the Dallas police of targeting black citizens for years and demanded the firing of the chief of police (who eventually resigned). Ragsdale also blamed "institutional racism, the mode of thinking that when you rush into a poor black community, you shoot, you don't think."[29]

Although Ragsdale had the steadfast support of her constituents, she was often criticized about her communication style. Attorney T. A. Sneed blamed Ragsdale's confrontational and combative style as contributing to the blight of her district. Sneed suggested that her anger, unwillingness to negotiate, and the tendency for her to alienate those who were willing to compromise with her prevented improvements to her economically disadvantaged constituency. But Ragsdale's communication, as well as the communication styles of other African Americans on the Dallas City Council, resulted in advances for the city, such as a change in the Citizens' Police Review Board. In addition, a number of prominent local African Americans supported Ragsdale and her "confrontational" style.[30] Ragsdale argued that:

> I listen to people in my district, and I hear more than what they say. . . . I hear
> they are angry and frustrated and helpless, and I want everybody in this given
> city to know about those feelings. When I speak in a council meeting, I say
> what my constituents would say if they were there. And I say it exactly the
> way they would say it. That's why I get so mad. People elected me to speak for
> them, and I do.[31]

City leader Hugh Robinson proposed that people who disliked Ragsdale's confrontational style might not "understand the deep-rooted issues and frustrations involved" and that there "wouldn't be a need for some of the aggressiveness" if Dallas had addressed racial inequality a long time ago.[32] However, younger African Americans (such as T. A. Sneed) stated that Ragsdale and other black leaders, whose aggressive communication style inflamed tempers, should be replaced with more-conciliatory minority leaders.[33]

"Privilege" is evident in the criticism of Diane Ragsdale's communication style. "Privilege refers to any advantage that is unearned, exclusive, and socially conferred."[34] Some argue that rather than using the term *privilege*, we should use the term *advantage*, because privilege is less likely to change the thoughts and actions of others. *Privilege* concerns something that is deserved, while *advantage* concerns unearned characteristics, such as skin color and sexual preference. Furthermore, asking ourselves "What unearned advantages do I have that others do not?" is easier to answer than asking ourselves about our privilege.[35]

Recall that those with power get to choose discourse that is considered civil and that this discourse can support "special interests, institutions of privilege, and structures of domination." Diane Ragsdale claimed that she spoke on behalf of and in the same manner as her constituents, but she was criticized for her use of the African-American communication style. This illustrates that the unearned advantage associated with a white communication style is that it is considered correct and/or natural; therefore, all other styles deviate from what is thought of as civil.[36]

## White Privilege

On July 7, 2016, five Dallas police officers were killed by a gunman who sought revenge for the shooting of black men by law enforcement. In light of the violence, the annual Dallas Festival of Ideas included a forum on criminal justice to foster respect and understanding between racial and ethnic groups. Participants met in small groups and one-on-one sessions that fostered intimacy and the recognition of the necessity of connecting with, and feeling responsible for, one's community. The forum wasn't about policy; instead, it was about changing hearts and minds and creating a safe space in which to share ideas and experiences.

The result was sessions that ran overtime as participants shared their stories and attempted to understand the stories of others. Anton Lucky, a participant who works for a group focused on criminal justice reform, said that people of different races can only move forward when they communicate honestly, and other participants similarly suggested that we must stop thinking in terms of "they and us" and instead, think in terms of "we." The forum participants illustrated respect, restraint, and responsibility, and "the results were painfully honest. Tears were shed, previous biases were admitted, [and] the realities of white privilege were acknowledged."[37]

*White privilege* concerns having an unearned advantage that is exclusive to this skin color (such as the advantage of being perceived by police as law-abiding). White privilege is evidenced when we realize that white people hold most positions of power and that our culture defines "white" as the standard for people in general. For instance, we use the term "non-white," which tells us what others are *not* rather than what they *are*. Similarly, "ethnic studies" departments at universities typically are group-specific (e.g., African-American studies and Latin-American studies); this label suggests that some people are ethnic and others are not.[38]

"White" is also viewed as "of American descent"; white people can ignore their race/skin color, and white people tend to be unaware of white privilege.[39] White privilege is "something you would barely notice unless it were suddenly taken away—or unless it had never applied to you in the first place."[40] Examples of white privilege include growing up with role models with your skin color in education and mass media, and being able to move into a "nice" neighborhood without worrying about being accepted. Another example of white privilege includes not being perceived as someone who achieved success because an opportunity was taken away from a white person who "deserved it." Still another example of white privilege is not having to experience a defining life moment when you realize that your skin color alone causes others to hate you.[41]

There is disagreement as to whether white privilege exists. Some contend that not all white people are privileged; that is, rich and well-connected. But the "privilege" in white privilege refers to unearned and socially conferred advantages rather than to wealth and status. Others maintain that white privilege is used by those who want to shame white people by labeling them as "racist," or to "guilt" white people into silence (e.g., "Check your privilege at the door"). But pointing out white privilege, which very often is "unintentional, unconscious, and uncomfortable to recognize but easy to take for granted," isn't the same as accusing them of being racist and need not silence white people.[42] In particular:

> A reminder to acknowledge one's privilege is just a reminder to be aware— aware that you might not be able to fully understand someone else's experiences, or that the assumptions you were brought up with may be blinding you to certain concerns. That awareness is the key to any sort of civil discussion, about race, class, or anything else.[43]

White privilege enables those in power to perceive that non-European-based communication styles are inferior to the style used by white people. Think about how this view of communication can affect everyday incivility.

Studies illustrate that "affect, emotion, and passion are considered positive attributes of the [African-American] communication process because they indicate sincere interest and seriousness toward the material or subject matter, while objectivity and unemotional responses indicate insincerity and lack of connection."[44] Returning to our earlier example, words such as "confrontational, combative," and "aggressive" were used to describe Diane Ragsdale's communication style and her communication was judged as being inappropriate. White privilege is evident in this example because the communication style of the dominant white culture is perceived to be ideal.[45] Since Ragsdale didn't make use of the communication style of those in power, she was thought of as an uncivil firebrand.

## Male Privilege and Patriarchy

Barbara Barres was discouraged from attending MIT as a young woman just because she was female. Nonetheless, she was admitted to the university and performed so well that one of her professors insisted that her boyfriend must have solved a difficult math problem that her male classmates could not.[46] Barres eventually earned both an MA and a PhD, and is currently a professor of neurobiology, developmental biology, neurology, and neurological sciences.

In 1997, Barres began living as a man, changed his name to Ben, and changed his sex at age forty. Soon after transitioning, Barres recognized that others treated him differently. For example, a colleague once said that Barres's work was much better than his sister's. Barres also asserts that he's treated with more respect compared to when he was a woman and that he "can even complete a whole sentence without being interrupted by a man."[47] Additionally, he has conversations with others that would not occur if he were female, such as the one in which a male surgeon told him that "he had never met a woman surgeon who was as good as a man."[48] Furthermore, Barres contends that as a man, he is listened to more carefully and his authority is rarely questioned.[49]

Barres isn't the only female-to-male (FTM) transgender person who is taken more seriously by others when identifying as male. In *Just One of the Guys?*, sociologist Kristen Schilt interviewed many FTM transgender people who had similar experiences. One interviewee explained that when he identified as a woman, colleagues constantly questioned her credibility, even when she presented facts and other informational material. However, as a man, he doesn't have to defend himself and colleagues automatically write down his opinions during meetings. Another interviewee described how her "aggressive" personality was viewed negatively by others in her place of work. But now that he's perceived as a man, colleagues tell him that they love his "take-charge attitude."[50]

Both Ben Barres and Kristen Schilt believe that women are negatively affected by stereotypes and invisible bias. Barres suggests that women often don't realize that they're treated differently than men because they experience life only as a woman and it's all they know. He maintains that people are blind to their inherent biases, and from his experiences as a man, he asserts that "many men are unconscious of the privileges that come with being male."[51] Schilt also contends that gender stereotypes privilege masculinity.[52]

Male privilege affects our everyday interactions with others. Gender roles teach us that masculinity includes physical strength, authority, competitiveness, emotional distance, and independence. Gender roles also teach us that femininity includes physical attractiveness and being emotional, nurturing, and cooperative.[53] Girls are taught to resist interrupting, listen very carefully to others, take turns, and refrain from cursing. Boys are not.[54] Our culture rewards conformity to these roles and punishes those who deviate from them, which in turn upholds *patriarchy*, defined as "a social structure in which men have and maintain the dominant power."[55]

Not only do men have the most powerful and highest-paying jobs in our society, they also have access to and hold positions in our most powerful social institutions, such as law, medicine, higher education, and government. "A male-dominated society . . . means that men feel they have power or authority over women in personal situations as well as the workplace."[56] In fact, "the sense of entitlement and superiority that underlies male privilege is so entrenched that men don't have to know what they're doing" in terms of behavior that casts women as inferior.[57]

Male privilege is evident in communication in that men tend to dominate conversations. Additionally, male privilege allows men to deny the perceptions and interpretations of women's life experiences.[58] The influence of power, privilege, and patriarchy are evidenced in three types of everyday incivility: microaggressions, mansplaining, and politically correct communication.

## MICROAGGRESSIONS, MANSPLAINING, AND POLITICALLY CORRECT COMMUNICATION

Sean Blanda is an author, conference speaker, and former editor in chief and director of 99u.com, a Webby Award–winning website. In an online article titled "The 'Other Side' Is Not Dumb," Blanda writes that we tend to perceive those who don't share our beliefs as backwards and less intelligent than we are. We also have a tendency to mock, laugh at, and dismiss the "other side" and their opinions. This is true for people who hold what we consider to be "radical beliefs," as well as those who have sincere and well-thought-out reasons for an opposing opinion (or at least have reasons just as good as ours).[59]

Blanda contends that "this is not a 'political correctness' issue. It's a fundamental rejection of the possibility to consider that the people who don't feel the same way you do might be right." He argues that we should consider every controversial opinion or disagreement with others with the realistic possibility that we might actually be wrong. He also maintains that we can have real discussions about such opinions and disagreements only after we understand the reasons held by the "other side." Blanda further asserts that "we won't truly progress as individuals until we make an honest effort to understand those that are not like us. And you won't convince anyone to feel the way you do if you don't respect their position and opinions."[60]

In effect, Blanda is making a case for civility. He asks us to respect others' opinions, refrain from mocking and dismissing the other side, and to take responsibility for understanding the other side's reasons and consider the possibility that we may be wrong. The ability to concede that "the 'other side' isn't dumb" is particularly difficult when it comes to controversial topics, such as privilege and patriarchy. It may also be difficult when you read about three additional topics that concern power, patriarchy, and privilege: microaggressions, mansplaining, and politically correct communication. However, even an attempt to understand these topics (whether good or bad) is a first step toward creating a more civil world. And "attempting to understand" doesn't necessarily mean we must eventually agree that microaggressions and mansplaining exist, or that political correctness is a way to limit our freedom of speech. Lawyer and columnist Christine M. Flowers expresses this viewpoint when she writes:

> I'm sure that people who like to feel victimized are outraged by my failure to respect their victimhood. It is a powerful weapon, this need to make others feel guilty about possibly causing pain. . . . I will honor their lifestyles, their beliefs, their political affiliations, and even their right to hate me. That is the essence of America. But I will not be forced to legitimize their fears . . . 'Let me never fall into the vulgar mistake of dreaming that I am persecuted whenever I am contradicted.'[61]

## Microaggressions

Danielle Brooks, an African-American actor on the television show, *Orange is the New Black*, showed her ticket to the gate agent as all passengers do before they board an aircraft. Brooks later tweeted that the gate agent looked at her as if she had never flown before and said, "You're in First Class; lucky you!" Brooks interpreted this situation as an example of a microaggression in which the gate agent was making a condescending comment based on a racial stereotype. Those involved in the Twitterverse both mocked and supported Brooks's complaint. One Twitter user wrote that the gate agent was just doing her job and trying to be friendly, albeit in an awkward manner. In an online blog, another person wrote that Brooks didn't provide details and didn't complain to the airline, which proves that the event was probably "completely made up, highly exaggerated, a misunderstanding, or completely delusional."

Others supported Brooks's interpretation that the event was an example of a microaggression. An older white male wrote that the gate agent's comment is another way of saying, "Wow, we don't see many of your kind in First Class!" He additionally wrote that no one ever tells him that he is lucky to fly First Class because he's old and white, and that the gate agent made an unfounded assumption that a young black woman is "lucky" to fly First Class. Still another writer responded that any time we're surprised at something, the implication is that whatever happened isn't expected or is unusual. Therefore, the gate agent's surprise at seeing Brooks with a First Class ticket is a microaggression and it implied that Brooks somehow didn't belong in First Class.[62]

*Microaggressions* are defined as "brief and commonplace verbal, behavioral, and environmental indignities, whether intentional or unintentional, that communicate hostile, derogatory, or negative racial, gender, sexual orientation, and religious slights and insults to the target person or group."[63] Additional examples of microaggressions include the questions, "Is she yours?" uttered by strangers to a white woman and her black daughter; "Do you speak English?," asked by partygoers to a Hispanic college student raised in Dallas, Texas; the comment, "But you look so Aryan . . . you so would have made it through the Holocaust!," expressed by a non-Jew; and the observation, "But you look pretty," voiced by a straight male to a lesbian acquaintance.[64] Such comments and questions are based on implicit biases and stereotypical thinking, and those who commit microaggressions are typically unaware that their comments are demeaning and suggest something is not "normal."

While one microaggression may not have much impact, the cumulative impact of microaggressions that occur during a lifetime can cause major detrimental consequences. Although they may appear harmless, microaggressions cause low self-esteem; anger, frustration, and emotional turmoil; physical health problems; low work productivity and problem-solving ability; and contribute to a hostile campus or work environment. Microaggressions also trigger what social scientists call *attributional ambiguity*, which refers to the inability to make sense of a situation. In terms of microaggressions, attributional ambiguity makes it difficult to determine whether a comment is actually demeaning or based on stereotypes. This causes targets to question their interpretations and consider whether to address the perceived infractions and those who utter them. Unfortunately, dealing with this type of attributional ambiguity depletes or diverts energy that should be used to adapt and function in society rather than question perceptions, manage difficult emotions, and decide whether or not to confront a perpetrator.[65] Attributional ambiguity additionally causes some to perceive the targets of microaggressions as being too sensitive and/or defensive, and that microaggressions themselves are trivial and banal.[66]

Microaggressions also reflect societal assumptions about who has power and who is "normal." The differing interpretations of what may or may not be considered microaggressions are based on our life experience, and since each person's life experience is different, it's difficult to say whose perceptions and interpretations reflect "reality" and whose do not. Those in power have the ability to define and impose their reality on groups with less power, and it is those in power who often suggest that microaggressions are "pure nonsense" and that targets of microaggressions are "overly sensitive."

Others suggest that targets of microaggressions buy into a "culture of victimization" in which individuals "reject the idea that words can't hurt, that slights should be brushed off, and that even overt insults should be ignored."[67] Some believe that those who condemn implicit and unintentional slights do so because (ironically) they live in a society that is egalitarian and tolerant. However, those who contend that microaggressions are real and shouldn't be dismissed argue that people in power typically don't perceive the plight of marginalized groups or understand the impact of microaggressions that occur over the course of a lifetime.[68] The conundrum of microaggressions can be explained in regard to "confirmation bias," which occurs "when people would like a certain idea/concept to be true, [and] they end up believing it to be true." Confirmation bias also "suggests that we don't perceive circumstances objectively."[69] Writing in terms of racial microaggressions, ethicist Jack Marshall claims that:

> There are real racial microaggressions, and there are innocent interactions that race-baiters and grievance collectors complain about to place whites on the defensive. Too many social justice warriors are unable to make reasonable distinctions between the two, because confirmation bias leads them to the default position of being offended. For their part, critics of the race-grievance industry can't recognize real microaggressions, because of their *own* confirmation bias.[70]

We can work to overcome (mis)perceptions and (mis)interpretations associated with microaggressions by being willing to explore the possibility that we hold implicit biases and that we may act in a biased manner (even if unintentionally). In addition, we can be open to the idea that disempowered groups may have an accurate perception of their reality since it concerns *their* everyday life experiences, not ours. If we believe we are the target of a microaggression, we can withhold judgement and realize that a question such as "What country are you from?" may be based on a desire to learn about others rather than to "other" them. We can also seek social support and validation from our "group(s)" when faced with someone who denies communicating a microaggression and blames us for being oversensitive. Furthermore, targets of microaggressions must learn to deal effectively with the stress they produce by making use of coping skills, such as creating strong group identities, developing self-esteem, and by being resilient.[71] Finally, we can educate those who we perceive as communicating a microaggression by letting them know that in certain circumstances and among certain people, their comments may be interpreted as offensive.[72]

## Mansplaining

As author Rebecca Solnit prepared to leave a party, the host asked her to stay. After a short while, he said, "So, I hear you've written a couple of books." Solnit replied that she had, and in a somewhat patronizing voice, the host asked, "And what are they about?" Solnit began to tell the host about her seventh and latest book, which concerned Eadweard Muybridge, a Victorian-era photographer who captured movement on film. The host interrupted Solnit to ask "And have you heard about the *very important* Muybridge book that came out this year?"

Solnit was surprised that she had missed a book about Muybridge that had been published almost simultaneously with hers. The host had a smug look on his face as he informed Solnit in an authoritative manner about the very important book. At one point, Solnit's friend entered the conversation, and after a few moments, tried to interrupt the host to say that he was describing Solnit's book. However, the host continued on in a commanding manner, only realizing that he was talking about Solnit's book after hearing "That's her book" at least three times. He turned ashen as he realized that Solnit was the author of the very important book that he hadn't even read (but spoke about, based on a *New York Times* book review he had read a few months earlier).[73]

Solnit later wrote about this conversation in a 2008 essay titled "Men Explain Things to Me."[74] The term *mansplaining* was coined soon thereafter. Simply put, mansplaining occurs when "a man condescendingly lectures a woman on the basics of a topic about which he knows very little, under the mistaken assumption that she knows even less."[75] Solnit wrote that:

> Every woman knows what I'm talking about. It's the presumption that makes it hard, at times, for any woman in any field; that keeps women from speaking up and from being heard when they dare; that crushes young women into silence by indicating, the way harassment on the street does, that this is not their world. It trains us in self-doubt and self-limitation just as it exercises men's unsupported confidence.[76]

Mansplaining occurs when a more-powerful (male) person ignores, invalidates, and/or explains the life experience and perceptions of a less-powerful (female) person.[77] It occurs in politics, in the workplace, and in everyday life.[78] Mansplaining is experienced by women when men presume that their superiority, authority, and greater knowledge of a topic gives them the right to dictate to women.[79] For example, mansplaining occurred when a woman was told that her husband should be on the phone to obtain quotes for new windows and doors because doors are "tricky" (the woman is an architect and the sole owner of the home). Mansplaining was also evident when a man told a woman who worked at the Goddard Space Flight Center that he'd read the schematics because she obviously could not (and the woman subsequently pointed to where her signature was located on the legend).

Some argue that accusing men of mansplaining is a silencing tactic used by feminists against men who disagree with feminist orthodoxy.[80] Others contend that mansplaining isn't real because it only happens when a man acts like a "jerk"; that is, explains something authoritatively (and "jerks" aren't only males). Similarly, men sometimes use the term *womansplain* to demonstrate that women can also explain things to men in a condescending manner. Nevertheless, the term *mansplaining* was created to go beyond mere condescension; it was invented to uncover "the privilege men have to assume that they are right, that women are wrong, and that their responsibility is to explain something to the poor woman who just can't understand it."[81] Additionally, while "jerks" are everywhere, it doesn't mean that mansplaining is nonexistent. In fact, mansplaining is described as a form of *everyday* incivility in which women "are presumed ignorant, powerless, or just plain wrong because men know better."[82]

Mansplaining is thought by some to be so ubiquitous that the Swedish trade union Unionen set up a hotline to raise awareness of its occurrence. The hotline, open to women and men, allows both sexes to report instances of mansplaining at work and to seek advice regarding how to speak up during a mansplaining episode; how to help females whose comments are ignored; and how to address colleagues and clients who only speak to male employees. Although the hotline was developed to "visualize suppression techniques and talk about them" regardless of a target's gender, negative responses to the hotline were posted on the Unionen Facebook page. In response to the word "mansplaining," one man wrote "How would women react if you used words like 'old biddy chat' or 'female whining'?" Another man posted, "Just what we need in society, more polarization." However, one woman wrote, "Good initiative. Judging by the comments, it seems quite a lot of men feel this is aimed at them, so it shows how much this kind of work is needed."[83]

Mansplaining is said to be based on the same assumptions that cause women to be less frequently promoted or hired for jobs in male-dominated areas; that is, ingrained assumptions about the superiority of men's knowledge and opinions compared to women's. Therefore, we can't "fix" the problem by advising women to be more assertive.[84] We can, however, advise those with privilege to allow people who are marginalized to speak and be heard; acknowledge the lived experiences of those who differ from us in terms of gender, race, etc.; and pay attention to the assumptions we hold about the person we're talking with (e.g., it's not wrong to want to share our knowledge with others, but it's wrong to assume that our conversation partner doesn't know the subject or isn't smart enough to understand it).[85]

Workplace advice columnist Rex Hupke suggests that before a man interrupts or explains something to a female colleague, he should pause and ask himself, "Am I about to mansplain?" Hupke further comments that it takes no more than a pause of three seconds to prevent a man from demeaning a coworker, regardless of claims and excuses about not giving in to politically correct culture, promoting men's rights, etc.[86] But in the end, the only way to stop and prevent mansplaining is to "change the narrative that sets up male contributions as superior in the first place."[87]

## Politically Correct Communication

Near the end of the fall 2015 semester, Harvard University's Office of Equity, Diversity, and Inclusion distributed "Holiday Placemats for Social Justice" to students in the freshman dining halls and in a number of upper-level dining halls. The placemats were meant to facilitate the discussion of politics and social issues with family members during winter break. Topics included Yale student activism, Islamophobia and refugees, and police killings of African Americans. Another topic, changing the title of "House Master," specifically related to Harvard and Harvard students:

> **House Master Title:** "Why did they change the name? What does a House Master have to do with slavery? It's not related to that at all."
> **Response:** "For some, the term *master*, historically used to describe stewardship of a group of people (such as a house), is reminiscent of slave masters and the legacy of slavery. The title, 'House Master,' is no longer actively associated with its historical antecedents, nor is it used to address House Masters. Given [that] the name is offensive to groups of people, it doesn't seem onerous to change it. The mastery of a subject is an understandable use of the word. However, within our cultural and historical context, implying mastery of people feels inappropriate. There are other words we could use that other institutions have already adopted."[88]

Negative responses to the placemats appeared in the *Harvard Crimson* and elsewhere soon after their distribution. The *Crimson* staff specifically took offense at the elimination of the title "House Master," even though the dean of the college said that the change "makes sense on many levels" (but failed to explain why). Staff members wrote that the elimination of the House Master title wouldn't have any effect on race relations at Harvard, and rather than focus on a title that has no connection with slavery (negating the claim on the placemat—that the title at one time had a meaning associated with slavery), administrators should instead focus on racial inclusivity on campus. The *Crimson* staff members asserted that eliminating the House Master title could lead to changes of anything at which others take offense.[89] Idrees M. Kahloon, a *Crimson* editorial executive, wrote a subsequent article in which he expressed dismay at the "seemingly official and definitive 'responses'" and the "misguided decision to change the House Master title."[90] He also argued that:

> Presenting unglorified talking points not only wrongly attempts to stifle debate, but also stands in stark contradiction to the mission of the College to transform students "with exposure to new ideas, new ways of understanding, and new ways of knowing." Admissions officers often spin hagiographies of Harvard's dining halls and the conversations we have in them as the most formative portion of a Harvard education. Yet that is exactly what is threatened by such recklessness.[91]

Even Harvard alumni weighed in, with one alumnus writing that the Harvard placemats exemplify "political correctness" run amok and that "the placemats violate not just Harvard's values and mission but those of higher education. This is indoctrination."[92]

Harvard quickly moved to end the distribution of the placemats and offered a letter of apology to students. In the letter, the dean of student life and the dean of freshmen wrote that "academic freedom is central to all that Harvard stands for. To suggest that there is only one point of view . . . runs counter to our educational goals."[93]

## The Meaning of "Politically Correct" Communication

*Political correctness* means different things to different people, and being described as "politically correct" can be interpreted as an insult or as a compliment. History professor Jonathan Zimmerman contends that there are two types of political correctness. "Political Correctness 1" (PC1) focuses on using words that help us to communicate across differences because they reflect respect and decency.[94] PC1 entails "observing common decencies in the way we treat each other" and fosters civil communication.[95] Some believe that the label "political correctness" has been "misconstrued as censorship," but political correctness can be characterized as the careful, intentional language used by people who believe in basic human decency and equal rights . . . It's about tolerance and respect."[96] This was the goal of the

Harvard placemats: to provide a framework so that students could communicate across differences with loved ones.

On the other hand, "Political Correctness 2" (PC2) constrains communication because it imposes "liberal political orthodoxies" and maintains that there are right and wrong words we use when interacting with others.[97] PC2 is often considered a way to restrict free speech that "silences dissent for fear of giving offense to specific interest groups."[98] Those who define political correctness on the basis of PC2 may believe that "they can't say what they think, or even entertain views outside the boundaries laid down by elites."[99] This is the meaning of political correctness held by those who viewed the Harvard placemats as a means to indoctrinate students and stifle debate. Another way of distinguishing between PC1 and PC2 is that PC1 is based on respect, restraint, and responsibility (e.g., refusing to use derogatory terms associated with race, sex, and ethnicity) and PC2 is based on power and control.

*The Power of Words*

Whether or not one believes that political correctness focuses on equality or indoctrination, we cannot deny the power of words to shape thoughts and feelings. For example, what do you envision when you read the italicized words in the following sentence: "*An undeveloped fertilized egg* doesn't describe a baby any more than a seed describes a rosebush." How might the overall terminology used in this analogy influence your thoughts? Whether you agree or disagree with the analogy, you can see that words have the power to influence beliefs and behavior in our conversations with others.

Suppose you find yourself in a discussion about abortion. Would you use the label "pro-life" or "pro-choice" to describe yourself? How might you react upon hearing the word *murder* versus *prevention*? Would you use labels such as "fetus" or "zygote," or would you use labels such as "baby" or "pre-born child"? Even if you've never engaged in a discussion about abortion, you can probably understand how the phrases "eliminating a product of conception" and "fighting for the rights of the unborn" can influence thought.

The idea that words have the power to influence thought and behavior is the reason why some attempt to promote equality by changing word choice. For instance, for much of the twentieth century, those in power chose the word "Negro" to describe African Americans. In an attempt to wrest the power of words from white males, African Americans in the Civil Rights Movement sought to redefine themselves.[100] This struggle for self-definition is evidenced in a speech delivered by civil rights activist Stokely Carmichael to students at Morgan State College in 1967:

> The need of a free people is to be able to define their own terms and have those terms recognized by their oppressors. It is also the first need that all oppressors

must suspend. And so for white people to be allowed to define us by calling us Negroes, which means apathetic, lazy, stupid, and all those other things, it is for us to accept those definitions. We must define what we are and move from our definitions and tell them to recognize what we are. [101]

Similarly, the power of words is also evidenced in the sentence, "Christopher Columbus discovered America." Reflect upon this idea for a moment; how might the word *discovered* influence thought? This terminology suggests that Native Americans were invisible or insignificant until a European recognized their existence. Another example of the ability of words to influence thought concerns the term *minority group*. How does this label subtly affect our thoughts? Some people believe that *minority group* suggests insignificance, or something that is negligible. [102] Will US citizens of European ancestry accept this label when people of color outnumber whites in the year 2050? [103] In all, "Language is power. When you turn 'torture' into 'enhanced interrogation,' or murdered children into 'collateral damage,' you break the power of language to convey meaning, to make us see, feel, and care. But it works both ways. You can use the power of words to bury meaning or to excavate it." [104]

Whether or not we take a positive or negative view of political correctness, the power of words to influence thought and behavior should cause us to carefully consider our choice of words. There are those who contend that "Sticks and stones may break my bones, but words will never hurt me." However, everyday uncivil communication can contribute to even greater harms on a societal level. Specifically:

Hitler's "Final Solution" appeared reasonable once the Jews were successfully labeled by the Nazis as subhumans, as "parasites, vermin, and bacilli." The segregation and suppression of blacks in the United States was justified once they were considered "chattel" and "inferiors." The subjugation of "American Indians" was defensible since they were defined as "barbarians and savages." . . . [And] as long as adult women are "chicks, girls, dolls, babes, and ladies," their status in society will remain "inferior." [105]

## SUMMARY AND CONCLUSION

The ability to define what constitutes civil and uncivil behavior belongs to those who are powerful. Civil communication can be criticized as reflecting and maintaining a power hierarchy, particularly when the same behavior is prized when associated with the male gender (e.g., an "assertive" communication style) but is criticized when associated with the female gender (e.g., a "strident" communication style). It's important to note that we can't tell who is more or less powerful by examining the communication strategies used by conversation partners. Specifically, giving orders via a direct command or hinting via an indirect statement are strategies sometimes used by those with power and sometimes by those with little power. Moreover, interrupting others has different possible meanings and interpretations that don't necessarily correlate with who has power or who does not.

"Privilege" refers to any advantage that is unearned, exclusive, and socially conferred. "White privilege" concerns having an unearned advantage that is exclusive to this skin color. This type of privilege enables those in power to perceive that their communication style is ideal, while non-European-based communication styles are perceived as inferior to the style used by white people. The influence of power, privilege, and patriarchy are evidenced in three types of everyday incivility: microaggressions, mansplaining, and politically correct communication.

Microaggressions are brief and commonplace verbal, behavioral, and environmental indignities, whether intentional or unintentional, that demean a person or group of people based on their race, gender, sexual orientation, and/or religious beliefs. While one microaggression may not have much impact, the cumulative impact of microaggressions that occur during a lifetime can cause major detrimental consequences. Mansplaining occurs when a more-powerful (male) person ignores, invalidates, and/or explains the life experience and perceptions of a less-powerful (female) person. Political correctness can refer to the use of words that help us to communicate across differences because they reflect respect and decency. Political correctness can also refer to the imposition of liberal political orthodoxies and a restriction on freedom of speech. Whether or not one believes that political correctness focuses on equality or indoctrination, we cannot deny the power of words to shape thoughts and feelings.

---

**Box 5-1**
**Strategies for Change: Power and Everyday Incivility**

- We shouldn't automatically characterize direct or indirect communication as uncivil behavior. The perception and interpretation of direct and indirect communication styles as civil or uncivil is influenced by norms associated with culture, region, ethnicity, gender, and generation.
- We shouldn't judge interruptions as uncivil because "overlaps" that occur while someone else is talking may be meant to show enthusiasm and interest rather than to demonstrate power by taking over a conversation.

- Instead of labeling a group of people as "uncivil," we should consider that they may be adhering to conversational norms that differ from our own.
- If we believe we are a target of a microaggression, we can withhold judgement and realize that a question such as "What country are you from?" may be based on a desire to learn about others rather than to "other" them. We can seek social support and validation from our "group(s)" when faced with someone who denies communicating a microaggression and blames us for being overly sensitive. We can educate those whom we perceive as communicating a microaggression by letting them know that in certain circumstances and among certain people, their comments may be interpreted as offensive.
- To combat mansplaining, we can advise those with privilege to allow people who are marginalized to speak and be heard, and acknowledge the lived experiences of those who differ from us in terms of gender, race, etc.
- Our knowledge of the power of words should cause us to carefully consider our choice of words. Whether or not one believes that political correctness focuses on equality or indoctrination, we cannot deny the power of words to shape thoughts, feelings, and behavior.

*Part II*

# Everyday Incivility in Contexts

## Chapter Six

# Everyday Incivility at Work

> *When you're going into an employment environment that looks pretty scary, it is easy to lose your moral compass, your decency, your sense of civility, and your sense of community.* [1]
> —Henry Rollins, musician, actor, writer, publishing company and record label owner

When Ryan Block's wife phoned Comcast to cancel their bundle subscription, she wasn't prepared for the ensuing conversation. A "customer retention specialist" continued to aggressively repeat his questions despite the answers she offered and tried to get her to remain with Comcast. Mr. Block was listening to the conversation on speakerphone when his wife handed him the phone because she was no longer willing to continue the conversation. Block spoke to the "condescending and unhelpful" rep, and about ten minutes into the conversation, he began to record the interaction with his other phone. Block provided the rep with a number of reasons why he and his wife wished to cancel, but the rep continued to pepper Block with the same questions:

"You don't want something that works?"

"So you're not interested in the fastest Internet in the country?"

"I'm really ashamed to see you go to something that can't give you what we can."

Block remained calm and stopped giving the service rep reasons for discontinuing his subscription. His response to further questions was, "I'm declining to state; can you please go to the next question." The rep then suggested that since Block was no longer willing to provide an explanation, he should go to a Comcast store to cancel his service. The rep further commented, "You've been a Comcast customer for nine years . . . clearly the service is working great for you . . . All of a sudden you're moving and something is making you want to change. What's making you do that?"

Block replied, "That's none of your business. Your business is to disconnect us."[2]

Block's Comcast service was eventually canceled and he posted online his recorded conversation with the service representative. The recording went viral, and the transcript of the conversation was published in various print and online outlets. Dave Lieber, a consumer watchdog and columnist for the *Dallas Morning News*, described the Comcast service representative as "one of the rudest, most relentless customer retention specialists in the history of American consumerism."[3] The Comcast senior vice president of customer experience subsequently apologized and wrote that Comcast was embarrassed about the rep's unacceptable behavior. Comcast also stressed that the behavior was inconsistent with the training received by the customer service representatives. The Comcast vice president also stated that "we are using this very unfortunate experience to reinforce how important it is to always treat our customers with the utmost respect."[4]

Although this may be an extreme example of customer "disservice," it illustrates incivility in the workplace. The customer service representative failed to demonstrate respect, restraint, or responsibility. In addition, according to the Comcast vice president, the rep violated a company norm to always treat customers with respect. In terms of the Communication Competence model, this means that the rep failed to act in an appropriate manner. Problems such as poor customer service, managers who don't respond to employee complaints, and customers who berate employees are just a few of the many instances of workplace incivility that occur each day. In this chapter, you'll read about the characterization and types of incivility that occur on the job, the causes and consequences of workplace incivility, and strategies to cope with uncivil communication in our places of employment.

## CHARACTERISTICS OF INCIVILITY AT WORK

When top executives at Google wanted to find the secret to building more-productive teams, they spent a number of years interviewing hundreds of employees and analyzing statistical data for what they labeled "Project Aristotle." The executives believed that the best teams were comprised of the best people, or at least those who shared similar characteristics. Project Aristotle began when its researchers reviewed over fifty years of academic studies that focus on how teams work. They analyzed the Google teams based on the study results and looked for patterns; for example, whether teammates socialized outside of the office, had the same hobbies, possessed the same educational backgrounds, etc. Surprisingly, no patterns emerged and the data revealed that a combination of personality characteristics, backgrounds, or skills made no difference in influencing team productivity. While reviewing the academic studies, Project Aristotle researchers continued to come across findings about group norms, and subsequently spent more than a year combing through their data and looking for descriptions of "unwritten rules." The Project Aristotle team concluded that Google's team productivity could be improved by understanding and influencing group norms. However, they needed to discover which norms matter most.

At this point, Google's research identified dozens of norms but found no clear patterns; sometimes a norm associated with an effective team contrasted sharply with a norm in another equally effective team. Project Aristotle researchers then focused on a study that revealed that productive teams shared two characteristics: Its members spoke for roughly the same amount of time (i.e., no one dominated the conversation); and the members listened well and empathized by focusing on nonverbal communication (tone of voice, expression, etc.). These characteristics form the basis of what psychologists label "psychological safety," which describes a group climate based on mutual respect, trust, and the knowledge that members can speak up without being humiliated. While Project Aristotle found additional group norms that are critical for success—for example, having clear goals and a culture of dependability—psychological safety is the most vital component of making a team work.[5]

Project Aristotle illustrates that productive teams are less a matter of who is on a team than about how team members communicate with each other. Successful teams are comprised of members who contribute to a conversation equally and respect others' emotions. Negative consequences that affect employees, management, and the organization itself may result when team members don't have a sense of psychological safety. Furthermore, a sense of psychological safety will diminish, if not disappear completely, if workplace incivility robs employees of their human dignity.[6]

## Definition of Workplace Incivility

In terms of the workplace, incivility is defined as "low-intensity deviant behavior with ambiguous intent to harm the target, in violation of workplace norms for mutual respect."[7] Similar to a non-contextual and general definition of incivility, three important features of the workplace definition are norms, intent, and intensity.

Most organizations have *norms* for appropriate behavior on the job and often these are spelled out in civility codes, corporate etiquette policies, and/ or codes of ethics.[8] These civility, etiquette, and ethics codes specify what type of civil behavior is expected of employees and members of professional organizations. It doesn't matter whether we work for a company that manufactures semiconductors, peanut butter, or clothing, civility codes govern workplace communication.

In addition to norms, a second important feature of workplace incivility concerns ambiguity regarding the *intent* to harm others. It may not be clear to a target, observer, or even an instigator whether or not an uncivil act is designed to harm others. The ambiguous intent of workplace incivility distinguishes it from other forms of mistreatment on the job. In particular, intentional misbehavior is described as belonging in the category of workplace "aggression," which includes the goal to hurt others and/or an organization.[9] Furthermore, "unlike instigators of aggression, instigators of incivility can easily deny or bury any intent, if present, in ignorance of the effect, in misinterpretation by the target, or in hypersensitivity of the target."[10] Similarly, intent also distinguishes workplace incivility from bullying in that bullying involves abusive behaviors that are intended to cause harm and distress to others.[11]

The third key feature associated with the definition of workplace incivility is *intensity*. Uncivil behaviors in organizations are distinguished from intense behaviors such as workplace violence (which entails physical assault) and "petty tyranny," which refers to more-intense behaviors exhibited by someone who abuses her/his position of authority.[12]

## Magnitude of Workplace Incivility

Just as everyday incivility is considered pervasive, workplace incivility is perceived as ubiquitous. Statistics reveal that 96 percent of Americans have experienced uncivil communication at their place of employment, and 50 percent experience uncivil behavior at least weekly.[13] According to the Weber Shandwick–Powell Tate 2013 poll, *Civility in America: Corporate Reputation Edition*, 53 percent of Americans believe that large corporations are uncivil, and 31 percent of Americans who predict that incivility will increase during the next few years blame corporate America.

Moreover, 61 percent (six in ten) of Americans refuse to purchase goods from businesses which treat them in an uncivil manner, and 43 percent advise others not to buy from these businesses because of their uncivil experience.[14] Workers who are members of a racial minority group, younger in age, and who are judged as "disagreeable" tend to experience incivility on the job more frequently than others.[15] In addition, women report more uncivil experiences than men, and those who instigate uncivil behavior are three times as likely to have more power and/or higher status than the target.[16] Similarly, employees who lack power are more often the recipients of uncivil communication.[17]

## Forms of Workplace Incivility and Incivility Spirals

Furious that her car was towed, ESPN reporter Britt McHenry berated a towing company clerk with profanity and disparaging remarks. What McHenry didn't realize was that her tirade was caught on the company's security camera. Someone posted the one-minute video on the Internet and the video went viral. McHenry said aggressively:

> I'm in the news, sweetheart, I will #$%!ing sue this place. Yep, that's all you care about, just taking people's money. With no education, no skillset, just wanted to clarify that. . . . Do you feel good about your job? So I could be a college dropout and do the same thing? Why, 'cause I have a brain and you don't? . . . Maybe if I was missing some teeth they would hire me, huh? 'Cause they look so stunning . . . 'Cause I'm on television and you're in a #$%!ing trailer, honey.[18]

After she paid her fee and began to leave, McHenry sneered, "Lose some weight, baby girl."

ESPN responded by suspending McHenry for one week. McHenry responded by apologizing via Twitter: "In an intense and stressful moment, I allowed my emotions to get the best of me and said some insulting and regrettable things. As frustrated as I was, I should always choose to be respectful and take the high road. I am so sorry for my actions and will learn from this mistake."[19]

McHenry engaged in personal attacks against an attendant who was following procedures created by senior management. It's understandable that someone might vent in anger after her or his car is towed, but targeting the clerk's employment, education, and appearance can be described as going beyond incivility and illustrating verbal abuse.[20] Even without the personal attacks, McHenry's communication was uncivil, as it included profanity, accusation, and an aggressive nonverbal tone of voice. In addition to those just mentioned, there are many other forms of uncivil behavior that take place in the workplace.

### Forms of Workplace Incivility

Management professors Christine Pearson and Christine Porath write that workplace incivility includes:[21]

- Taking credit for others' effort
- Passing blame for our own mistakes
- Checking e-mail or texting during a meeting
- Sending bad news through e-mail so that we don't have to face the recipient
- Talking down to others

- Not listening
- Spreading rumors about colleagues
- Setting others up for failure
- Not saying "please" or "thank you"
- Showing up late or leaving a meeting early with no explanation
- Belittling others' efforts
- Leaving snippy voice-mail messages
- Forwarding others' e-mail to make them look bad
- Making demeaning or derogatory remarks to someone
- Withholding information
- Failing to return phone calls or respond to e-mail
- Leaving a mess for others to clean up
- Consistently grabbing easy tasks while leaving difficult ones for others
- Shutting someone out of a network or team
- Paying little attention or showing little interest in others' opinions
- Acting irritated when someone asks for a favor
- Avoiding someone
- Taking resources that someone else needs
- Throwing temper tantrums

Additional forms of workplace incivility include making condescending and demeaning comments, overruling decisions without offering a reason, disrupting meetings, giving public reprimands, talking about coworkers behind their backs, not giving credit when credit is due, and giving dirty looks or other negative eye contact.[22] Similarly, walking out of meetings due to lack of interest, pointing out employee character flaws or personality quirks in front of others, reminding workers of their "role" and "title" in the organization, and pointing the finger at coworkers when problems occur, are also examples of incivility on the job.[23]

A final type of incivility on the job is workplace ostracism. Workplace ostracism occurs when an employee is left off an e-mail thread, isn't allowed to break into a conversation, is ignored when making suggestions, or discovers that s/he is not invited to a party. Surveys illustrate that workplace ostracism occurs more frequently than other forms of workplace incivility because organizations are less apt to recognize and respond to covert forms of uncivil behavior. Ostracism on the job differs from other forms of workplace incivility because it can threaten our innate need for belonging, which results in stress, poor health, and low psychological and physical well-being. Ostracism is less risky for perpetrators because it is ambiguous, subtle, and intangible and perpetrators can easily claim lack of intent. However, like other forms of workplace incivility, the perception of ostracism is dependent on the context, intent, and norms for appropriate behavior.[24] This means that "any two organizational members facing the same experience can interpret it quite differently, with one viewing it as ostracism and the other viewing it as something else or not noticing it all."[25]

In all, co-cultures such as culture, ethnicity, gender, and generation influence the perception of and the expression of uncivil communication in the workplace. In particular, a lack of knowledge about culturally based values and norms affects what is interpreted as on-the-job incivility. In fact, culture more strongly influences the expression and perception of workplace incivility than personality characteristics do. One study found that the strength of an individual's motivation to achieve and the ability to engage in direct conflict are less predictive of uncivil workplace behavior than is the influence of culture. Specifically, employees from more collectivist cultures are less likely to communicate in an uncivil manner compared to employees from more individualist cultures. Consequently, employees from more individualist cultures may be perceived as "uncivil" by employees from more collectivist cultures, even though the individualist employees communicate in a manner that is appropriate in their culture.[26] Culture also affects whether the perception of workplace behavior is considered uncivil. For example, Pakistan is described as a collectivist "honor culture" in which a person's worth is highly dependent on the evaluation of others. On the other hand, the United States is described as an individualist "dignity culture" in which a person's worth is based more on self-appraisal than other-appraisal. For Pakistanis, ostracism on the job is a type of direct aggression that may result in severe humiliation. Ostracism is also considered a serious assault on one's honor and self-worth. However, social exclusion in the United States is perceived an indirect act of aggression that doesn't significantly damage one's core sense of self. This is because people from the US culture place the utmost importance on self-generated rather than other-generated evaluations of worth.[27] Therefore, excluding a Pakistani employee may be considered a minor slight by a US manager; however, the Pakistani employee may perceive the exclusion as uncivil, threatening, and a situation in which the manager should intervene and take corrective action.

Gender and generation also affect the perception and expression of uncivil communication in the workplace. Women typically report higher levels of workplace incivility compared to men, while women who are members of sexual minority groups report even higher levels on incivility at work. Interestingly, men who are members of sexual minorities report the lowest levels of incivility on the job. This is possibly due to the power and social status that is associated with being male, which outweighs the potential for mistreatment based on sexual orientation.[28] In terms of working with members of various generations, researchers suggest that "the ever-accelerating pace of technological change may be minting a series of mini-generation gaps, with each group of children uniquely influenced by the tech tools available in their formative stages of development."[29] Similarly, each generation has their own norms that influence workplace behaviors.[30] For example, Boomers and members of Generation X complain that Millennials are uncivil because they demand constant praise and spend too much time using technology.[31] Members of Gen Z expect instant responses from those with whom they communicate and become impatient if they don't receive a quick response. This is because members of Gen Z have grown up with technology that provides them with "answers at their fingertips."[32] The intergenerational tension and many complaints about uncivil Millennial and Gen Z employees often stem from competing norms and a lack of understanding between generations. Therefore, managers are advised to "face the future" and provide additional feedback beyond an annual review to younger workers. Managers can also create "reverse mentoring" programs in which employees from different generations exchange information and at the same time, learn about generational norms. For example, younger workers can teach older workers about technology and older workers can advance corporate knowledge to younger workers.[33]

### Incivility Spirals

When workers believe that others have violated one or more norms related to respect or restraint, they subsequently perceive that they are being treated unfairly, which in turn creates a desire to reciprocate with further unfairness. The response may then lead to similar perceptions on the part of the instigator, and s/he may react with further incivility. Thus, a potential spiral is formed.

One reason we may react to incivility with further incivility is because other stressors sap the energy we need for self-control. Today's workers must contend with downsizing, increased pressure to "produce more with less," autocratic work environments, and the hiring of more part-time and temporary employees who may need extra attention. Additionally, targets of uncivil behavior expend energy when they attempt to understand why they are targets and how to respond. This causes a reduction in the energy needed for self-control and results in the target becoming the instigator of uncivil behavior. However, employees can avoid the creation of a cycle of incivility by ignoring a perceived uncivil action; choosing not to respond (i.e., because the injured party decides to release emotional energy in a different way, give the instigator the "benefit of the doubt," or believes that the instigator is not worth further attention); or by apologizing for, denying, or offering an excuse for the perceived incivility.[34]

If an incivility spiral is not ended, it may result in intense aggressive behaviors specifically enacted to harm others and/or the development of secondary spirals. Secondary spirals occur when norms for civil workplace behavior erode due to the experience or witness of primary spirals. Secondary spirals can spread incivility throughout an organization and influence the creation of a new organizational norm based on uncivil communication.[35] The spread of incivility and the creation of secondary spirals can be likened to catching a cold or virus. Similar to catching a cold, workplace incivility can be widely dispersed, easily caught (e.g., even after one exposure), can be caught from anyone in an organization, and result in symptoms that alter behaviors.

This also means that the consequences of incivility affect those with whom a target or witness communicates, and, "like a true virus, the effects of even a single act of rudeness may manifest themselves in multiple parties within the organization."[36] As incivility spreads within an organization, employees become negative, fearful, and mistrusting of other employees. Employees then become unwilling to display even the most minimal type of civil communication, such as the polite use of "please" and "thank you," which has the potential to create even more spirals of incivility. When dozens of incivility spirals are triggered at once and feed off the other, causing employees to believe that an organization is "out to get them," an organization can be characterized as "uncivil."

## CAUSES AND CONSEQUENCES OF WORKPLACE INCIVILITY

Senior vice president of Korean Air and head of in-flight service Heather Cho sat in the First Class section of a plane heading to Incheon and was served a snack of macadamia nuts. Flight 86 was already on the runway when a flight attendant placed a small bag of nuts in front of her instead of serving them in a small dish, according to protocol. Cho lost her temper and screamed at the attendant to bring her the company's in-flight service manual, which includes instructions for the proper presentation of nut snacks. When the attendant failed to find the manual, Cho demanded that the plane return to a gate at the airport so the attendant could leave the aircraft. Confusion ensued at JFK as the flight crew and airport officials discussed expelling the attendant at the gate and whether or not to replace him. The pilots gave in to Cho's demands, and without warning the plane, with 250 passengers on board, left the runway to drop off the attendant.

After Cho, the eldest daughter of Korean Airlines chairman Cho Yang Ho, delayed the flight, the incident came under the scrutiny of the Korean transport minister. The ministry announced that it would investigate whether Cho had violated the Aviation Safety Law, which prohibits passengers from creating disturbances for reasons of safety. Cho subsequently stepped down from her position as vice president and her father reported that she was being removed from all other posts. In addition, Cho apologized publicly and her father also apologized for the trouble caused by his daughter's "foolish conduct."[37]

Cho's uncivil behavior may, in part, be due to the fact that she was a vice president of Korean Air and the chairman's daughter. However, a transportation ministry official said that even though Cho was a company vice president, "she was a passenger at that time, so she had to behave and be treated as a passenger."[38] Unlike Cho, most of us can't say that our uncivil communication is caused by our senior status within an organization, or because we are the offspring of the chairman. However, there are other causes of on-the-job incivility that may influence us to engage in uncivil communication.

## Causes of Workplace Incivility

The causes of workplace incivility are many and varied. One source is the uncivil communication in society that carries over to the workplace. Some have described modern society as coarse, tough, and one in which we believe that we don't need to communicate in a civil manner. This occurs because we no longer connect with neighbors and community groups as frequently as we did in the past. We are also disconnected from friends and family members in that we have fewer face-to-face interactions with our loved ones. Other societal forces that impact workplace incivility include politics, the media, and the hectic pace of modern life. The nastiness of the 2016 presidential election found its way into classrooms across the country and it's easy to imagine that name-calling, taunts, and personal attacks were also evidenced in places of employment. In addition, the media is criticized as sensationalizing and magnifying controversy and conflict. The media also is described as condoning and showcasing vulgar language, lewd topics, and offensive commentary, therefore contributing to uncivil communication in the workplace.[39]

In addition to cultural and societal forces, the fast pace of modern life is stressful and may cause us to neglect to communicate civilly, or "forget to be nice."[40] We struggle to keep commitments related to family, friends, and our occupation. Increasing the speed at which we complete tasks is often suggested as a way to solve the problems caused by a busy life. However, 95 percent of Americans believe they don't have enough time to accomplish all they need to do.[41] Twenty percent of respondents in an Associated Press–Ipsos poll admitted they're rude to service workers if they are made to wait too long for service. We become impatient after five minutes "on hold" on the phone and won't tolerate a wait of fifteen minutes in line.[42] We also typically think about our own need to be on time and fail to consider how our self-interest may cause harm to others.[43]

Additionally, Americans are described as overworked; the amount of time spent on the job has increased during the past few decades. The increase in work hours has occurred in both white-collar and blue-collar jobs and our modern-day time crunch contributes to an increase in uncivil behavior. "Longer work days, longer working weeks, and more weeks at work, coupled with less leisure and vacation time, may in part explain a rise in incivility at work."[44] The longer hours at work are correlated with the findings that employees don't sleep well or long enough. Over two-thirds of employees get less than the recommended eight hours of sleep per night and one in five admit that the lack of sleep interferes with their performance on the job. Employees who don't get enough sleep are typically more irritable and more prone to act out in an uncivil manner, whether or not they intend to harm a coworker.[45]

Furthermore, the economic forces mentioned earlier which impact the workplace, such as downsizing, budget cuts, and autocratic work environments, can create an organizational climate in which uncivil behavior can flourish.[46] These economic forces, in addition to reorganization and rapid growth, result in four types of stress which cause us to communicate uncivilly:[47]

- **Role stress:** Employees find it increasingly difficult to juggle their responsibilities to their employers, their families, and others.
- **Change stress:** Companies undergoing changes tend to cause more stress.
- **Relationship stress:** This stress can range from an inability to get along with the boss or other coworkers, to marital problems that affect productivity.
- **Workload stress:** This has become fairly acute in many organizations today. Companies are stretched thinner and people are being asked to do more with less.

Two additional causes of workplace incivility include the idea that our jobs should fulfill our emotional needs, and the influence of informal corporate climates. Some argue that people focus on their jobs to fill an emotional vacuum in their life. However, because such workers expect their employment to satisfy basic emotional needs that would have been met by family and community groups in an earlier era, they feel betrayed and vulnerable when it does not provide the central meaning in their life. Unfortunately, "when our workplace fails us, we are disappointed, angry, depressed, and even hostile, the familiar causes and consequences of incivility."[48] Moreover, increasing numbers of organizations have "gone casual" and this has limited the cues that provide us with information about norms for appropriate behavior in the workplace. Informal corporate climates may actually encourage disrespectful behavior, as the approved casual clothes and casual communication imply that it's acceptable to behave unprofessionally and impolitely. "Without the trappings of formality, it can be difficult for some employees to discern acceptable behavior from unacceptable behavior."[49]

Finally, workplace incivility may occur in response to employees who "blow the whistle" and/or raise legal or ethical problems at their place of employment. Although we may think about retaliation in terms of actions that are dramatic and obvious, it is sometimes evidenced in "mild" behaviors, such as providing few opportunities for advancement, smaller raises, and petty slights. Mild retaliation also occurs when employees are selectively left out of e-mail threads and sometimes excluded from social events. This type of retaliation is subtle, indirect, and is drawn out over time. And similar to other forms of uncivil behavior, it enables the instigator of retaliation to deny any responsibility for uncivil behavior and may be impossible to prove in a court of law. [50]

## Consequences of Workplace Incivility

During a Repertory East Playhouse production of Tennessee Williams's *Cat on a Hot Tin Roof*, an inebriated member of the audience and his friend began catcalling and whistling at the actress who played Maggie, the female lead. The heckling continued up to the moment that the male lead, Brick, was asked why he had rejected Maggie's kiss. Before the actor could respond, the heckler shouted, "Because he's a fag!" At this point, the actor who played Big Daddy, John Lacy, charged into the audience to confront the heckler. The heckler's friend attempted to physically assault Lacy, but he and others subdued the heckler and his friend and forced them to leave the theater. The audience applauded, and Lacy asked, "Is everybody okay? Do you want us to continue?"

The play continued, although management later fired Lacy for going into the audience and confronting the heckler. There were no producers or security guards inside of the building, and one theatergoer asserted that "an audience member shouldn't have to protect actors from an attack." Anton Troy, the actor who played Brick, quit the production, stating, "I support my cast mate; no John Lacy means no Anton Troy. I will not support homophobia or an establishment that doesn't support its talent. . . . It should never escalate to a point where the talent has to handle an unruly drunk in the audience themselves regardless of the outcome. The producers dropped the ball."

Other actors quit the production and the theater announced that the run of the play was suspended because the cast "revolt" had left the producers with no time to recast the parts. In the end, the entire run of the play, which included a tour, was canceled. [51]

The example of the heckler illustrates that if not stopped by upper-level management, uncivil communication will continue to result in negative outcomes. This example also illustrates that negative consequences are experienced not only by those directly involved in an uncivil situation, but by those who witness it. Specifically, audience members were not able to fully appreciate the performance because of the loud heckling; actor John Lacy was fired by management and lost a source of income; other actors quit the show, which caused the production to fold and the producers to lose money; and the actors were denied the opportunity to go on tour.

In general, incivility affects performance on the job in two ways: a decline in employee motivation, and a decrease in ability. Workers stop performing well (or stop performing altogether), job satisfaction declines, and anger at the organization increases. The low level of employee motivation is evidenced when they reduce effort, time, and the quality of their job performance.[52] Findings from a large national study of managers and employees reveal that incivility in the workplace was dealt with in the following manner by respondents:[53]

- 48 percent intentionally decreased work effort;
- 47 percent intentionally decreased time at work;
- 38 percent lost work time worrying about the incident;
- 63 percent lost time avoiding their offender;
- 66 percent said their performance declined; and
- 78 percent said their commitment to the organization declined,

Workplace incivility also negatively affects employee health. Workers exposed to uncivil behavior for a long period of time and/or too often may find that their immune system is compromised. Similarly, major health problems such as cardiovascular disease, diabetes, ulcers, and cancers are associated with having to contend with workplace incivility.[54] Moreover, workers who are targets or who witness uncivil communication in their organization may suffer emotional and psychological harm, including hurt feelings, depression, feeling disappointed, lowered self-esteem, and feeling disrespected.[55]

Workplace incivility additionally takes a toll on family life. Hostile experiences at work increase the potential for employees to be angry or withdrawn when they return home to their families. One study had employees report on workplace incivility and other emotional states on the job over a ten-day period. At the same time, daily reports about the employees' marital behavior after returning home from work were provided by their spouses. The study found a "spillover effect" in which uncivil behavior at work affected the home environment. Specifically, the experience of workplace incivility is associated with feelings of hostility, which subsequently increases the potential for employees to be angry at family members. Feeling hostile as a result of workplace incivility also can influence employees to withdraw from the family after returning home from work.[56]

Some argue that workplace incivility can produce positive results. David Yamada, professor of law and director of the New Workplace Institute at

Suffolk University Law School, suggests that "some forms of incivility may be necessary toward building a psychologically healthy workplace. After all, honest expressions of emotion, including anger, can be a first step in resolving differences."[57] Yamada also claims that there are situations during which uncivil communication understandably results from a difference of opinion or disagreement. The harsh words and rude behavior that occur in such an exchange may actually clear the air and lead to a healthy resolution. However, we need to exercise self-control in these instances so that a workplace encounter doesn't turn into an emotional shouting match. We also need to be aware of power relationships so that a more-powerful employee doesn't enact retribution on a less-powerful employee during a conversation that includes uncivil communication.[58]

## MANAGING WORKPLACE INCIVILITY

"Will" works for a small company that makes graphic material for print media. The operations manager, rather than the owner/boss, is responsible for the day-to-day workings of the company. The nature of the work is heavily dependent on meeting deadlines, some of which are regular and others that occur at the last minute. Unfortunately, the operations manager's uncivil communication increased as each deadline approached. Specifically, the manager shouted orders, failed to utter "please" or "thank you," and called employees by their last names or just "you" (which communicated that they were dispensable and that he didn't need to know them). Will claimed that he never got used to the uncivil communication and that it was embarrassing when the manager spoke to him in that manner in front of coworkers and friends.

One day, an employee who was somewhat new asked Will and his colleagues, "Why do we take it?" The following week, side-by-side photos of the manager appeared on the company's website along with descriptions of the manager's behavior. One example included a photo of the manager and was described as "Here is manager 'X' calmly chatting and at his desk, working." The second photo was described as "It's manager 'X' pointing, and even from behind you can see how red he gets." Three photo pairs were posted the first week and more were posted in subsequent weeks.

Will contends that the owner/boss of the company was either unaware of the operations manager's uncivil behavior or simply ignored it. However, Will noticed a change after the photos were posted on the website, and he believes that the owner/boss and the manager met to discuss the manager's on-the-job incivility. The result is that the operations manager now has civil conversations with his employees. Will says that the manager even responded to the photos in a good-natured way; he held up his hands and said, "Okay, I get it!"[59]

Will's experience with the uncivil manager is one example of how employees cope with workplace incivility; that is, targeted retribution designed to end the uncivil behavior. There are other ways that employees can contend with uncivil communication in an organization. These coping strategies include avoiding conflict, minimizing the uncivil behavior, challenging the person who behaves uncivilly, and seeking social and organizational support.

## How Targeted Employees Can Manage Workplace Incivility

Because uncivil communication on the job is low-intensity and ambiguous in intentionality, employees tend to use coping responses rather than taking their grievances to management. Consequently, the unreported uncivil communication continues uncorrected and can result in extensive harm.[60] Typically, employees who are the targets of workplace incivility cope by doing one (or more) of the following:[61]

- Avoiding conflict (they try to avoid the person who communicates uncivilly, put up with the uncivil behavior, and/or try not to make the person angry);
- Minimizing the uncivil behavior (they tell themselves that "it's not important," try to forget it, and/or assume the person means no harm);
- Challenging the person who communicates uncivilly (they confront the person, ask the person to leave them alone, and/or let the person know they don't like what is happening);
- Seeking informal social support (they talk to a friend for advice and support, talk to someone they trust, and/or talk with family members);
- Seeking formal organizational support (they talk with a supervisor or someone in management).

Although the coping strategy of seeking support from family members has merit, this strategy doesn't always work and can result in additional harm. Turning to a family member for support may result in advice that is counterproductive, such as aggressive retaliation. On the other hand, a family member may influence a targeted employee to believe that the situation is not as bad as it seems. Seeking support from a family member may also lead to "taking it out" on the loved one, because it's safer and more convenient to express frustration with loved ones than at work. One study of work–family incivility found that targets of uncivil communication on the job experience negative outcomes when they receive a high amount of family support. This is because family members themselves may be a source of tension and communicating with them can trigger additional stress that a target must deal with.[62]

An additional coping strategy used by targets of uncivil behavior concerns "payback" or retaliation, especially when the instigator has more authority than the target. Retaliation is usually successful when it is specifically aimed at the person who commits uncivil acts; when it's well-timed (i.e., it occurs at times when a connection can be made between the incivility and the payback); and when it is motivated by a desire to end the uncivil communication rather than to punish the instigator.

In the example of Will and the operations manager, the retaliation was successful in that it ended the uncivil behavior and created benefits for the employees and the organization itself. However, retaliation most likely won't be successful if it is aimed at vulnerable factors within an organization rather than at the person who communicates uncivilly. Retaliation also won't work if it is poorly timed (i.e., it occurs at times when it won't highlight a person's uncivil behavior) and if it is ill-tempered, aggressive, and/or designed to inflict punishment rather than end the workplace incivility.

An example of unsuccessful payback occurred when a programmer at a major bank sabotaged the organization's payroll program because his supervisors were uncivil. Once the payroll program began to fail, all of the other programs began to fail as well. Consequently, although a number of his supervisors were fired, the bank employees and customers also suffered because of the employee's uncivil desire to punish rather than remediate.[63] The bank programmer's retaliation was disrespectful, failed to show restraint, and, more importantly, disregarded the welfare of his "community"—the bank employees and customers.

Therefore, before deciding whether or not to retaliate against a superior who communicates in an uncivil manner, employees should ask themselves whether:[64]

- the payback will specifically target an instigator of uncivil behavior or harm others (the payback should be well-targeted);
- the instigator will realize the connection between the retaliation and their behavior (the payback should be well-timed); and
- the retaliation is designed to inflict revenge rather than to end the uncivil behavior (the payback should be well-tempered).

## How Senior Executives Can Manage Workplace Incivility

An Amazon customer contacted a customer service representative via an online chat to complain that the book he ordered didn't arrive in the mail. The customer service representative introduced himself as Thor, and the following conversation ensued:

**Customer:** Greetings, Thor. Can I be Odin?

**Amazon:** Odin, Father, how art [thou] doing on this here fine day?

**Customer:** Thor, my son. Agony raises upon my life.

**Amazon:** This is outrageous! Who dares defy The All Father Odin! What has occurred to cause this agony?

**Customer:** I am afraid the book I ordered to defeat our enemies has been misplaced. How can we keep Valhalla intact without our sacred book?

**Amazon:** This is blasphemy! Wherever this book has been taken to, I shall make it my duty to get it back to you! I fear it is Loki, but I dare not blame him for such things. I shall have your fortune returned to you, and thereafter we can begin to create a new quest in order to get the book back to you.[65]

The role-play conversation continued for quite some time, and finally the customer asked, "Role play aside, can I have my money back and reorder the book?" Amazon responded affirmatively and placed the order for the customer. The customer continued:

**Customer:** I've heard Amazon had great customer service, and this just proves it! Thanks, man.

**Amazon:** No problem. Is there any other issue or question that I can help you with?

**Customer:** Nah, that was it. Really appreciate it.

**Amazon:** Anytime, bro. Have a great day. Good-bye, Odin.

**Customer:** Bye, my son.[66]

The online conversation was posted on various websites and garnered much attention. On Imgur, comments included the following:

- That was some Thor-ough customer support.
- This is why you don't outsource customer service.
- Awesomeness!
- I dream of meeting people like this when talking to customer service.
- 9/10 are ordering stuff on Amazon right now in an attempt to have a similar experience.[67]

Amazon's successful customer service is partially due to its emphasis on teams. Studies about successful teams reveal that there are eight characteristics associated with team excellence. While Amazon's customer service department meets all eight characteristics, of particular interest is "collaborative climate," which focuses on civil behavior: "Team members can stay focused on goals, listen and understand each other, feel free to take risks, and be willing to compensate for one another."[68] Not only are Amazon customer service representatives taught to be civil with one another, management communicates to employees that they are valued. One reader of the "Thor–Odin" interaction commented:[69]

> I once read a book about leadership from the office library . . . about approaching customer service from the perspective of large companies like Amazon and Apple, and how their strategy and approach differ from other companies. From what I remember, the focus was always on valuing the employees highly . . . so that they would feel most invested in the work they were doing, and in turn offer customers better outcomes based on their positive attitudes towards their work. Based on your post . . . it seems to be working excellently for them, and they are always recognized as one of the top companies for customer service in the world.

The author of the comment above is correct in assuming that employees treat customers well when they are valued and treated civilly by upper management. However, if senior executives are unaware of or ignore incivility within their organization, the uncivil communication will spread to vendors, clients, and customers alike.

Although individual employees may take various steps to contend with workplace incivility, there is general agreement that the way to stop such behavior is to "begin at the top." Experts typically recommend that higher-ups respond to uncivil behavior by creating zero-tolerance policies that spell out the consequences for incivility on the job and by providing training and opportunities for feedback.[70] Organizations can attempt to prevent incivility by taking it seriously when it does occur and by assisting the targets of uncivil behavior with support as they attempt to cope with incivility.[71]

Although one can find a variety of "pop-psychology" suggestions for managing incivility in the workplace, the following guidelines for organizations and CEOs are based on interviews, survey results, and focus-group discussions:

- Set zero-tolerance expectations for employees: An organization's culture and climate are powerfully shaped by those at the top.
- "Practice what you preach": Managers and supervisors should communicate civilly, evaluate their behavior, and solicit honest feedback from others.

- Teach civility: Use experiential training programs which include role-playing and information about listening, dealing with difficult people, stress management, and conflict management.
- Recognize signals that may indicate the presence of incivility: Because uncivil workplace communication is rarely reported, managers and employees should learn to spot incivility and know how to respond to it (e.g., note employees who refuse to work with others, complaints that flow through the "grapevine," feedback from exit interviews, and absentee and turnover rates).
- Don't tolerate incivility, period: This holds true for customers, vendors, and contractors, as well as employees; take complaints seriously and don't make excuses for those who are habitually uncivil. [72]

Overall, organizations should handle uncivil incidents by attempting to prevent them in the first place. Employees at all levels of an organization should understand the characteristics and negative consequences associated with uncivil behavior. Hiring personnel should complete thorough reference checks on all prospective employees and expectations about behaviors should be modeled and communicated to potential workers. Similarly, expectations about civil behavior should be communicated and reinforced during new-employee orientation sessions. [73]

## SUMMARY AND CONCLUSION

Incivility on the job is typically defined as low-intensity behavior that may or may not be intended to harm a target. Uncivil behavior in organizations is pervasive and statistics reveal that 96 percent of Americans experience uncivil communication at their place of employment. Instigators of uncivil behavior typically possess more power than targets, and employees who lack power are more often the recipients of uncivil communication. The various forms of workplace incivility range from texting during a meeting and not saying "please" or "thank you" to belittling others' efforts and engaging in ostracism.

The causes and consequences of workplace incivility are many and varied. A major influencing factor is society itself; in particular, the uncivil communication that permeates the larger culture carries over to the workplace. Similarly, the fast pace of modern life is stressful and may cause us to neglect to communicate civilly or "forget to be nice." Economic forces additionally create a stressful work environment in which uncivil communication can flourish. Incivility affects performance on the job in two ways: a decline in employee motivation and a decrease in ability. Workplace incivility also negatively affects employee health.

Employees can cope with incivility on the job by putting up with or minimizing the uncivil behavior, challenging the instigator, seeking informal social support, and seeking formal organizational support. Employees can also engage in well-aimed, well-timed, and well-tempered retaliation designed to end the uncivil communication rather than punish the instigator.

**Box 6-1**
**Strategies for Change: Incivility at Work**

Although individual employees may take various steps to contend with workplace incivility, experts agree that change must occur at the highest levels to influence the overall climate of an organization. Employees can cope with uncivil communication on the job by:

- avoiding conflict (try to avoid the person who communicates uncivilly, put up with the uncivil behavior, and/or try not to make the person angry);
- minimizing the uncivil behavior (tell yourself that "it's not important," try to forget it, and/or assume the person means no harm);
- challenging the person who communicates uncivilly (confront the person, ask the person to leave you alone, and/or let the person know you don't like what is happening);
- seeking informal social support (talk to a friend for advice and support, talk to someone you trust, and/or talk with family members);
- seeking formal organizational support (talk with a supervisor or someone in management); or by
- engaging in retribution that is well-aimed, well-timed, and well-tempered (that is, used to end the uncivil behavior rather than to punish the instigator).

Supervisors and managers can "cope" with incivility on the job by preventing it (i.e., by educating employees about the characteristics and negative consequences of workplace incivility and by establishing and enforcing a zero-tolerance policy). Management can also:

- communicate civilly, evaluate their own behavior, and solicit honest feedback from others;
- teach civility by using experiential training programs, which include role-playing and information about listening, dealing with difficult people, stress management, and conflict management;

- recognize and respond to signals that may indicate the presence of incivility; and
- refuse to accept uncivil behavior from customers, vendors, and contractors, as well as from employees.

## Chapter Seven

# Everyday Incivility Online

*The speaker [at the commencement ceremony] was speaking and the cell phones kept going off and the parents were taking calls and saying, "I can't hear you." It got so disruptive . . . that the superintendent stood up and said, "Can everyone please turn their pagers and cell phones off? We're honoring the senior class."*
—*A survey respondent's comment in "Aggravating Circumstances: A Status Report on Rudeness in America"*[1]

Justine Sacco, the thirty-year-old senior director of corporate communications at media company InterActive Corp (IAC), was flying from New York to South Africa to visit relatives during the holidays. Becoming somewhat frustrated with the discomfort of travel, Sacco began to send sarcastic tweets about fellow travelers and destinations to her 170 Twitter followers. Her tweets included the following:

"Weird German Dude: You're in First Class; it's 2014. Get some deodorant." —*Inner monologue as I inhale BO. Thank God for pharmaceuticals.*

"Chilly—cucumber sandwiches—bad teeth. Back in London!"

"Going to Africa. Hope I don't get AIDS. Just kidding. I'm white!"[2]

Sacco slept most of the time during the eleven-hour flight from London to South Africa. She turned on her phone after the plane landed and received a text from a high school friend she hadn't heard from in years: "I'm so sorry to see what's happening." Sacco had no idea about the meaning of the tweet. She next read a tweet from her best friend, Hannah: "You need to call me immediately." Sacco was bombarded with text alerts and tweets, and then her phone rang. It was Hannah, who had called to tell her that she was the number-one trend on Twitter.

Unknown to Sacco, her tweets had been retweeted. Sam Biddle, the (former) editor of *Valleywag*, a tech-industry blog, had retweeted Sacco's AIDS tweet to his 15,000 followers. He also posted it on *Valleywag* with the text, "And now, a funny holiday joke from IAC's PR boss." Biddle said that "the fact she was a PR chief made it delicious" and that he wanted to "make a racist tweet by a senior IAC employee count."[3]

Although Sacco's AIDS tweet wasn't meant to be taken literally, many interpreted it as racist. Others interpreted her tweets as flaunting her wealth and privilege. The responses were immediate and harsh; Sacco was still mid-flight when the avalanche of tweets and texts began. The tweets included the following:

"How did @JustineSacco get a PR job?! Her level of racist ignorance belongs on Fox News. #AIDS can affect anyone!"

"I'm an IAC employee and I don't want @JustineSacco doing any communications on our behalf ever again. Ever."

And from her employer, IAC: "This is an outrageous, offensive comment. Employee in question currently on an intl flight."[4]

Sacco touched down in South Africa not knowing that tens of thousands of angry tweets had been sent in response to her AIDS tweet. She later explained that her tweets were never meant to be taken literally and were written to amuse her small circle of Twitter followers. But the damage had been done. Sacco's South African family told her, "This is not what our family stands for. And now, by association, you've almost tarnished the family."

Sacco cut her vacation short and issued an apology. Hotel employees threatened to strike if she booked a room and she was told that her safety couldn't be guaranteed. She was fired from her job and she stopped dating, aware that people conduct Internet searches on dating partners. Sacco had been Google-searched thirty times in November, the month before she traveled to South Africa. However, from December 20 through the end of the month, she was googled 1,220,000 times.[5]

Although Biddle claimed that he had never set out to ruin Sacco's life, the responses she received after he retweeted her tweet changed her life forever. She traveled to Addis Ababa, Ethiopia, to do volunteer PR work for an organization working to reduce infant mortality rates. She then returned to New York and was hired at an Internet dating site. Nonetheless, Sacco continued to cry and lose sleep, feel confused and anxious, and claimed that "They've taken my name and my picture and have created this Justine Sacco that's not me and have labeled this person a racist." Sacco currently avoids all publicity and wants to put the incident behind her. However, one Twitter user tweeted "Sorry @JustineSacco, your tweet lives on forever."[6]

Justine Sacco's situation illustrates that although social media can be used to promote community and social causes, it can also be used to publicly shame others and change their lives in ways never imagined. Although most of us won't find ourselves publicly shamed via social media—at least not to the extent of Justine's Sacco's public humiliation—the technology that is supposed to make our life easier can also make our lives more difficult when we are forced to contend with cyber incivility. In this chapter, you'll read about the need for ethically based standards for civil online communication; the types, magnitude, and negative consequences associated with cyber incivility; the causes of and how to contend with incivility online; and cell-phone incivility.

## ETHICS AND CIVIL ONLINE COMMUNICATION

Because Internet posts, tweets, and text messages defy the limits of time and space, it's especially important to consider the necessity of civil communication online and its ethical base. In particular, the Internet celebrates the individual because it enables anyone, not just journalists and communication specialists, to tweet, blog, post on Facebook, etc. But the downside is the risk that anyone who uses social media can act on the basis of his/her own ethical standards. According to William Lawrence, a professor of historical theology at Southern Methodist University, when social media readers and writers create their own ethical standards:

> [Forms of] social media are not managing to connect us as a society. Instead, they are managing to disconnect us from one another. It is not simply that new ethical standards need to be written in our age. It is also that we need to determine how to establish ethical standards that apply to more persons than solely the individuals who write them. [7]

Lawrence's comments suggest that we need to emphasize responsibility to the community rather than responsibility to the self. One way we can accomplish this goal is by using restraint each time we engage in various forms of social media. We can also make sure that we reflect on our Internet-based message before we post or send it (e.g., we can ask ourselves if our message will keep a conversation going or stifle further interaction). [8] In addition, we can demonstrate respect by focusing on information and logical reasoning rather than relying on name-calling and "othering" those with whom we disagree. By remembering to be respectful, refraining from posting or sending immediate and emotional knee-jerk responses, and reflecting on the welfare of our online community, our online behavior will be both effective and appropriate, the necessary conditions for competent communication.

## INCIVILITY ONLINE: TYPES, MAGNITUDE, AND NEGATIVE CONSEQUENCES

Cyber incivility can be defined as "rude [and] discourteous behaviors occurring through Information and Communication Technologies (ICTs) such as e-mail or text messages.[9] We can broaden this definition to include social media (e.g., Twitter, Instagram, Facebook, Tumblr, etc.) and cell phones, which are often used to send messages and post on social media sites.

### Types of Incivility Online

Dani Mathers, a *Playboy* "Playmate of the Year," secretly photographed an older woman showering at the gym and posted the photo to Snapchat with the spiteful caption, "If I can't unsee this, then you can't either." The young and curvaceous Mathers was referring to the woman's bulges and lumps that are a natural by-product of aging. Despite a hasty public apology, Mathers was the target of intense public outrage. She was banned from the gym and suspended from her radio talk show.

Unexpectedly, women across the country engaged in an outpouring of mutual support for their "well-worn" bodies. For example, Christine Blackmon, Florida wife, mother, and army veteran, posted on Facebook a revealing yet discreet photo of herself while changing clothes. The woman described herself in all her "lumpy, bumpy glory," writing, "You may have been a *Playboy* model, but not all of us work out to be 'hot.' I bet I could get 100s of women to post their beautiful bodies, and regardless of size, shape, or color, they will ALL be more beautiful than the ugliness you showed in that post." Blackmon's post was shared more than 7,000 times and received approximately 65,000 views and 3,000 comments. Women of all shapes and sizes posted photos of themselves, stretch marks and all.[10]

Body shaming is just one type of cyber incivility. Other common types of online incivility include:

- Flaming: An online argument that becomes nasty or derisive, where insulting a party to the discussion takes precedence over the objective merits of one side or another.[11]
- Trolling: Internet users who hide behind their anonymity to play pranks, harass, or threaten other Internet users.[12]
- Doxxing: Publishing personal information, such as Social Security and bank-account numbers.[13]
- Swatting: Phoning in a fake emergency and providing a target's home address for the SWAT team.[14]

- Sexting and revenge porn: Sending sexually explicit images of oneself or others via cell phone or computer. The images may later be used to cause harm, humiliate, and shame the person in the images. [15]
- Calling out: "The tendency among progressives, radicals, activists, and community organizers to publicly name instances or patterns of oppressive behavior and language used by others." [16]

## Magnitude of Incivility Online

According to the 2016 Digital Future Project, *Surveying the Digital Future: Year Fourteen*, 90 percent of Americans use the Internet and spend an average of 23.5 hours per week online. [17] Even though the majority of Americans are connected to the Internet, their feelings about social media sites are complicated. This is because social media posts, for a variety of reasons, are perceived as uncivil. In particular, 36 percent of Facebook users "strongly dislike" people who share too much information about themselves and people who post photos of others without first obtaining their permission. Facebook users also dislike the ability of others to access posts or comments that they aren't meant to see, and the pressure to comment on content posted by Facebook friends. [18]

Moreover, 73 percent of adult Internet users have seen someone targeted for online incivility and 40 percent have personally experienced online incivility. Specifically, 60 percent of those who witnessed online incivility observed someone being called offensive names and 53 percent saw attempts to purposefully embarrass others. Similarly, 27 percent of users who experienced cyber incivility have been called offensive names and 22 percent had someone try to embarrass them purposefully. [19] According to the Pew Research Internet Project *Online Harassment* report, respondents said they experienced uncivil communication after expressing political or religious opinions. Here are a few examples:

- "Through social media, and especially when commenting on controversial issues, often my difference of opinion from others would result in those who do not agree insulting and berating instead of arguing their point respectfully."
- "While commenting on a sensitive religious feminist issue, I was attacked because of my opinion, and some other commenters resorted to name-calling in their anger."
- "On Facebook, a few days ago, I expressed my feelings about present issues and was harassed and called names. Of course there were no substantive arguments—just judgmental, harsh name-calling." [20]

Uncivil communication may be directed toward us even if we don't engage in political or religious discussions, as reported by 70 percent of eighteen- to twenty-four-year-olds who don't text, tweet, post, etc., about controversial topics, but have nonetheless experienced online harassment.[21] Similarly, those who witness online incivility say they have observed insults, name-calling, and lack of respect for differences of opinion:

- "I have seen all types of inappropriate comments that people make to harass, demean, and belittle others. I don't understand why people are so disrespectful and uncaring, and just plain mean."
- "I have observed condescending and antagonistic remarks about people in an online discussion group about . . . social issues."
- "[I've witnessed] rude put-downs relating to disagreements on . . . religion."[22]

Chris Perry, president of Digital Communications at Weber Shandwick, asserts that "we prefer to communicate through social networks the same way we do in everyday social settings. . . . [I]f there is a difference of opinion, we expect respectful dialogue. If not, we tune out."[23] In particular, 45 percent of social media users have blocked or defriended someone because of uncivil comments and/or behavior; 38 percent stopped visiting an online site because of its incivility; and 25 percent left an online community because it had become uncivil.[24]

## Negative Consequences of Incivility Online

Three rookie Florida police officers were joking around in a group chat with other officers about using mostly black neighborhoods for target practice. The rookies said they weren't trying to offend anyone and they were just commenting on what they'd seen during their training. However, their remarks occurred during a time when the department was under supervision by the US Department of Justice. Police department leaders concluded that the officers' comments made them a liability and the rookies were fired.

Miami's police union president said that even though the rookies' messages were in poor taste, they shouldn't have been fired. The rookies' attorneys similarly stated that they were young reckless kids who were off duty when they made their comments. Nonetheless, the rookies were found to have "violated multiple police department policies that involve social media, courtesy, and responsibility."[25]

Cyber incivility can result in a variety of harms that are experienced by instigators such as the rookie police officers, as well as specific targets and those who witness the uncivil communication. Facebook, Twitter, newspaper comment sites, and sites that encourage rants negatively affect the mental health of those who write angry posts or tweets. In particular, instigators may experience additional negative emotions, participate in verbal fights, engage in self-harm and substance abuse, and damage property and harm relationships after posting or sending uncivil communication.

Although those who post angry rants may feel an initial sense of catharsis, long-term emotional effects include an increase in anger. Specific targets of online incivility also experience negative consequences. For example, those who are the targets of name-calling or who experience embarrassment resulting from uncivil online behavior claim that they feel "very" or "extremely" upset as a result.[26] Similarly, when supervisors engage in incivility online, employees are likely to report increased levels of burnout, miss work frequently, and consider quitting their jobs more often than employees who experience low levels of cyber incivility.[27]

Additionally, "witnesses" experience harms that stem from online incivility. In particular, those who read online rants may experience a decrease in happiness and an increase in sadness as a result.[28] Negative effects of incivility online also result for "lurkers" who read online discussions but don't participate in them.[29] Furthermore, the incivility produced by trolls negatively affects members of marginalized groups and young users:

> When sites are overrun by trolls, they drown out voices of women, ethnic and religious minorities, gays—anyone who might feel vulnerable. Young people in these groups assume trolling is a normal part of life online and therefore self-censor. An anonymous poll of the writers at *Time* found that 80 percent had avoided discussing a particular topic because they fear online response.[30]

Finally, one in four people say that "electronic displays of insensitivity" (EDIs) have caused a serious rift with a friend or family member. Joseph Grenny found that of the more than two thousand respondents who participated in his *Digital Divisiveness* study, "89 percent reported damaged relationships due to friends and family ignoring them for technology, a phenomenon that 90 percent of respondents witness every week."[31]

## CAUSES OF AND CONTENDING WITH INCIVILITY ONLINE

Yik Yak, a mobile app aimed at college students, allowed users to post short anonymous messages within a 1.5-mile radius. Founded by Millennials Tyler Droll and Brooks Buffington, the app was designed to help college students "create a more democratic social media network where users didn't need a large number of followers or friends to have one's thoughts read widely."[32] Buffington stated that the app was developed to "level the playing field and connect everyone," and asserted, "When we made this app, we really made it for the disenfranchised."[33] The majority of posts, labeled "yaks," concerned topics familiar to most college students; for example, anxieties that result from living away from home, difficulties trying to fit into a social group, relationship complications, etc. Users responded with encouragement and advice regarding how to solve such problems. However, because posts were completely anonymous, students and others who used Yik Yak weren't held accountable for bullying behavior and uncivil messages. They also couldn't be held responsible for posts that were clearly racist, misogynistic, and homophobic. Consequently, universities found it difficult to contend with uncivil posts because the app's privacy policy mandated a subpoena, search warrant, court order, or an emergency request from law enforcement in order to identify users.

In response to the persistent incivility on Yik Yak, students created their own ways to fight back. At Boston College, students posted a video of classmates who read sexist and racist Yik Yak posts out loud. The students then gazed at the camera with a look that implied, "Is this for real?"[34] At Kenyon College, in response to Yik Yak posts about sexual assault, students started a project on Facebook called "Respectful Difference." According to Kenyon University president Sean Decatur, Respectful Difference "uses social media to positively assert the values of civility and respect and the importance of dialogue to bridge different views."[35] President Decatur's statement was reinforced by a student-authored article in the *Kenyon Collegian* in which the project was described as helping everyone move away from the cycle of "hearing disrespectful things and saying them back."[36] Respectful Difference spread across campus, was adopted by other colleges, and circulated throughout the world, thanks to Kenyon's alumni.[37]

Yik Yak eventually lost its popularity and its founders shut it down in 2017.[38] Before making the app unusable, Yik Yak introduced the option of using first names in posts. Subsequently, Yik Yak required first names and verified users' phone numbers to further reduce the anonymity of "Yakkers." Higher education consultant Eric Stoller asked, "Why use Yik Yak when you can use other platforms that have user profiles? Yik Yak was always about user location and anonymity." Similarly, Colgate College communication strategist Matt Hames claims that the app died on college campuses because it was no longer anonymous.[39]

Although anonymity is the most often cited reason for cyber incivility, there are additional factors that promote uncivil online behavior. These causes range from feelings of powerlessness or anger to mirroring offline incivility.

## Why People Engage in Incivility Online

Steven Fink received an e-mail from someone he didn't know. The e-mail contained nude photos of a woman whose ex-boyfriend wanted to embarrass her. The boyfriend wanted the private photos to go viral, which they eventually did. In the days before the Internet, the boyfriend may have torn up photos of his ex-girlfriend or mounted them on a dartboard and thrown darts at them. But these days, vindictive and vengeful behavior can easily be spread across the globe in a matter of seconds. Some even wonder if we've become a more angry and malicious society because of the powers of technology. Jonathan Bernstein, a crisis consultant, asserts that:

> Human nature hasn't changed. There have always been people whose aim in life was to cause pain to others. If they saw people embarrassing themselves, they got pleasure in sharing that information. Before the Internet, they had to gossip with their neighbors. Now they can gossip with the world. [40]

However, others assert that changes in technology have made us cynical, nasty, and mean-spirited. Reality television, divisive politics, and violence in sports also fuel cyber incivility, as does:

- A sense of community among online commentators who may not be so mean-spirited as individuals;
- A growing tolerance for outrage, making those who want to be heard even more uncivil;
- Social media, which rewards impulsive emotions while spreading them at lightning speed; and
- A sense of powerlessness, often economic, which can fuel righteous outrage. [41]

Those who feel powerless post their outrage on comment forums and other platforms as a way to adjust to changing times. [42] In addition, unclear norms and "etiquette-free zones" on the Internet encourage people to post uncivil comments. [43] Moreover, the perception of time/space remoteness on the Internet is cited as influencing online incivility, and those who post uncivil messages may also feel entitled to challenge norms for appropriate behavior that exist offline. [44]

An additional factor that is associated with uncivil online behavior is uncivil offline behavior. One study about incivility online revealed that more than half of the over one thousand respondents admitted to misrepresenting themselves or others on online forums or to other Internet users. When respondents were asked why they engaged in this type of behavior, only 6 percent agreed with data collected in the initial half of the study that illustrated offline and online uncivil behaviors are comparable. However, the research clearly showed a "striking congruence between online and offline misbehavior . . . [which] suggests that online misbehavior closely replicates and reinforces existing misbehavior." [45]

It's interesting to note that users who self-identify as "trolls" tend to possess a number of alarming personality traits, such as narcissism, Machiavellianism, and psychopathy. But individuals who self-identify as trolls may engage in a small amount of actual trolling. Although trolls are often depicted as "aberrational" and "antithetical to how normal people converse with each other," trolls can be described as "normal people who do things that seem fun at the time that have huge implications."[46] And it's easy for "normal" people to engage in online incivility when they can remain completely anonymous.

## Anonymity

Recall that anonymity is the major reason why users post uncivil messages on social media sites. Anonymity also facilitates a lack of accountability and responsibility for the community.[47] Social scientists contend that anonymity contributes to a feeling of "deindividuation" which involves lowered social inhibitions and increased impulsivity.[48] Technology contributes to deindividuation in that its users may dehumanize other users in the same way that drivers dehumanize other drivers in incidents of road rage (i.e., drivers rage against "*that car* rather than *that driver*," which in turn makes it easier to engage in acts of aggression).[49] Anonymity also provides users with a sense of invisibility, invincibility, and the belief that they can easily escape the consequences of what would be considered offensive behavior offline.[50] Subsequently, we perceive that "we have a screen that protects us, [and] we feel we can talk about anything and say whatever thoughts come to mind."[51] And even if users are required to sign in, trolls can make up names and post uncivil comments, causing thoughtful contributors to turn away from a site.[52]

## Contending with Incivility Online

Former Red Sox pitcher and ESPN commentator Curt Schilling sprang into action when he discovered that his teenage daughter was the target of obscene anonymous tweets. He tracked down the identities of the anonymous tweeters and exposed them and their cyber incivility on his personal blog. He also apologized to his daughter for prolonging her embarrassment, but maintained that there is no situation in life that calls for any man to talk to her or other women with language that includes obscenities. The consequences for the tweeters included being suspended from college and being terminated as ticket sellers for the Yankees. Additionally, a number of athletes were punished by their coaches for sending the uncivil tweets.[53]

Although we may not have the time or resources to identify those who engage in online incivility, there are steps we can take to prevent and minimize uncivil behavior online. In fact, some claim that a "civil online culture is achievable, with the right mind-set, willingness, and tools."[54] A number of websites have adopted these strategies to reduce incivility online. For example, Twitter has a "Report Abuse" button and is suspending the accounts of users who engage in abusive behavior. Twitter is also preventing them from creating new accounts.[55] Facebook set up a review process to determine if content is too offensive for advertisements, and Gawker instituted a system that rewards users who receive high marks from the site's readers and editors (their comments receive preferred placement). Reddit banned a number of discussion groups, including one with more than 150,000 subscribers.[56] In addition, the gaming company Riot Games created new participation standards and the ability for users to police each other.[57]

In addition to website management, those who use social media have various ways to contend with cyber incivility. For instance, we can ensure that we send civil e-mails by paying special attention to our messages and taking the time to rephrase wording that may be misperceived as rude. When using Google's Gmail, we can use the "Undo Send" function that will stop messages from being sent up to thirty seconds from the time that we hit "send." The Undo Send function allows us to reread our messages and cancel them if we perceive them to be uncivil.[58]

We can also turn to the Internet for guidance about appropriate "netiquette." It's possible to access YouTube videos that provide advice about using emoticons in professional and personal e-mail; suggestions for using discretion when posting on someone's Facebook wall; and recommendations about retweeting Twitter messages and juggling various online chats.[59]

Jim Printup, president of the Upper Midwest chapter of the Employee Assistance Professionals Association, has developed a creative technique for online self-policing. Printup instructs his clients to assemble an imaginary board of directors with people they learn from and try to impress. (Printup's own imaginary board of directors includes his family, a few friends, and the 1970s *Kung Fu* TV character, Kwai Chang Caine, a monk who fights for justice with martial arts.) Printup says that prior to sending an e-mail, text, or posting a comment, we can curb our online incivility by thinking about how our board of directors would advise us to communicate in the situation.[60]

If we're the target of online incivility, we may be able to alert the company for whom a troll works. For example, a feminist writer in Australia was called an uncivil name on her Facebook page by a man she didn't know. She accessed his Facebook page and saw that he listed his employer. The writer contacted his employer and shared his comment. According to numerous media reports, the employee was fired.[61]

## CELL-PHONE INCIVILITY

Communications professor Andrew F. Wood wanted his students to slow down a bit and critically analyze the information he presents in class. He also wanted to be sure to listen to his Millennial students to try to understand exactly how they learn. In an attempt to increase his overall knowledge, Wood enrolled in an art history course, where he found himself "a forty-something among kids young enough to be my daughter, and observing how roughly one-third of my fellow students seemed more interested in updating their Facebook pages than in attending to the professor's lecture." [62]

This situation influenced Wood to impose a strict antitechnology zero-tolerance policy in his classroom. Later in the semester, Dr. Wood noticed a student tapping on her cell phone, her brow furrowed in concentration, while he was delivering a lecture. Wood stared angrily at the student and asked, "Just what do you think you're doing?" The student looked up, held up her cell phone so that Wood could see her dictionary app, and stammered, "I didn't understand that word you used. I was looking it up!"[63] Wood felt "battered" at that moment and knew right then and there that he'd have to change his classroom cell-phone policy. Wood concluded, "How many times, after all, have I used my phone for the same reason? Why would I deprive her of the same resource?"[64]

Wood's experience illustrates that the use of mobile devices can be distracting to some and can be a source of information to others. Similarly, Wood's situation highlights the lack of clarity about what is considered appropriate cell-phone use. Even so, the number of people who use cell phones continues to increase, along with the problems associated with their use. Whether used for phone calls, texts, or to connect to the Internet, cell-phone use is commonly perceived as uncivil.

### Annoying Cell-Phone Use

Eighty-three percent of Internet users use their cell phone as the preferred way to connect to the Internet, an increase of more than two-thirds (67 percent) since 2000, and 80 percent more than in 2008. Additionally, over 50 percent of cell-phone owners use their device to text messages, send and receive photos and videos, use apps, and use GPS mapping services.[65] Interestingly, "most cell owners are likely to get complaints that they are not responding quickly enough to calls or contacts, than to get complaints that they are spending too much time with their devices"[66] According to the PEW Internet and American Life Project, *The Best (and Worst) of Mobile Connectivity,* uncivil cell-phone use is still a persistent problem, but the frequency with which we encounter loud and annoying cell-phone users is decreasing. Additionally, only 6 percent of cell-phone owners report that they have received dirty looks or drawn criticism in response to how they use their cell phone in public.[67]

Nonetheless, while most cell-phone owners know that they need not shout into their phones to be heard, they may be so involved in their conversation that they don't realize they're holding up a line or blocking a sidewalk.[68] Furthermore, when the US Department of Transportation considered a 2014 proposal to allow cell-phone use on airplanes, they were flooded with thousands of comments, such as:

- "I think this is a terrible idea. In fact, I would pay extra to be in the 'quiet cabin' section."
- "Please, NO use of cell phones on aircrafts for voice calls. Narrow seats, no leg room, and screaming children are bad enough."
- "If these people are SO important they have to be plugged in 24/7, let them quietly text if they must."[69]

Currently, airline passengers can use cell phones and tablets on flights within the United States, as long as they're in "airplane mode." However, the FCC has proposed that airlines allow passengers to use their phones to converse with others. If the proposal is adopted, individual airlines will have the final say about in-flight cell-phone use.[70] Some individuals equate the "second-hand intimacy" that accompanies listening to loud cell-phone conversations with secondhand smoke. These individuals suggest that since there are laws against smoking in public (including on airplanes), there should be laws that limit cell-phone use in additional public places.[71]

There are a variety of reasons why cell-phone users and their conversations are considered exceptionally uncivil. Some researchers suggest that cell-phone use can be ego-enhancing at the expense of others. "[Cell-phone users are] telling people around them, 'You don't matter, and I must be very important.' "[72] Furthermore, cell phone conversations are often viewed as uncivil because users feel insulated from people around them. People who use cell phones in public often speak about intimate topics that are normally discussed in private, which can make those people who are "forced" to listen feel uncomfortable.

Moreover, studies reveal that people judge cell-phone conversations to be more intrusive and annoying than face-to-face conversations, even when the volume and content of both are the same. This is because the listener hears only one side of a conversation which leads to discomfort, irritation, and distraction. Listening to only one side of a conversation hijacks attention, which also occurs in face-to-face conversations when only one person is audible.[73] In other words, "people pay more attention when they hear only half a conversation. It's apparently easier to tune out the continuous drone of a complete conversation, in which two people take turns speaking, than it is to ignore a person speaking and falling silent in turns."[74]

## Cell Phones and Norms

Consider the following situations and ask yourself whether you believe that norms for appropriate cell-phone use were violated:

- Sandie sent her husband an e-mail during dinner asking if they could talk. Even though he was sitting across the table, it was the only way she could get his attention as he buried his nose in his smartphone.
- While discussing a very personal matter with her pastor, he interrupted the private discussion to take a social phone call.
- While attending a funeral for a friend, another attendee's phone went off just as the casket was leaving the service. The ring tone was "Gentlemen, Start your Engines!"[75]

While it may seem obvious to us that a husband should speak to his wife during dinner, a pastor shouldn't answer a social call during a confidential face-to-face interaction, and a funeral attendee should silence his cell, others may perceive that it's acceptable to use a cell phone at the dinner table, take a call in the middle of private discussion, or even fail to silence a cell phone during a funeral. The *Digital Divisiveness* study reveals that 90 percent of respondents agree that norm violations occur when people answer text messages or check their social media profiles while at the dinner table, while driving a car, while at church or school, or during a customer-service interaction. However, these norms are commonly violated.[76]

In addition to the common violation of cell-phone norms, norms for and the perception of appropriate cell-phone use may differ by culture, gender, and generation. For example, text-messaging norms in the United States are different from those in India. In the United States, both females and males are more likely than Indian women and men to send and read texts in public places, such as restaurants, shops, and movie theaters. However, it is not as appropriate for women and men in India to send and receive texts in these public places because Indians can't confidentially send or read texts in such densely crowded public areas. Additionally, Americans and Indians have conflicting ideas of what constitutes impolite texting behavior:

> U.S. Americans report significantly more types of impolite texting behavior than do Indians and, in particular, find impolite—more than Indians—texting in a classroom, movie theater, at dinner, loud text alerts, and while conversing with others. Indians, however, report swearing in texts as impolite more than do Americans who infrequently indicate that this is impolite behavior. . . . Indians may text in settings that U.S. Americans find inappropriate, like movie

theaters, and may not be conscious of the volume of the texting alerts, which could also be considered impolite.[77]

In addition to cell-phone norms that are influenced by culture, the perceptions of uncivil use of cell phones is affected by gender, especially within the workplace. Although the use of mobile phones during meetings is becoming more acceptable, it is still considered inappropriate, rude, and/or distracting. In particular, employees in one study overwhelmingly perceived that taking or making calls during meetings is disrespectful, followed by writing or reading text messages or e-mails. When asked whether the employees had recently observed uncivil cell-phone use in their workplace, more than one-half said that they had recently witnessed others taking or making calls, and one-fourth of the employees had observed others checking incoming calls or allowing their phones to ring. Furthermore, at informal meetings (such as off-site lunch meetings), two-thirds of the employees perceived that writing and sending text messages or e-mails, answering a call, and browsing the Internet are behaviors that are rarely or never appropriate. Compared to the male employees, more female employees perceived the use of cell phones at informal meetings as uncivil behavior. In addition, compared to the female employees, men were approximately twice as accepting of behaviors such as checking text messages, sending text messages, and answering calls at meetings.[78]

Not only do cell-phone norms differ by culture and gender, norms for appropriate cell-phone use differ in regard to generation. For example, according to a 2016 Associated Press–NORC survey, most Americans agree that talking on a cell phone in restaurants is inappropriate. However, based on the survey, the director of the AP-NORC Center asserts that, "There are clear differences between what older Americans and younger Americans consider to be generally rude behavior." In particular, almost half of the Millennial generation respondents indicated that it's appropriate to use cell phones in restaurants, while only 22 percent of respondents over sixty indicated that cell-phone use in restaurants is acceptable.[79] Furthermore, with the exception of the workplace, members of Gen Z believe it's appropriate to use a phone during a family dinner, on a job interview, during a religious service, and at a wedding.[80] It may be that "technology does not just provide a different method of communicating from what was available for previous generations in early adulthood; it forces a rewriting of etiquette rules."[81] This means that although we may perceive a cell-phone user to be violating a norm of appropriate behavior, others may not. Therefore, it's important to remember that we may hold different ideas of what constitutes civil behavior, especially as it relates to cell-phone use, and that we shouldn't be quick to judge others as uncivil when we think they're using a cell phone in an inappropriate manner.

## Cell-Phone Etiquette

Kevin Williamson is a theater critic and *National Review* blogger who was attending a Broadway production. Much to his dismay, a member of the audience was ruining the performance for him by using her cell phone during the play. Williamson complained to the management, but they did nothing to stop the woman from using her phone. Finally, Williamson had had enough. According to Williamson: "I asked her to turn it off. She answered, 'So don't look.' I asked her whether I had missed something during the very pointed announcements to please turn off your phone, perhaps a special exemption granted for her. She suggested that I should mind my own business."[82] Williamson subsequently grabbed the phone from her and flung it against the wall. She slapped him and Williamson once again complained to management, after which he, not she, was escorted from the theater.[83]

Although the uncivil audience member appeared to disregard everyone around her and interfered with their theatergoing experience, Williamson's response to the woman's incivility was to be uncivil himself. While some maintain that we have a duty to confront uncivil behavior, we should do so in a respectful, restrained, and responsible manner. *Digital Divisiveness* author Joseph Grenny states that:

> Technology allows us to quickly and effectively communicate with a large network of friends and acquaintances we would not have access [to] otherwise. However, these benefits should not trump social norms of respect, courtesy, and politeness—especially with those we care about. It's time we learned [how] to speak up and confront electronic displays of insensitivity so that civility and technology can peacefully coexist.[84]

Even though there are no universally agreed-upon norms to guide us on the appropriate use of mobile devices, we can practice what we *believe* to be appropriate cell-phone behavior and be sensitive to others' perceptions of appropriate behavior, even if they differ from our own. We can also use effective and appropriate communication (that is, communication that is perceived as competent) to point out norm violations to others. However, it's important to consider the people with whom you are speaking (e.g., work colleagues, family members, friends, acquaintances, or strangers), the topic, the setting, and the others' culture, ethnic and regional background(s), gender, and age before deciding whether or not to communicate about a norm violation. We should therefore choose the message that we believe will be perceived as the most effective and appropriate in light of the characteristics just mentioned.

In terms of our own cell-phone behavior:

- We should respect others' personal space. If possible, we should move to a private space when using a cell phone and speak softly in a location from which people can escape our conversation, should they wish to do so.
- We shouldn't interrupt a face-to-face conversation when the cell phone rings. Having a phone conversation in front of someone who is physically present tells the person that the phone is more important than s/he is.
- We should refrain from speaking about private matters on a cell phone, if at all possible. This information may not only be annoying to others, but it can be used against us (e.g., we may leak confidential information while talking in public). [85]

To prevent the uncivil use of cell phones in our presence, we can:

- **Set expectations:** Talk about and display rules for cell-phone use during meetings.
- **Remove the temptation:** Store cell phones in a basket outside of the dining room until the meal is finished.
- **Impose consequences:** Let children know that we will take away their cell phones if used inappropriately.
- **Model good behavior**: Start an interaction by stating our intention to put our phone away and enjoy quality time with our conversation partner(s). [86]

And finally, to communicate with an uncivil cell-phone user "in a way that restores civility without damaging common courtesy," we can: [87]

- **Take the high road:** Assume the best of our conversation partner's intentions and remember that some calls or texts are urgent. We can say, "That sounds important. I can wait if you need to respond to that call or text."
- **Spell it out:** Rather than making a vague request, we can say something like, "We need your full attention at this meeting, so please turn off your cell phones."
- **Illuminate the impact:** Describe the consequences of the behavior rather than engaging in name-calling or judging the other's behavior. We can say, "Your screen light is disturbing my experience of the performance. Would you please turn off your phone?"
- **Take heart:** Even if others fail to comply with our requests for civil behavior, our communication may help in the slow establishment of new norms for appropriate cell-phone use.
- **Let it go:** If we perceive that our safety is at risk, we should move on. [88]

# SUMMARY AND CONCLUSION

Because Internet posts, tweets, and text messages defy the limits of time and space, it's important to consider the necessity of civil communication and its ethical base when communicating online. By remembering to be respectful, refraining from posting or sending immediate and emotional knee-jerk responses, and reflecting on the welfare of our online community, our cyber behavior will be both effective and appropriate, the necessary conditions for competent communication.

Online incivility can be defined as rude and discourteous behaviors that occur via e-mail, text messages, posts on social media sites, and cell-phone use. Flaming, trolling, doxxing, swatting, sexting, and "calling out" are examples of incivility online. In addition, insults, name-calling, and showing disrespect for differences of opinion are commonly observed as uncivil communication. Unfortunately, many social media users are targeted or witness online incivility whether or not a controversial topic is at issue. Incivility online can result in a variety of harms that are experienced by instigators, targets, and by those who witness the uncivil communication. The negative consequences associated with cyber incivility include mental health and emotional problems, embarrassment, and relationship issues. People engage in incivility online for a variety of reasons, the most common being anonymity and the lack of accountability for uncivil behavior. We can contend with incivility online by reporting abuse on social media sites, taking time to rephrase wording in e-mails that may be misperceived as rude, accessing and making use of "netiquette" information, and creating an imaginary board of directors to advise us about our online behavior. As a target of incivility online, we may be able to alert the company for whom an instigator works.

Whether used for phone calls, texts, or to connect to the Internet, cell-phone use is commonly perceived as uncivil. Although users no longer shout into their phones as much as they have in the past, they may be so involved in their conversations that they don't realize they're holding up a line or blocking a sidewalk. In addition, cell-phone users and their conversations may be considered uncivil because users feel insulated from people around them (and speak about topics that are normally discussed in private) and because hearing only one side of a conversation is a primary cause of listeners' discomfort, irritation, and distraction.

Furthermore, norms for appropriate cell-phone use are unclear and even those norms with which most people agree are often violated. Norms for appropriate cell-phone use are also influenced and may differ by culture, gender, and generation. Therefore, it's important to remember that we may hold different ideas of what constitutes civil behavior, especially as it relates to cell-phone use, and we shouldn't be quick to judge others as uncivil when we think they're using a cell phone in an inappropriate manner. We can illustrate civil cell-phone use by respecting others' personal space, not interrupting a face-to-face conversation when the cell phone rings, and not speaking about private matters on our cells, if at all possible. We can also take steps to prevent the uncivil use of cell phones and to point out others' uncivil cell-phone behavior in an effective and appropriate manner.

---

**Box 7-1**
**Strategies for Change: Everyday Incivility Online**

To contend with cyber incivility, we can:

- report abuse on social media sites;
- use an "Undo Send" function on e-mail, if available;
- rephrase wording in e-mails that may be misperceived as rude;
- access and make use of "netiquette" information;
- create an imaginary board of directors to advise us about our online behavior;
- and, as a target of cyber incivility, we may be able to alert the company for whom a troll works.

In terms of our own cell-phone behavior:

- We should respect others' personal space; if possible, we should move to a private space when using a cell phone and speak softly in a location from which people can escape our conversation.
- We shouldn't interrupt a face-to-face conversation when the cell phone rings. Having a conversation in front of someone who is physically present tells the person that the phone call is more important than s/he is.
- We should refrain from speaking about private matters on a cell phone. This information may not only be annoying to others, but it can also be used against us (e.g., we may leak confidential information while talking in public).

To prevent the uncivil use of cell phones in our presence, we can:

- **Set expectations:** Talk about and display rules for cell-phone use during meetings.
- **Remove the temptation:** Store cell phones in a basket outside of the dining room until the meal is finished.
- **Impose consequences:** Let children know that we will take away their cell phone if it's used inappropriately.

---

- **Model good behavior:** Start an interaction by stating our intention to put our phone away and enjoy quality time with our conversation partner(s).

To communicate with an uncivil cell-phone user in a civil and competent manner, we can:

- **Take the high road:** Assume the best of our conversation partner's intentions and remember that some calls or texts are urgent. We can say "That sounds important. I can wait if you need to respond to that call or text."
- **Spell it out:** Rather than making a vague request, we can say something like "We need your full attention at this meeting, so please turn off your cell phones."
- **Illuminate the impact:** Describe the consequences of the behavior rather than engaging in name-calling or judging the other's behavior. We can say "Your screen light is disturbing my experience of the performance. Would you please turn off your phone?"
- **Take heart:** Even if others fail to comply with your requests for civil behavior, your communication will help in the slow establishment of new norms for the appropriate use of cell phones.
- **Let it go:** If we perceive that our safety is at risk, we should move on.

# Chapter Eight

# Everyday Incivility at Home

*I have been far more impressed by the bad manners of parents to children than by those of children to parents. Who has not been the embarrassed guest at family meals where the father or mother treated their grown-up offspring with an incivility which, offered to any other young people, would simply have terminated the acquaintance?*
—C. S. Lewis, The Four Loves[1]

Rachel Canning wasn't the best-behaved teenager, nor was she the worst. Her parents also demonstrated good and bad behavior. However, this family's story became international news when Rachel sued her parents for financial support after they refused to pay for her college tuition. In court filings, she alleged that her parents were abusive, contributed to an eating disorder, and forced her to get a basketball scholarship. Canning also said that her parents kicked her out of their house when she turned eighteen because they didn't like her boyfriend.[2] Rachel subsequently moved in with the family of her best friend, the Inglesinos. Her parents, however, painted a different picture of the conflict they had with their daughter. Sean and Elizabeth Canning maintained that Rachel left home on a voluntary basis because she defied authority and refused to abide by reasonable household rules. These rules included keeping a curfew, doing chores, communicating in a respectful manner, and breaking up with her boyfriend, who the Cannings believed was a bad influence on Rachel.[3]

The Cannings' troubled relationship with their eldest daughter took a turn for the worse a few days before Rachel's eighteenth birthday, when they'd had just about enough of her wild behavior. The conflicts between Rachel and her parents centered on her weight, her drinking, and her boyfriend. In court papers, Rachel contended that her mother complained about her weight and called her names such as "fat" and "porky." But her parents said that

Rachel was spinning out of control—that she'd started to cut school and engage in excessive drinking every weekend. Sean and Elizabeth Canning maintained that they supported their daughter and tried to help her through her eating disorder.[4] They also claimed that the family she had moved in with was irresponsible and that they'd allowed Rachel to have her first taste of alcohol a few years earlier. It was the Iglesinos who eventually funded and filed the lawsuit on Rachel's behalf.[5]

Rachel lost the first round of her lawsuit when Judge Peter Bogaard suggested that her suit could lead to teens who "thumb their noses" at their parents, leave home, and then ask for financial support. Judge Bogaard asked, "Are we going to open the gates for twelve-year-olds to sue for an Xbox? For thirteen-year-olds to sue for an iPhone?"[6] Unexpectedly, Rachel Canning moved back home to her welcoming parents prior to the next hearing. In addition, she formally dropped her lawsuit. Judge Bogaard ordered the dismissal of the case, ruling that Rachel's request was voluntary and that no one coerced her to dismiss her complaint. Neither members of the Canning family nor those who represented them in court revealed the motive for the familial reconciliation and for the dismissal of the lawsuit. However, during the initial hearing, Judge Bogaard cited a letter that Rachel had written during the conflict in which she apologized for her actions. She wrote, "I really need to realize there are consequences for the things I do. I do miss you guys. I am trying to turn over a new leaf."[7]

The story of Rachel Canning and her lawsuit against her parents illustrates various aspects of incivility. Rachel was uncivil when she used disrespectful communication while conversing with her parents. She refused to restrain her impulse to defy parental authority and showed no responsibility toward her "community" (i.e., her family). Some news outlets labeled Rachel "the spoiled New Jersey teen."[8] But Rachel's mother was also uncivil when she called her daughter "fat" and "porky." And if we believe the Iglesinos encouraged Rachel to sue her parents, they were disrespectful, failed to restrain their opportunity for "payback" (knowing that the Cannings believed they were reckless for giving Rachel alcohol), and were irresponsible regarding their "community" (that is, the psychological and emotional damage they inflicted on Rachel and her parents).

Incivility and conflict within the family can be commonplace and rarely leads to lawsuits. However, incivility at home results in negative consequences that can affect the entire extended family. In this chapter, you will learn about family norms and disconfirming communication, causes of everyday incivility at home, familial relationships and incivility, and how to manage everyday incivility at home.

# CHARACTERISTICS OF EVERYDAY INCIVILITY AT HOME

Research reveals that communication in the family differs from communication in other contexts in several ways. For example, family conflict is frequent and more difficult to escape than conflict in other contexts, especially because of the close physical proximity and experiences shared by family members. Additionally, because family members are interdependent, communication between two members of a family may very well affect all other members. [9] Another way that family communication differs from communication in other contexts is that families establish norms that influence interaction and the perception of incivility.

## Family Norms

Gabriele Kembuan is of Chinese descent and writes that although her family prays to her ancestors during the *Ching Ming* festival, they have adopted colonial Dutch family norms. These norms include obedience to parents, accepting objects only with the right hand, saying *danke* for thank you, and refraining from smacking one's lips at the dinner table. A powerful norm in Kembuan's family is financially supporting all members of the extended family whenever needed. An unusual Kembuan family norm is the restriction against eating mackerel. This norm comes from a family story that says her great-grandfather would have died in a shipwreck if it weren't for a school of mackerels that saved his life. Family folklore says that Gabriele's great-grandfather swore that his descendants would not eat mackerel in gratitude for saving his life. Even today, Kembuan's grandmother forbids her to eat mackerel. [10]

Family norms concern the expected behaviors that everyone in the family is aware of, and they range on a continuum from explicit to implicit. [11] Explicit family rules define the degree of freedom of expression in the family; that is, what we can talk about, when and where we can talk about it, and to whom we can talk. Explicit family rules may be communicated with the sentence, "We should/shouldn't discuss such subjects / use those words in our family!"

Similarly, family stories, such as the one involving Kembuan's great-grandfather, can include both explicit and implicit rules that affect behavior. An implicit rule associated with the "mackerel story" is that Kembuan family members should express gratitude across many generations if helped by others (including fish) in a life-or-death situation. Shared stories communicate the family's history, expectations, and identity; they instruct, warn, and communicate issues that matter to a specific family. [12] Stories about births and deaths, immigration and foreign travel, and triumphs and tragedies can communicate implicit rules about the importance of helping others, what it means to live a moral life, and how to deal with adversity.

In terms of the Communication Competence model, what one family considers appropriate behavior, another may not. We may find that our behavior is considered "uncivil" by families whose norms differ from the norms in our family. For example, one family may enjoy loud storytelling and arguing at family meals just for the fun of it. Another family may follow a norm that says it's okay to burp out loud so that other members of the family can tease the burper and come up with creative put-downs for the rest of the evening. Still another family may allow their cat to jump on the table while they're eating dinner and pretend not to notice when family members sneak food under the table to feed the dog.

What might the perception be if someone from a family that adheres to strict dinnertime etiquette is invited to have dinner with any of the three families described above? In all probability, the dinner guests would describe the behavior of these family members as inappropriate and uncivil. However, just as norms differ among cultures, ethnicities and regions, gender, and generation, so do norms differ among families. We should be careful when we judge other families to be uncivil because the behavior that is considered appropriate in *our* family may be perceived as inappropriate by members of other families.

## Disconfirming Communication

Harlan Cohen is a nationally syndicated advice columnist and author of six books. His overall goal in giving advice is to get people "comfortable with the uncomfortable." Cohen's goal is evidenced in his response to the following request for advice:

> Dear Harlan:
> My grandmother always brings up my weight when we get together for holidays. She has no filter. She says whatever comes to mind. This happened again over Thanksgiving. I've struggled with my weight for my entire life. She knows how much it bothers me, but continues to keep hurting my feelings. I've respectfully asked her not to ask me about this, but she doesn't listen. I will see her again during the holidays. What should I do? I'm already dreading the upcoming holidays. [13]

Cohen advised the granddaughter to become comfortable with the uncomfortable, because Grandma will most likely continue to speak to her in an uncivil manner:

Dear Grandma Problem:

Grandma roasts a ham and the guests. No, it's not nice. You can lose the weight, but you'll never lose your grandma's unsolicited advice. Even if she stops with the weight comments, she'll find some other way to get under your skin. She wants a reaction. She will never stop giving you her opinion. Don't try to manage her. Manage your reactions. Acknowledge her comments and move on. You can talk to her again about it, if you want, but that will just give her a bigger reaction. She likes the attention. The best approach is to love yourself even more. This can mean changing what you don't love or loving what you can't change. When you love yourself, stupid comments from family members roll off your back. [14]

Grandma's comments are an example of disconfirming communication which is uncivil and fails to respect others. We communicate disconfirmation when we ignore people, fail to acknowledge their thoughts and feelings, and refuse to accept their opinions and emotions. On the other hand, we communicate confirmation when we respect others even though we may disagree with their thoughts and feelings. Saying "I disagree with your opinion but I understand your reasons for thinking the way you do" respects a conversation partner. However, saying "You're wrong!" or "That's a stupid thing to say!" is disconfirming and uncivil. [15]

*Three Levels of Disconfirming Communication*

In general, there are three levels of communication that are considered disconfirming:

- **Not recognizing others:** Maybe a partner or member of your family once gave you the silent treatment. Perhaps you've written an e-mail or texted a family member and requested a response ASAP. However, you don't receive a response and later find out that the family member "just didn't get around to it." If so, you know that being ignored is uncivil and disconfirming.
- **Not acknowledging others:** Suppose you tell a family member about a difficult romantic relationship or about a serious problem you're having at work. In the middle of your story, the family member interrupts and says, "You just reminded me that I have to phone my friend. I better do it now before I forget." This response is disconfirming because it fails to acknowledge your thoughts and feelings.
- **Not endorsing others:** We fail to endorse others when we don't accept their thoughts and feelings. How might you feel if a partner or member of your family responds with "You are not!" after telling her/him that you felt angry and upset about something s/he did? Maybe you were once chastised for thinking a certain way because there were "more important things to think about." These examples illustrate that failing to endorse

others' thoughts and feelings communicates disrespect and lack of affir-
mation.[16]

## Disconfirming Gift-Giving

A wife described purchasing clothes for her husband in the style and colors
he doesn't like. When asked why she buys him clothing that she knows he'll
dislike, she explained:

> I buy a lot of clothes [for my husband] because he has horrible taste in
> clothes. . . . I usually buy him dress clothes. We really don't have the same
> taste. I got him a silk shirt that was a little too loud for him. He's very, very
> conservative; strictly blue, gray, black . . . I bought him burgundy pants, really
> dark burgundy pants and a silk shirt, which was really nice, and he's worn it
> twice because I forced him to on an occasion. It looks really good, but that's a
> little bit more than he usually likes.[17]

Most people assume that gifts that fail to reflect a recipient's preference
are given unintentionally. However, some gift-givers deliberately give
presents because they know the recipient won't like the gift and/or they want
to send a specific message that the gift will convey. Unwanted presents are
sometimes given in an attempt to gain control or to impose a particular
identity on the recipient. In the example above, the wife is disconfirming her
husband's clothing preferences and imposing her own fashion style and identity. In essence, her gift of clothing is a gift to herself because *she* wants him
to dress differently to meet her idea of what is stylish. The gift is an example
of uncivil and controlling nonverbal behavior because it disrespects the husband's preferences and is a threat to his self-concept.[18]

Other examples of disconfirming and uncivil gifts that threaten a recipient's self-concept include:

- Those that attempt to force someone into a particular social role. For
  example, a mother-in-law repeatedly gave pregnancy tests to her daugh-
  ter-in-law for Christmas. The disconfirming message the gift communicated was that it was time for her to become a mother. Another mother
  bought her daughter, a stay-at-home mom, a new business suit. The underlying disconfirming message was that she should go to work rather than
  stay at home.
- Faith-oriented gifts based on the gift-giver's own religion, which differs
  from the recipient's. Recipients typically believe that such gifts represent
  an imposition of faith and they complain about these gifts on social media.
  One recipient posted that he or she had received a "guilt-laden" religious
  book to help him or her "come home to the faith." Another recipient

posted that she or he had received a "Jews for Jesus" Bible, even though the recipient is neither Jewish nor Christian.

- Traditional gendered gifts when recipients want egalitarian cross-gender gifts. For example, a grandmother asked her daughter what her little girl (the granddaughter) wanted for her birthday. The girl's mother explained that her daughter liked "boy things." The grandmother then bought her granddaughter a frilly dress because she wanted the little girl to like "girly things." This gift is disconfirming because it disrespects the preferences of and imposes a gender identity on the recipient.
- Collections of special objects ("collectibles") which can be an extension of the gift-givers' self-concept. Collectibles provide us with the opportunity to be remembered after our death and to achieve "immortality" if the recipient continues to add to the collection. Collections that are contrary to a recipient's self-concept are disconfirming since they don't respect the recipient's preferences. One woman described this type of present in a post on Babycenter.com: "I have this one aunt who buys my daughter a Precious Moments collectible for . . . every occasion. . . . She told my mom once: 'I don't care what Sophie likes; I buy what I want to buy.' "[19]

Uncivil gifts can also be given to communicate aggression. These spiteful presents are given to deliberately offend the recipient and may reflect a deteriorating relationship. For example, after a teenager had a fight with her parents just before Christmas, her mother gave her a pocketknife, a chocolate bar, and a card that said "Good luck in the wild." The underlying disconfirming message of this gift is that the daughter will not be able to survive on her own without her parents.

Still other presents are given because the gift-giver wants to brag and/or "out-gift" other gift-givers. Some gift-givers post on social media sites about the wonderful gifts they purchase to send an underlying message about their "generosity." Similarly, grandparents may purchase "big toy" gifts for their grandchildren to out-gift the parents, even when the parents tell the grandparents not to give these types of presents to the grandkids.[20]

## CAUSES OF EVERYDAY INCIVILITY AT HOME

Claire is a successful piano teacher who was elected vice president of her music association. She and her mother, Maureen, typically have pleasant and supportive conversations. During one phone call, Claire mentioned that she was extremely tired and said, "I was up half the night last night writing up my evaluations of the students who applied for our association's music scholarship, and tonight I'll be up late again typing up the minutes from our last meeting."

Maureen replied, "You take on too much, Claire! Why can't some of the other officers do that? You shouldn't be typing minutes anyway; you're not the secretary, you're the vice president! I hate to see you allowing yourself to be taken advantage of."

Claire responded angrily, "You know how much I love working with the music teachers' association! I was thrilled to be elected, and it was my choice to continue as chair of the scholarship committee. I like being a judge because it helps me prepare my students for competition. And I volunteered to take minutes this time because the secretary couldn't make the meeting. Why are you putting me down? Why can't you just be supportive?"

Feeling unfairly attacked, Maureen defended herself by saying, "I'm not putting you down. I *am* being supportive!"[21]

Although Claire and Maureen were involved in the same conversation, they interpreted it very differently. Claire "heard" her mother say that she doesn't think she makes the right choices and can't handle the responsibilities she's taken on. Maureen "heard" that Claire failed to appreciate her support by encouraging her to stand up for herself and demonstrating that she is "on her side." Maureen's advice was meant to show that she cares, but Claire's interpretation of the advice was that her mother disapproves of what she's doing. Both Maureen and Claire's interpretations weren't based on the words actually used in their conversation, but on the underlying or the hidden meaning of the words, their relationship, and their past history.[22] Without explicit mention, a single message can communicate information not only about a topic, but also about the association between the conversation partners.

## Underlying Messages

Studies of "relational communication" demonstrate that we not only interact about the content of communication, but also about our association with a conversation partner. These messages are described as occurring at the content and relationship levels of communication.[23] A major reason for the perception of incivility at home is the misinterpretation of the underlying, implicit, and unspoken message associated with the words that are actually spoken.

The *content-level meaning* of a message refers simply to the content of the words and sentences that are communicated. The *relationship-level meaning* of a message concerns meaning that can be ascertained, in part, from nonverbal communication, such as the way something is said, eye contact, facial expression, and/or gestures. In addition, the interpretation of relationship messages are influenced by the past experience and personal associations that we bring to a conversation.

For example, suppose a sibling says, "Please get off the computer." The meaning on the content level is obvious: The sibling wants us to get off the computer. If the sibling communicates this message with a smile and a calm tone of voice and places a hand on our shoulder, the underlying message is that our relationship is based on connection and respect. Similarly, we are more likely to interpret the relationship-level meaning as positive if our sibling has made previous requests to spend time away from the computer so he or she can engage in an activity with us.

On the other hand, if the sibling communicates this message with a frown and an angry tone of voice, crossing her or his arms, the sibling may be communicating that our relationship is based on control and a power differential; in other words, she or he believes s/he has the right to tell us what to do. In addition, we are more likely to interpret the relationship-level meaning as negative if our sibling has previously demanded that we cease engaging in particular activities.

Because relationship-level meaning is based on our subjective interpretations, our perceptions of others' nonverbal messages and intentions may be incorrect.[24] For instance, the sharp tone of voice our sibling uses to tell us to get off the computer may have nothing to do with us; it may just reflect a hard day at work or extreme fatigue. It may even be that a relationship-level meaning interpreted as control (e.g., "Drive carefully!" or "Put on your jacket") may be an expression of affection and an attempt to establish connection. The misinterpretation of underlying connection and respect messages as control and disrespect messages is one reason why we perceive our family members to be uncivil.

## Connection, Control, and Respect

Have you ever found yourself feeling angry with a family member and not knowing exactly why? It may be that the reason for your anger is based on your interpretation of an underlying message on the relationship level of meaning. Relationship-level messages focus on connection, control, and/or respect.

*Connection* is the force that drives us to become close with a relational partner, and *control* is the force that drives us to gain dominance; both are communicated implicitly at the relationship level of meaning. In addition to connection and control, respect is considered a relational message. *Respect* involves acknowledging others by listening well and affirming their point of view (without necessarily agreeing with it). You may feel disrespected if you are speaking with a family member and see that she or he is riveted to the television screen, even though the family member doesn't utter disrespectful words. In addition, you may become upset when a family member tells you to put out the dog, pick up the mess, or turn off the light. You don't become upset at the request (whether it deals with the dog, the mess, or the light); you become upset because that family member feels entitled to tell you what to do (control) and doesn't think you're capable of dealing with household issues on your own (disrespect). As a result, you say, "Don't tell me what to do!," and you begin to argue about the family member's uncivil communication and whether s/he has the power to control your actions.

People react more strongly and emotionally to underlying relationship messages and meanings than the content of a conversation. This occurs even with the knowledge that interpretations of nonverbal communication and others' motivations may be incorrect.[25]

Let's return to the example of a sibling asking you to get off the computer. Based upon your sibling's nonverbal communication, you may interpret the underlying relationship message as one in which your sibling is trying to spend more time with you. Since you want to be sure that your sibling understands that your relationship is based upon love and affection, you may respond with happiness and a click on the mouse to get off the computer. On the other hand, based upon your sibling's nonverbal communication, you may interpret the underlying relationship message as one in which your sibling is trying to control you and disrespects your needs and choices. Since you want to be sure that your sibling understands that your relationship is based upon an equal distribution of power (that is, your sibling can't tell you what to do), you may respond with anger and a refusal to get off the computer. In either case, it's not the content of the message but the underlying relationship-level meaning of the message that influences your perception of incivility and determines whether or not you decide to get off the computer.

## FAMILIAL RELATIONSHIPS AND INCIVILITY

When partners in an intimate relationship decide to end their association, their talk frequently consists of insults, accusations, and recrimination (in other words, uncivil communication). However, relationships don't have to end in this manner. In June 2011, Jack White, the former front man of the band White Stripes, and his wife, model and singer Karen Elson, announced their plans to divorce. Instead of sending a press release that implied blame or a plea for privacy, the couple released a statement about a party to celebrate their six-year wedding anniversary and their impending divorce. The couple stated that they intended to honor their time together with a divorce party designed to confirm their friendship and celebrate the past and future with friends and family.[26] Invitations to the party asked guests to celebrate a new anniversary and breaking the bonds of marriage. The public announcement of the un-nuptial celebration also included the statements that they will continue to be trusted friends and that they appreciate the time they shared together, as well as the time they will share together in the future.[27] One marriage and family therapist summarized the White-Elson divorce as an example of respect—not only for each other, but for others who know and care about them.[28]

After learning about White and Elson's civil communication during their divorce, you may be tempted to wonder why they divorced in the first place. You may think that White and Elson must have shared compatible views and rarely, if ever, fought while they were together. However, research demonstrates that even more important than having like-minded beliefs and attitudes is how couples handle conflict, which is inevitable in any relationship. Marriages that last "must have at least five times as many positive as negative moments together," and partners must avoid four uncivil interaction strategies that will sabotage their attempt to communicate in a civil manner.[29]

## Married Couples

According to *Public Discourse*, an online publication that makes academic scholarship on various issues available to the public, the major determinants of a couple's risk of divorce include:

- **Cohabitation:** Cohabitating couples have a 50 to 80 percent higher likelihood of divorce than couples who do not cohabitate.
- **Race:** The general lifetime risk of divorce is 1.3 percent higher for African-American couples than for whites.
- **Age and age difference:** Couples who marry after age eighteen have a 24 percent reduced risk of divorce, and the risk of divorce for spouses with a significant age difference is twice that of partners who are close in age.
- **Education:** Only 27 percent of college graduates will divorce by middle age.[30]

Other risk factors include family background, marital history, income, beliefs, religion, child-bearing and desire for children, sexual history, and smoking.[31] Interestingly, spousal communication is not included in this list of factors that place couples at risk for divorce. This absence is egregious, especially since specific types of uncivil marital communication can predict divorce with a 94 percent accuracy rate.[32]

### The Four Horsemen

Eric and Pam's marital communication was a disaster. She was extremely accusatory and attacking, and as a result, Eric stopped listening to her. Each argument ended with Pam screaming that he shut her out by not saying anything. The few times that Eric did respond to Pam, he'd say something like, "I can't get anywhere with you," and he'd leave the room. One day Eric bought flowers for Pam after working late. He had been stuck in traffic and feared that Pam would be angry because being late for dinner was one of her frequent complaints about Eric.

Pam had had a rough day as well, which included babysitting a spoiled six-year-old niece and having to take her to the emergency room because of an asthma attack. There had been no time to make dinner.

Pam took her frustrations out on Eric as soon as he walked through the front door:[33]

**Pam:** Once again, you're very late!

**Eric:** Got caught in traffic. Sorry. What's for dinner?

**Pam:** I have had it up to my eyeballs today with stress and disappointments. This has been a terrible day. Don't you think you could have the consideration to call me if you know you're going to be late? We've been over this a hundred times.

**Eric:** There was no chance to call you. [*Eric picks up the paper and starts to read it.*]

**Pam:** You worked late, didn't you? It wasn't only traffic that made you late.

**Eric:** [*After a long pause in which Eric is trying to control his temper*] Yes, I worked late, and yes, I'm inconsiderate; but I'm also hungry and tired. What's for dinner?

**Pam:** I've got news for you, mister: We're going out. I've made reservations at Arnie's at eight. [*Pam grabs Eric's newspaper and crumples it up.*]

**Eric:** I've got news for you: I'm not going to take this crap. I need a drink. See ya. [*Eric storms out of the house, on his way to a local tavern.*][34]

Eric's behavior is an example of "stonewalling," which often happens when partners are in conflict. Stonewalling describes minimal, if any, responses; the use of props (such as a newspaper) to take oneself out of a conversation; and physically walking away from a conversation partner. Although stonewallers may engage in this type of behavior to remain "neutral," stonewalling communicates disapproval, distance, and disrespect. Stonewalling is an uncivil interaction strategy included in sociologist John M. Gottman's "Four Horsemen of the Apocalypse."[35]

Gottman began his studies of married couples by watching newlyweds interact in his "Love Lab" at the University of Washington. He also hooked couples up to electrodes and measured their blood flow, sweat, and heart rates as they spoke. Gottman followed up with the couples six years later to discover whether they were still married. He found that the group of couples he labeled "masters" were married and happy after six years. The group of couples he labeled "disasters" had divorced, separated, or were together, albeit chronically unhappy. Compared to the masters, the disasters were more physiologically active in the Love Lab; their heart rates were quick, they sweated a lot, and their blood flow was fast. The masters had low levels of physiological arousal because they had created a climate of trust and intimacy. However, the disasters displayed signs of the "fight or flight" syndrome, which prepares the body to flee from danger or to face danger and fight. These couples were prepared to attack and to be attacked, even when they talked about pleasant aspects of their relationship.[36]

Gottman next focused on happy couples and how they created a climate of trust and intimacy. He found that happy couples make "bids for connection" throughout the day. Bids go beyond mere comments in that they request a response from the conversation partner. The conversation partners who turn toward their spouses and respond by engaging the bidders are involved in happy marriages. The partners who don't support their spouses fail to meet their partners' emotional needs.

Those who had divorced after the six-year follow-up had only three out of ten of their bids for emotional connection met with intimacy. Studies demonstrate that civil communication within a relationship promotes intimacy, as well as empathy and authenticity.[37] Gottman believes that the "masters" couples very purposefully built a culture of respect and support in which they communicated appreciation for their spouse by creating a climate of trust and intimacy.[38]

The marital partners whose bids for connection were not met received specific types of disconfirming communication which Gottman labeled "the Four Horsemen of the Apocalypse." These messages not only contribute to marital dissatisfaction but also predict divorce with a 94 percent rate of accuracy.[39] Taken as a whole, these disconfirming messages communicate disrespect, a lack of restraint, and the shirking of responsibility—in other words, uncivil communication:

- **Criticism:** Whereas complaints are aimed at specific actions and behaviors, criticism involves negative words about a partner's personality or character. Criticism is common in most relationships, but can usher in the other three types of disconfirming messages if pervasive.
- **Contempt:** Contempt is based on long-simmering negative thoughts about a partner and is evident in sarcasm, name-calling, hostile humor,

and mockery. Nonverbally, contempt is communicated by eye-rolling, sneering, and "tsking." Contempt is described as the most poisonous disconfirming message because it communicates disgust with a partner.

- **Defensiveness:** Defensiveness occurs when we believe that our self-concept is under attack. Communicating defensively is a way to blame a partner (e.g., "You're the problem, not me!") and typically escalates a conflict.
- **Stonewalling:** Also labeled "withdrawal," stonewalling occurs when a partner physically and/or mentally disengages from a situation. A stonewaller fails to give verbal and nonverbal feedback during a conversation and may act as if she or he doesn't care what a partner has to say. Stonewalling typically occurs when the other three disconfirming responses become overwhelming and it is perceived as a way out.

Gottman can predict the occurrence of future divorce by assessing whether couples use these four types of disconfirming messages; how partners recall their relational history; and by the amount of their physiological stress.[40] He advises that to avoid divorce, marriages should be based on love and respect, "the direct opposite of—and antidote for—contempt, perhaps the most corrosive force in marriage."[41]

*Covert Verbal Abuse*

Sometimes we may fail to recognize that communication directed toward us is disconfirming and uncivil. Consider Ellen's story:

> I spent several weeks going through the papers and old household files that Ernie and I had accumulated for more than twenty years. After extensive sorting, I categorized everything and made color-coded files: "Business, Medical, Insurance, Personal," etc. The result was three drawers of files in a new file cabinet. It was a long and tedious job. Occasionally I had mentioned to Ernie how the work was progressing. Finally, after a couple of weeks' work, I was glad to be done. I said, "Ernie, I finished the files. It was really a job." I opened the drawers and showed him what I'd done. He said, "Wow! I'm impressed." I didn't remember him acknowledging me like that ever before. With a smile I said, "You are?" He answered in a strange voice, "I'm impressed with how you got those names to fit on all those little itty bitty labels." I said, "Oh, Ernie, I just typed them on. That wasn't the hard part." He looked seriously at me and said, "Well, I think it was."[42]

Ellen felt frustrated and depressed after her conversation with Ernie but didn't quite know why. Ellen was the target of covert verbal abuse, which is so subtle that we often don't realize we're the victim of such abuse. Covert verbal abuse is subtle and not as intense as verbal abuse and is a type of uncivil communication because it is disrespectful, illustrates lack of restraint, and demonstrates responsibility to the self rather than the "community" (that is, the marriage). In addition, similar to reactions to other forms of uncivil communication, targets of this behavior question whether the covert abuse messages are truly disconfirming and uncivil.

Covert verbal abuse causes pain and confusion, especially since we may even feel insulted in response to communication that appears "nice" on the surface.[43] One reason for the confusion is that we assume the person who communicates the covert verbal abuse interacts in a rational manner. The reality of the situation is that the instigator has no rational explanation for the abuse and her/his communication is not grounded in reason. Therefore, when a target communicates with the instigator about the covert verbal abuse, s/he believes that there must be a reason for the abuse. However, it's highly likely that the instigator responds with additional abuse and blames the target for the disconfirming communication (e.g., "Stop being so sensitive!").[44]

People who are victims of covert verbal abuse often feel disoriented and off balance because their perceptions of reality are constantly challenged. The abuser's ability to undermine a partner's sense of self and reject her/his perception of reality creates the emotional and physical toll that results from covert verbal abuse.[45] In addition to emotional and psychological consequences, physical deterioration can result, since "a prolonged state of emotional stress—especially if you feel out of control, overwhelmed, and helpless—literally undermines and breaks down your tissues and body systems."[46] The subtle nature and resulting harmful consequences of day-to-day covert verbal abuse are the reasons why this type of communication can be more damaging than overt forms of verbal abuse.[47]

Covert verbal abuse consists of:

- Hurtful remarks that are delivered in a caring and sincere manner (e.g., "I'm only telling you this for your own good, but you look ridiculous in those clothes").
- Messages that judge or deny the validity of a partner's thoughts, perceptions, or feelings (e.g., "You don't know what you're talking about!" or "You twist things all around").
- Jokes that criticize or put down a partner (which an abuser can defend by saying that the partner "can't take a joke, has thin skin, and overreacts").
- Verbal messages that are incongruent with nonverbal behaviors (such as saying, "I'm listening" while watching TV or constantly interrupting with topic changes).
- Messages that trivialize a partner and/or a partner's accomplishments (e.g., "Yes, I'm happy that you received an A on your term paper; the professor must have really liked the expensive notebook that you used to turn in your report").[48]

It's difficult to contend with covert verbal abuse because it's insidious and difficult to recognize. The first step in dealing with it is to recognize that the covert verbal abuser aims to confuse and weaken a partner to make her/ him easy to control. It's natural to believe that differences can be talked out in a reasonable and loving manner, but this assumption holds true for partners who are psychologically healthy. Unfortunately, dealing with covert verbal abuse by defending, explaining, compromising, apologizing, and negotiating are typically ineffective because these tactics work only when a partner is rational.

## Parents and Children

Larry Venable was happy for his eight-year-old grandson, who was excited to finally wear shoulder and knee pads while playing for his youth football league. Venable looked forward to the Saturday football games and thought they would be relaxing, fun, and even educational. However, he was shocked at the behavior of the parents who attended the game. One mother stood up and shouted "Do it again!" when her son jumped on another player after the whistle. Parents also screamed at the coaches for their decisions and yelled at the parents of the opposing team's players when their own team lost the game. Venable was confused because he "did not know for sure if the eight-year-olds were on the field or in the stands." He wrote, "Surely these people are not citizens of a civilized society."[49]

According to an AP/Ipsos poll, 70 percent of those questioned believe that Americans are ruder in the twenty-first century than they were twenty or thirty years ago. Sixty-nine percent of the respondents blamed celebrities, athletes, and public figures who behave rudely and are poor role models for the increase in rudeness. Similarly, 73 percent of those questioned pointed to TV shows and movies that include rude behavior as the cause for the increase in incivility. However, 93 percent of the respondents placed the blame on parents who fail to teach civility to their children.[50]

Although parents may believe that their children learn rude and disrespectful communication from their friends, many children learn uncivil behaviors from their parents, such as the behaviors Larry Venable witnessed at the youth football game. At home, parents don't recognize that interrupting and talking over their children's messages communicate disrespect and that children learn to model their disrespectful behavior.[51] Children are also disrespected when they're on the receiving end of messages that disconfirm them, such as being ignored.[52] Furthermore, parental discipline characterized by commands (e.g., "Turn off that TV now!"); threats ("I'll ground you for a week if you don't turn the TV off right now!"); and imperatives ("Why? Because I told you so, that's why!") is correlated with greater aggression and incivility in children's behavior.[53] Additionally, children watch and mimic their parents when they bicker and fight, shout obscenities at drivers whose skills aren't up to par, and engage in sideline rage during athletic activities.[54]

Although some school districts encourage "character education," experts maintain that instilling respect for others is a process that must begin early in life, in the home. In fact, in one survey of the more than two million American families that homeschool their children, it was found that parents want to avoid exposing their children to the ill manners and incivility found in public schools.[55]

One way that parents can teach their children civil behavior is by setting aside their own interests for "the larger good." For example, parents who openly bicker in front of their children teach the lesson of thinking only of themselves, whereas postponing an argument until the children are no longer in earshot (and resolving it in a civil manner) is a choice made for the sake of civility. Parents should make a conscious effort to disagree with an attitude of mutual respect so children learn that adults can demonstrate respect and love even when they aren't in agreement. Teaching respectful behavior also means that parents must be civil when they communicate with rude shop-keepers, bad drivers, and intrusive telephone salespersons. Parents should additionally teach their children about civil communication by not saying behind people's backs what they wouldn't say to them face-to-face. Children who see their parents set aside their own concerns for the larger good are more likely to do the same when they reach adulthood.[56]

It is possible for parents to reduce disrespectful behavior from their children. However, this task is not an easy one, since children grow up in a culture in which they learn that it's okay to disrespect their parents (thanks to the smart-alecky kids portrayed in mass media, including the Disney Channel); other kids (e.g., evidenced by wearing T-shirts that say "I don't like you!"); and themselves (e.g., believing that sexting is "no big deal").[57] Parents can teach their children to be respectful in this "age of awfulness" when they:

- Emphasize "character" (e.g., restraint, humility, and interest in others) rather than "looking out for number one." Instruct children to think before they speak and refrain from "hogging the stage" during conversations (and model these behaviors).
- Prioritize the family by joining together at the dinner table at home and scheduling "family dates" instead of "play dates." Communicate about the day's activities and ask family members about their day.
- Stress respect for authority by demanding respectful communication at all times and enforcing negative consequences when children are disrespectful.

- Teach and model the art of face-to-face conversation, which can be accomplished by limiting technology use and communicating without distractions. Ban the cell phone from the dinner table.[58]

## Siblings and Others

Vicky's sister always thought that Vicky was the favorite child and "got more" than she did. Her sister carried her grudge against Vicky into adulthood and was extremely angry at Vicky, especially on her wedding day. Vicky was marrying a loving, caring, and responsible man, but her sister was in the middle of separating from her alcoholic husband. On the day of Vicky's wedding, her sister showed up in an ugly dress and no makeup. Vicky described her sister's clothing by saying, "It was as if everyone else had been in black tie and she showed up in gym shorts!"[59] Some relatives wanted to know the reason for the shabby clothing, but Vicky didn't want to reveal the "family secrets" about her sister's anger. Vicky explained in an interview that her sister, via her clothing, was saying, "Look at me! She's got everything; I've got a miserable life! I have no job, I'm living on alimony!" Vicky concluded: "You'd think she was talking about me as if we were six years old."[60]

As is the case with Vicky and her sister, childhood sibling relationships and competition for attention and status often persist and form the basis of adult sibling relationships. The habitual ways that siblings communicate provide evidence of their place within the family. For example, older siblings tend to express concern and offer advice even if younger siblings object. If an adult older sister suggests to a younger brother that he make some time in his busy life to work on finding a partner, the younger brother may perceive her underlying attempt at connection as an attempt to control. In other words, she offers advice because she cares, but he believes that she's trying to direct his behavior.

Relationships among siblings may be close but competitive. Sibling hierarchies within the family may be based on birth order, parental favoritism, or communication style. In terms of birth order, older siblings typically realize that their power derives from their physical size, knowledge, and overall rank within the family. It's not unusual for older siblings to tease, torment, and communicate uncivilly with younger siblings. Older siblings may frighten younger ones by informing them of the monster in the closet, or how the "bad guys" are waiting for them behind the bushes in the front yard. But woe to the family outsider who mistreats a younger sibling; while older siblings may have the right to torment younger brothers and sisters, they also have the obligation to protect them from outsiders. "Both childhood memories of being mistreated (or of mistreating) and of being protected (or of protecting) can contribute to the sense of being linked forever as members of a family."[61]

In regard to members of the extended family, the same problems associated with communication-style differences among strangers, acquaintances, and friends (see chapter 3) also occur within the family. However, the problems become more acute since they occur among family members, whom, at the very least, we must tolerate. Recall that to a large extent, communication style refers to pacing and pausing, volume and pitch, directness and indirectness, and even topics of conversation. Communication style is influenced by our culture, ethnic group and regional background, gender, and generation. Unfortunately, we tend to blame others' negative personality characteristics and uncivil behavior for our discomfort rather than differences in communication style.[62]

Perceptions of incivility also occur when we're not familiar with the customs and traditions associated with different ethnic groups in the United States. For example, suppose during a wedding reception the groom's parents are surprised to see the bride greeting her guests while carrying a small satin bag. The new in-laws are shocked as they watch the guests place cash inside the bag. They believe this is rude behavior that shames guests into donating money to support the newlyweds.

What the groom's parents don't know is that the bride's family, who are Italian Americans, is following a custom called *buste*. This tradition helps the bride's family to defray wedding costs, and the satin bag, called *la borsa*, is typically used to collect money at the reception. Wedding guests willingly place money in the bag because they know that their hosts will do the same when members of their own families get married.[63] This example illustrates that "with more and more families blended from different backgrounds, opportunities abound to feel misjudged—or to feel that your relatives are misjudged."[64] Therefore, it's especially important to remember that communication-style differences and different customs are just that, *differences*, rather than evidence of rude and uncivil familial behavior.

## MANAGING EVERYDAY INCIVILITY

What can we say or do in response to family members who communicate in a disconfirming manner (both verbally and nonverbally); speak to us based on underlying messages of control and disrespect; deal with conflict by using criticism, contempt, defensiveness, or stonewalling; or reply to us with covert verbal abuse? Using metacommunication and setting boundaries are two ways we can respond to these uncivil behaviors.

## Metacommunication

One way to improve interpretations of underlying relationship messages is to use a communication skill known as *metacommunication*, which is "communication about communication." Suppose a mother and father ask their teenage daughter who plans to drive to a party to text them when she arrives at her destination. Rather than responding automatically on the basis of an underlying relationship message of control and disrespect (i.e., "We need to know where you are at all times because we don't trust you"), the daughter can pause and consider whether the underlying message might be that of connection (i.e., "We care about you and want to know that you are safe"). She can then respond by communicating about communication: "Why are you asking me to text you?" This response is civil because it asks the parents about *their* meaning of the message.

Similarly, we can change the way we perceive current-day communication among siblings, even as it continues to be influenced by those childhood relationships. The knowledge that our perceptions of underlying control messages may actually be connection messages enables us to reflect on whether our knee-jerk reaction to a sibling's comment is rooted in recollections of childhood inequities. This insight allows us to "change the way we interpret what our [adult] siblings say, or change the way we speak, to reshape and improve relationships with our brothers and sisters."[65]

Metacommunication also comes in handy during family gatherings in which political and/or controversial topics are discussed. Rather than responding to a contention with which we disagree by saying "What a bunch of crap!" (which includes an underlying relationship message of disrespect), we can instead say "I can understand why you say that, but I disagree with your opinion," which communicates our respect. Nonverbally, metacommunication can communicate our feelings of connection and respect with focused eye contact, head nods, and vocalizations that suggest understanding and acknowledgment ("Uh-huh"). However, even the best attempt at metacommunication may be perceived as disrespectful if it's accompanied by a sarcastic tone of voice, rolling eyes, or laughter.

## Setting Boundaries

We can also manage everyday incivility at home by setting boundaries. A boundary is an edge or limit that defines us as being separate from others and lets others know that we have limits to what we believe is appropriate.[66] Boundaries can be flexible and they can vary from person to person. For example, we may decide after the fact that we are uncomfortable with someone's words or actions and subsequently create a new boundary with revised standards for appropriate communication. Boundaries enable us to limit the actions of people who intend to hurt us, but we can additionally set boundaries for people we love and who we believe to be trustworthy.[67]

Boundary violations occur when others knowingly or unknowingly cross our limits. Such violations may be committed based on malice, ignorance, thoughtlessness, or even with the intention of kindness. Boundary violations are illustrated in disconfirming messages such as personal questions, inappropriate behaviors, and communication that attempts to control how we should think and feel.

We can use assertive metacommunication to respond to boundary violations, which enables us to stand up for our beliefs, rights, and needs in a respectful manner. Examples include:

- "I don't want to answer that question / talk about this subject."
- "That's private information."
- "I don't feel comfortable talking about this."
- "I don't know you well enough for me to talk about this / answer this question."

Creating and maintaining boundaries is also a way to counteract covert verbal abuse. An appropriate response to covert verbal abuse should enforce limits. Comments such as "I will not allow your criticism to influence my feelings" and "I refuse to listen to your comments any longer" will communicate our boundaries. Similarly, we can set limits by saying "I don't accept that," or "I'm going to end this conversation and leave if you don't stop trivializing my accomplishments" (and then do it). However, it's important to remember that appropriate boundary-setting messages may not be effective against a covert verbal abuser because such abusers tend to be irrational.

## SUMMARY AND CONCLUSION

Family norms concern the expected behaviors that every member of the family is aware of, and family stories may include explicit and implicit rules that affect behavior within the family. However, what one family considers appropriate behavior, another does not, and we may find that our behavior is perceived as "uncivil" by families whose norms differ from the norms in our own.

Disconfirming communication is uncivil and fails to respect others. There are three levels of communication that are considered disconfirming: not recognizing others, not acknowledging others, and not endorsing others. Nonverbal disconfirming communication may occur in the form of giving gifts, especially when gifts threaten a recipient's self-concept, communicate aggression, or are purchased to "out-gift" another family member.

Relational communication includes the subject of an interaction and the implicit information about the participants' relationship. A major reason for the perception of incivility at home is the misinterpretation of the underlying unspoken message associated with the words that are actually spoken. We react more strongly and emotionally to underlying relationship messages and meanings based on connection, control, and respect rather than to the content of a conversation. This occurs even with the knowledge that interpretations of nonverbal communication and others' motivations may be incorrect.

Marriages that last require at least five times as many positive as negative moments together and partners must avoid four types of uncivil communication that sabotage a marriage: criticism, contempt, defensiveness, and stonewalling. Disconfirming marital communication also includes covert verbal abuse, which, because of its subtle nature and resulting harmful consequences, can be more damaging than overt forms of verbal abuse.

Although parents may believe that their children learn rude and disrespectful communication from their friends, many children learn uncivil behaviors from their parents. However, experts believe that children should learn within the family to respect others and how to communicate in a respectful manner. Childhood sibling relationships and competition for attention and status often persist and form the basis of adult sibling relationships. In regard to members of the extended family, customs may differ and the same problems associated with communication-style differences among strangers, acquaintances, and friends may occur within the family. Therefore, it's especially important to remember that different customs and communication-style differences are just that, *differences*, rather than evidence of rude and uncivil familial behavior.

We can use metacommunication and set boundaries in response to uncivil communication within the family. Metacommunication is "communication about communication," and setting boundaries entails setting limits that let others know what we consider to be appropriate and inappropriate communication.

**Box 8-1**
**Strategies for Change: Everyday Incivility at Home**

- Parents can teach children to be respectful by making a conscious effort to disagree civilly so children learn that adults can demonstrate respect and love even when they aren't in agreement. Teaching respectful behavior also means that parents must be civil when they communicate with rude shopkeepers, bad drivers, and intrusive telephone salespersons. Parents should also teach their children about civil communication by not saying behind people's backs what they wouldn't say to them face-to-face.
- Because children grow up in a culture in which they learn it is okay to be disrespectful, it's difficult for parents to teach their children to be civil. Parents can teach their children to be respectful in this "age of awfulness" when they emphasize character rather than "looking out for number one"; prioritize the family; stress respect for authority; and teach and model the art of face-to-face conversation.
- One way to improve interpretations of underlying relationship messages is to use metacommunication, which is "communication about communication." Metacommunication enables us to ask about our interpretations of underlying relationship messages about connection, control, and/or respect.
- We can also manage everyday incivility at home by setting boundaries. A boundary is an edge or limit that defines us as being separate from others, and lets others know that we have limits to what we believe is appropriate.

## Chapter Nine

# Promoting Everyday Civility

*'Humane' humans are and probably always will be a minority. Yet it is this very fact that challenges each of us to join the minority; things are bad, but unless we do our best to improve them, everything will become worse.* [1]
—*Viktor Frankl, Austrian neurologist, psychiatrist, and Holocaust survivor*

John Hall and Connie Cullen are running buddies who train for the latest marathon with a group of Dallas runners. They met over ten years ago in a training class and became close as they ran together and shared stories about their life. Hall, a Republican, and Cullen, a Democrat, refuse to allow political differences to divide their friendship. They've felt this way since 2008, when Cullen canvassed for Barack Obama. Cullen planned to attend an Obama campaign visit in Dallas by herself, but Hall said he wanted to join her because he was interested in what Obama had to say. Although Hall enjoyed Obama's speech, he voted for Republican John McCain. Hall invited Cullen to a Trump campaign stop eight years later. Cullen attended the rally but voted for Democrat Hillary Clinton.

Although Hall and Cullen disagree about politics more often than not, they listen to each other and wish others would do the same. Cullen stated, "The rhetoric that's come up [makes] the other person 'the other.' Just the intolerance level and the crassness; I've never seen anything like it. It makes me nauseous because of the way people talk at each other. No one listens. They're so entrenched." Hall agrees, and asserted, "It's very caustic on both sides. It's literally 'burn the place down.' And the message isn't so much to make things better. It's, 'How bad can I make the other person look?' " Hall also said that people will see each other's side if they talk long enough. People will realize that they want the same thing, and that the only difference is how to get there. As for Hall and Cullen, "the two might never agree on politics, but they respect each other's views." [2]

John Hall and Connie Cullen exemplify Victor Frankl's quote about join-ing "the minority of the humane" in order to improve the world—in this case, by behaving civilly. In addition to self-help, which includes finding our own ways to promote civil communication, there are a number of available strate-gies that can be used to encourage everyday civility. These strategies include:

- Making physical spaces less prone to uncivil behavior—through signage, distraction, etc.;
- Legislation and policies, which enforce what normally would be governed by customs and norms;
- Education, including K–12 and higher education;
- Workplace interventions, including programs which can transform uncivil communication in organizations to civil communication; and
- Initiatives adopted by communities and schools to promote civility.

## PHYSICAL SPACES

The gas station is one place where drivers know they may have to wait in line before they get to the pump. Jack Marshall found himself waiting for what seemed like an eternity during a snowy day in January. Finally he had only one car ahead of him. However, according to Marshall, the lady in the car in front of him dithered, paused, disappeared, and returned. He wrote, "She punched in so many characters at the pump that her debit card password must have been a chapter of *Martin Chuzzlewit*." It was as if she had never filled a gas tank in her life. The lady finally replaced the pump "after pausing and contemplating it like it was Yorick's skull," walked around to the driver's-side door, then decided to creep back to the side of her car to make sure she had replaced the gas tank cap, then again slowly walked to back to the driver's-side door. By this time, the line of cars behind Marshall appeared to be endless. The lady stared at her car door, slowly unzipped her coat, slowly began to take it off, changed her mind, and then paused to think about what to do next. Marshall was almost to the point of screaming: *FOR GOD'S SAKE, LADY, GET IN YOUR DAMN CAR AND GET OUT OF HERE! EVERYBODY'S WAITING ON YOU—STEP IT UP!!! SHOW A LITTLE UR-GENCY!!! I DON'T WANT TO CELEBRATE MY NEXT BIRTHDAY BE-HIND YOU, AND EVERYONE BEHIND ME MIGHT HAVE SOME PLANS FOR VALENTINE'S DAY. MOVE IT!*[3]

But he didn't. Marshall exhibited restraint in a situation that was extreme-ly frustrating to him, and no doubt to others in the cars behind him. Perhaps this situation could have been avoided with additional pumps or signage with step-by-step instructions regarding how to pump gas and reminders about gas station etiquette.

One way that we can promote civility is to better design and manage physical spaces, especially when they become crowded. For example, sports stadiums can hire personnel to direct fans of opposing teams in different directions when a game ends. Similarly, studies have found that music affects people's moods and can be used in public places to lessen the likelihood of uncivil behavior.[4] Sociologists suggest that "Spaces and places need to be thought out so that tempers do not snap, people do not collide, those with baggage can get out of the way or are somewhere else, interpersonal space is maintained, and behavioral externalities, such as smoking or talking on mobile phones, do not bother other people."[5]

To encourage civility, the Transportation Security Administration (TSA) researched ways to make air travel less stressful, especially after screening activities. The TSA concluded that "composure benches" to help passengers put shoes back on and rearrange items in carry-on bags would maintain passenger dignity and promote civil behavior.[6]

Signage can also be used to promote civil behavior in public places. Signs can make clear the norms that are in place in particular areas, such as restaurants that post signs which request courteous cell-phone conversations.[7] Another example of a sign meant to encourage civility is one used to reduce an interesting type of uncivil behavior called *manspreading*. Not limited to men, this occurs when a passenger takes up more than one seat with his/her body and/or with large backpacks while on a subway. Ads in the New York subway system carry the slogan, "Courtesy Counts: Manners Make a Better Ride." One of the posters shows cartoon images of riders forced to stand because a man takes up two seats. The caption on the poster reads, "Dude . . . stop the spread, please. It's a space issue."[8]

Women are also targeted in the "Courtesy Counts" campaign. One sign shows cartoon images of a man forced to lean sideways because a woman takes up space brushing her hair and looking in a handheld mirror. The caption reads, "Clipping? Priming? Everybody wants to look their best, but it's a subway car, not a restroom."[9] Orange stickers that urge passengers to avoid manspreading have also appeared in Seoul, South Korea, where over five million people ride the subway each day. The stickers, created by a college student for a marketing contest, are currently being used on two of the nine subway lines in Seoul.[10]

## LEGISLATION AND POLICIES

Olivier Odom and her wife, Jennifer Tipton, looked forward to a day of family fun when they visited the Dollywood amusement park with friends and their friends' children. Odom didn't expect to be stopped at the theme-park entrance because of what was deemed an "offensive" T-shirt. However, an attendant asked Odom to turn her "Marriage is so gay" T-shirt inside out to avoid offending others at the family-oriented theme park. Odom agreed so as not to make a scene in front of the children, but she entered the park feeling offended. In fact, Odom contends that the situation reflects discrimination about the LGBT community and wonders what was specifically uncivil about the shirt—the word *gay* itself, or the fact that it was used in conjunction with the word *marriage*.[11]

Dollywood spokesperson Pete Owens said that while Dollywood is open to families of all shapes and sizes, the park's dress-code policy requires front-gate hosts to ask guests to cover up clothing or tattoos that can be considered offensive or uncivil. Owens maintained that the purpose is not to discriminate against specific groups of people or particular belief systems, but to prevent any guest from being offended by an item of clothing. However, Odom said that she was offended not only by the request to turn her shirt inside out, but because the reason for the request was that Dollywood is a "family park" (and she was with *her* family, after all).

Once they'd entered the park, Odom noticed guests whose tattoos and T-shirts she deemed offensive and uncivil, such as those sporting the Confederate flag and other political sayings. Dollywood management replied that these visitors would have been asked to cover up if another patron had complained. Odom and Tipton have subsequently asked Dollywood to make their policies clear and to train employees about determining what is or isn't "uncivil."[12]

The clothing-related civility policy at Dollywood illustrates that what is offensive and uncivil to one person is neither offensive nor uncivil to another. Even though what is perceived as uncivil is a subjective interpretation, a number of US cities have passed legislation that outlaws uncivil communication. For example, the Brighton, Michigan, city council approved a public conduct code that includes fining someone up to $500 for insulting, accosting, or otherwise annoying any person in public.[13] Some restaurants have sections that restrict cell-phone use, and in an attempt to improve the manners of Louisiana children, the state senate unanimously passed the "Yes Sir, No Sir" bill that requires students to address all school employees in a courteous fashion.[14] Additionally, Middleborough, Massachusetts, passed an ordinance that grants police the ability to issue tickets and impose a fine on people who use profanity in public.[15] Middleborough officials assert that the purpose of the ordinance to is limit loud, profanity-laden language used by teens rather than to censor private conversations. The ordinance gives police the discretion to ticket based on whether they perceive a violation of the cursing ban.[16]

It's not just US cities that pass laws prohibiting uncivil behavior. The Beijing city government has authorized fines up to one thousand *yuan* for subway riders who exhibit uncivilized behavior. According to the Legal Affairs Office of the People's Government of Beijing Municipality, uncivil behaviors include lying across the seats in subway cars, jumping over a crowd-control guardrail, jumping over the admission auto-gate, and walking the wrong way on up or down escalators.[17]

Similarly, England outlaws uncivil communication in certain circumstances. For example, after posting "jokes" about two kidnapped girls on Facebook, Matthew Woods of Chorley, England, was arrested and sent to jail. Another man was ordered to perform 240 hours of community service for posting "All soldiers should die and go to hell" on Facebook. Kirsty Hughes, chief executive of the London-based nonprofit group, Index on Censorship, is concerned that the criminalization of speech is occurring for distasteful comments which anyone might say in their favorite pub without fear of arrest. A communications law passed in 2003 makes it a crime to send messages that are "grossly offensive or indecent" through a public electronic network in Britain. The 2003 law actually stems from a law passed in the 1930s meant to protect telephone operators from abusive language. The 2003 act was passed before social media became a routine form of communication.[18]

Most organizations have written policies that include the need to communicate civilly. The National Alliance for Youth Sports convened recreation representatives from thirty-four states to create a policy to enforce civil behavior at youth sports events. Describing youth sports as a "hotbed of "mean-spiritedness, physical and emotional abuse of children . . . and total disrespect for opponents," the National Summit on Raising Community Standards in Children's Sports developed a number of guidelines, including the following:

- Leaders should adopt a resolution to ensure that youth sports programs are held to the highest standards and conducted in an appropriate manner.
- All programs should be led by a youth sports administrator, who will be responsible for high-quality programming, making participants aware of behaviors that are appropriate and inappropriate, and policing and enforcing standards for acceptable behavior.
- Youth sports programs should require a parent orientation to create a positive youth sports experience and to hold them accountable for their behavior.[19]

Additionally, some school districts require parents to enroll in sportsmanship courses before their children can participate in athletics. A number of high schools in California give parents "warning cards" and they are escorted from a game if they verbally harass officials or other fans. Furthermore, the Los Angeles chapter of the California Interscholastic Federation requires student athletes to sign a code of conduct before they are allowed to play in any school-related sports activities.[20]

In addition to youth sports organizations, some companies post civility policies and teach their content at new-employee orientation sessions. Although the majority of the policies emphasize the importance of mutual respect, they fail to spell out what "mutual respect" entails. However, there are some organizations whose policies are direct and specific. For example, McDermott, Will and Emery, an international law firm, employs a rule which states that "you're not allowed to yell at your secretary or yell at each other." The policy at Xilinx, a semiconductor firm, mandates that "employees should respect and support each other even if they don't like each other." Included in the list of company values held by the Men's Wearhouse is "We respond immediately if any individual degrades another, regardless of position." Additionally, SuccessFactors, a talent management software company, expects adherence to a rather blunt core company value—"respect for the individual; no assholes—it's okay to have one, just don't be one."[21]

## EDUCATION

Professor Adolph Brown was scheduled to present an anti-bullying program to Grand Prairie High School's 2,600 students. However, prior to his presentation, the school had already received national attention for an act of civility by two seniors whose friend had been nominated for homecoming queen as a joke. Lilly Skinner was told that she had been nominated for homecoming queen in a "cruel prank." The seniors, Anahi Alvarez and Naomi Martinez, describe their best friend Lilly as "an amazing girl" and one of the nicest people they've ever met. Lilly's life motto is inspired by her mother, who says that inner beauty is more important than outer beauty, and that we shouldn't judge people by their looks.

Both Alvarez and Martinez had also been nominated for homecoming queen, and they decided they would give Lilly the crown should either of them win. Lilly was on the field taking photos during halftime at the homecoming football game, and she took one of Alvarez when she was named homecoming queen. But Alvarez said, "The crown is yours" and placed it on Lilly's head. The story went viral and was featured on numerous media outlets. At the end of the anti-bullying rally, Lilly, Anahi, and Naomi held up a banner that read, "Because it's the right thing to do." Students were asked to sign the banner only if they were serious about stopping bullying. Students then crowded around the three friends and squeezed their names on what was left of the white space on the banner.[22]

While Lilly Skinner's story is more powerful and inspiring than typical anti-bullying and civility programs, civility courses and training programs do make a difference when presented to students. However, civility is difficult to teach and the impact of civility programs is limited. Some argue that the demographic composition of schools creates a barrier to teaching civility in that students learn less about civility from posters that celebrate diversity and more from socializing with those from different cultural and socioeconomic backgrounds. Additionally, learning about civil communication can't compensate for the overwhelming amount of uncivil behavior we are all exposed to on a daily basis. Furthermore, few teachers have been trained to teach civility in addition to their respective subject areas, and students may not be able to retain and practice civil communication once they leave school. [23] Nonetheless, "Just as we know that high-quality learning instructional practices and good school organization can affect learning in more standard academic subjects, we have every reason to believe that educating in civility, well done, will have real effects." [24]

## K–12

One way to teach civility in K–12 classrooms is for teachers to explain and model civility. Teachers can also create a classroom experience that requires civility from all students at all times. [25] Additionally, there are programs and lessons about civility that are specifically aimed at elementary and secondary students. These programs are adopted by public schools and school districts, in addition to private schools.

### Public Schools

"Character Counts," an initiative of the nonprofit Josephson Institute, provides the framework for various programs across the nation that teach civility to elementary, middle school, and high school students. [26] Character.org is one such program that provides resources and lesson plans to teachers. In particular, Plattin Primary School in Festus, Missouri, teaches "The Golden Rule: Do Unto 'Otters,' " a lesson plan for K–3 students that helps them learn to treat others as they would like to be treated (students listen to the read-aloud book, *Do Unto Otters,* by Laurie Keller). [27] Brentwood Middle School in Missouri teaches "Words Hurt!" so that students learn that comments meant to be "funny" can impact others negatively. [28] "Me and We: A Mix it Up Activity" is used by Rosa International Middle School in Cherry Hill, New Jersey, to teach students to express opinions in a respectful and nonthreatening manner and to respectfully listen to others. [29] Finally, Hinsdale Central High School in Illinois teaches "Conflict Resolution Skills Training," a lesson plan that teaches students to respond appropriately to interpersonal challenges. [30]

*Private Schools*

Some private schools also include civil communication in their curriculum. The Dallas, Texas, Akiba Academy, a private religious school, added a secular program about civility that aims to decrease bullying in public schools. The Akiba Academy adopted this program, called "R Time," because it fits in well with the Modern Orthodox Jewish curriculum. R Time occurs once a week when students are randomly paired, interact with each other, and describe their conversation to the entire class. Discussion topics may be either religious-oriented or secular, and rules include the requirement to show good manners and care for everyone. Additionally, paired students agree to shake hands and maintain eye contact. After the students share their conversations with the class, teachers use these examples to reinforce the need for civility and kind behavior. Students demonstrate this behavior soon after they learn it, not only among themselves but with others outside of the Akiba Academy.[31]

Similarly, Premier Charter School in St. Louis, Missouri, partners with "school families" to teach students about respect, responsibility, and caring for others. The families include everyone who works at Premier Charter School—administrators, secretaries, teachers, and custodians. The families meet on a regular basis and engage in team-building activities to foster a sense of community and to reinforce the school's core values. Premier Charter School has also created student groups to improve the climate of the school. "Tight 20" and "Teen 10" groups of students meet regularly to plan and manage activities with their peers. One year, as a result of "trust issues" among some middle-school girls, the activities focused on fostering trust and preventing unkind behavior.[32] In 2011, Premier Charter School was named a "National School of Character," an award that recognizes schools and districts that "have demonstrated through a rigorous evaluation process that character development has had a positive impact on academics, student behavior, and school climate."[33]

## Higher Education

Some university professors believe that those in higher education have a duty to teach civility to students since universities typically include information about civil behavior and citizenship in handbooks and official documents.[34] Furthermore:

> As stewards of the tools of public discourse, academics have an obligation not only to model polite and reasoned interaction in the classroom, but to . . . treat students with respect, to demand that they treat each other with respect, to display the discipline of clear reasoning in our classrooms, and to help students

understand why shouting other voices down should not be allowed as a strategy to make one's point. [35]

However, others warn that when teaching civility at the university level,
we should make clear that there is disagreement about what constitutes civility (e.g., in terms of its norms and as a general concept), and that civility is
sometimes used to prevent marginalized voices from being heard. [36] Therefore, "When we teach civility to students, we also must help them understand
the relative—as opposed to the absolute—value of civility. There are plenty
of cases in which civility has less value than some competing value." [37]

## Colleges and Universities

One way we can teach civility to college students is by teaching argumentation and debate. Collegiate debate entails learning to make a reasoned argument, providing evidence either for or against the argument, and rebutting
the argument. Debate also involves asking questions, equal time, and effective listening. These skills are not limited to the university setting and can be
used effectively at city hall, in the workplace, or at PTA and other commu-
nity-oriented meetings. Aside from developing courses in argumentation,
college programs such as the Model United Nations provide students with
experience in respectful argumentation and how to argue for positions that
may not align with their personal beliefs and values. Moreover, debate, logic,
and reasoning skills can be integrated into core courses in which all students
are required to enroll. [38] Civility education can also be introduced in courses
specifically designed for first-year university students. One method used to
accomplish this goal is to discuss an academic civility code which illustrates
that a class is a "community" with norms of appropriate behavior that are
transferable to other communities. Faculty members also have a responsibility to model academic civility for their students. Additionally, the reasons for
an academic code of civility should be explained to students (e.g., to foster
cooperation, facilitate discussion, etc.). [39]

## Institutes

Universities are also home to institutes devoted to the study and teaching of
civility. For example, in 2011, the University of California–Davis Humanities Institute launched a yearlong "Civility Project" to discover or refine a
shared notion of civility. The project incorporated research in the social
sciences, humanities, and the arts and included the development of a "limits
of civility" website to explore goals that are often in conflict on college
campuses: free speech, and the promotion of tolerance. "Paper Takes: The
Power of Uncivil Words" was comprised of "extreme" pamphlets in the
United States that were displayed to identify what motivates intolerant be-

liefs and opinions; how these beliefs become credible; the tactics used to draw readers in; what enables further dissemination; and what can be done to combat their circulation. In addition, a theater piece called "Uncivil (Dis)Obedience" explored the uncivil moments and hate-based incidents that took place on the UC Davis campus in 2009 and 2010.[40] "Through a series of public events open to the campus community and concerned citizens, the Civility Project . . . [focused on] concrete ways in which the study of history, the practice of listening, and the creativity of the arts can contribute to a better understanding of how we define and enact civility, its role in enabling the productive exchange of ideas, and the role of public institutions in shaping our ideas about and participation in democratic society."[41]

Unlike the UC Davis Humanities Institute, which focuses on a variety of issues, some institutes are devoted solely to the study of civility. The Janet Neff Sample Center for Manners and Civility at Penn State Behrend offers town hall meetings and lectures, and provides grants for campus organizations that create civility-related programs and/or conduct civility-related research. Faculty members associated with the center have developed college courses about communication and civility, and inventories to measure civil behavior. The Center also provides outreach services to Erie-area schools and organizations.[42]

Similarly, the National Institute for Civil Discourse at the University of Arizona, Tucson, is a nonpartisan center for advocacy, research, and policy. The inspiration for the Institute was the Tucson shootings that took place at a political rally during which congresswoman Gabrielle Giffords was wounded. Its mission is to support elected officials who can cooperate and work together to solve major problems facing our country; a public that demands civil public discourse; and a media that provides information in a manner that is fair and responsible.[43] Although the Institute focuses on public and political discourse, it also makes available information regarding everyday incivility. For example, the Institute created a web page titled "Post-Election: Your Civility Survival Guide for Thanksgiving" to help reduce uncivil family communication about the contentious 2016 presidential election. Suggestions included perceiving a discussion about politics as an opportunity to listen to ideas and understand others' viewpoints; responding to snide comments about political beliefs by respectfully agreeing to disagree; focusing on what all dinner guests have in common (e.g., the best for the county); and making the Thanksgiving table a "politics / election-free zone."[44]

## WORKPLACE INTERVENTIONS

Southwest Airlines is known for its low-cost, creative advertising and civil organizational climate. The airline's mission statement emphasizes that regardless of their job, all employees are to be treated with respect: "Above all, employees will be provided the same concern, respect, and caring attitude within the organization that they are expected to share externally with every Southwest Customer." Southwest employees share knowledge and goals, and they improvise and adapt to help each other and complete tasks. Flight attendants and pilots have been observed folding blankets and picking up trash to prepare a plane for the next set of passengers. This approach to civil teamwork has worked well for Southwest Airlines in that turnaround time is 20 percent below industry standards. Moreover, they receive less than the average amount of complaints filed by customers against airlines.[45]

Not all organizations stress civil communication to the extent of Southwest Airlines. Similarly, not all organizations employ workers who behave civilly to their customers and coworkers. In their book *The Cost of Bad Behavior*, authors Christine Pearson and Christine Porath highlight a number of organizations that implemented interventions to promote civil behavior when faced with challenges and perceptions of employee incivility. Two of the organizations are Starbucks and Microsoft.

### A Workplace Intervention to Cope with Growth

Starbucks promotes civility in its mission statement, which includes the need to "provide a great work environment and treat each other with respect and dignity."[46] The challenge for Starbucks was to adhere to their values associated with product and service delivery in the midst of massive expansion. With an average of five new stores opening and the addition of two hundred employees each day, Starbucks needed to build and sustain a climate of civility. This was accomplished by teaching the mission statement to all new employees and training them to put the mission statement into action. Store managers serve as role models to junior employees and the managers receive training in behavioral skills that are partner-centric and customer-centric. Additionally, Starbucks sends store managers to an annual leadership conference during which the guiding principles about communicating respectfully with coworkers and customers are reviewed and reinforced. To make sure that uncivil behavior is dealt with in a timely manner, Starbucks initiated "Mission Review," a tool that enables employees to provide anonymous feedback to management about behaviors that go against the guiding principles.[47] In 2016, Starbucks was ranked number six in *Fortune*'s top fifty "World's Most Admired Companies."[48]

## A Workplace Intervention to Improve Customer Relations

Microsoft also implemented an intervention to encourage civility and im- prove customer relations. In response to the perception that the company had become arrogant and uncivil, leaders knew they had to train employees to better serve their customers. Management began by conducting a corporate culture assessment that included projections thirty years into the future. The assessment was used to develop a "leadership blueprint" to create new values and develop a culture of civility. Microsoft now hires new employees who:

- Listen to understand others' perspectives without interrupting;
- Integrate diverse perspectives when making decisions;
- Communicate critical feedback respectfully;
- Consider the experience and knowledge of others;
- Do not disparage others;
- Assume the best motives in others;
- Ask difficult questions to discover answers, but never to demean;
- Never act in a manner that can be perceived as threatening, intolerant, or discriminatory;
- Demonstrate more interest in finding the right answer than in defending a position; and
- Maintain objectivity when conflict arises. [49]

Microsoft has also updated its learning and development program that places civility at the core of respectful interaction. For example, in the "Pre- cision Questioning" class, employees learn how to question their ideas, man- age their emotions, and remain calm in high-intensity conversations. Other courses teach employees how to listen well and how to appreciate construc- tive criticism. The focus on civility is also evidenced in Microsoft's new- employee orientations, during which participants are provided with an over- view of Microsoft's culture of respect and where employees of three months or less share their experiences to establish a friendly and civil climate. Addi- tionally, "at all levels, evaluation and rewards reflect respect and civility from 'confidence' to 'interpersonal awareness.' Employees are rated for 'challenging others respectfully when [they] disagree with them.' They're evaluated on their abilities to listen, understand, and appreciate others' per- spectives and behavior." [50]

## Workplace Interventions in Health-Care Organizations

Uncivil communication also occurs in health-care organizations. One survey of nursing staff showed that the approximately one thousand respondents frequently experienced the following uncivil behaviors: complaining about a coworker rather than engaging in conflict resolution; belittling and/or making hurtful comments in front of others; listening to harsh criticism without hearing both sides of the story; and raising eyebrows or rolling eyes at a coworker.[51]

In response to uncivil communication at a health sciences hospital, a three-part educational intervention was developed to improve the work environment and reduce the occurrence of uncivil behavior. Prior to the intervention, information was collected about perceptions of uncivil communication that occurred in specific units. Part one of the educational intervention included a presentation and discussion about incivility. Part two consisted of lectures, discussion, and role-playing situations that were created to mirror staff and nurses' perceptions of incivility. The session also included setting unit-based norms and learning how to deal with uncivil communication. The participants received a toolkit that included conversation strategies, sample responses to incivility, and commitment cards. Part three involved practicing the strategies and modeling effective and appropriate communication. Post-intervention reviews found that the three-part intervention decreased the perceived incivility in the units and increased the perceived ability of nurses to contend with uncivil communication at the hospital.[52] In addition, "Because they shared the camaraderie of the intervention experience, interviewees noted that staff talked more readily and sometimes even joked about the uncivil acts after the intervention. That is, staff called out the potential for incivility when they recognized it and changed the behavior before it went further."[53]

Similarly, a nationwide intervention was implemented at Veterans Health Administration (VHA) hospitals when the VHA National Leadership Board endorsed civility as an essential feature of an ideal workplace. A survey of former employees who voluntarily left the VHA revealed that they perceived a lack of respect and fairness across all jobs. Additionally, 67 percent of the employees said they were exposed to verbal abuse. Therefore, the CREW ("civility, respect, engagement in the workforce") intervention model was instituted in an attempt to change the VHA's culture toward increasing workplace civility.

The distinguishing feature of the CREW intervention was its flexibility in that the intervention was responsive to local needs and localized definitions of civility. Rather than a general workplace improvement intervention, CREW was led by facilitators who supported the VHA employees' thinking and planning.[54] At each site, employees "learned about the damage that aggression does, used role-playing exercises to 'get in the shoes' of bullies and victims, and reflected before and after they acted. Action team members and local VA leaders also made a public commitment to model civilized behavior."[55] Each VHA site held meetings during which employees defined civility, articulated needs, and devised plans; therefore, the interventions were customized to each site and changed along with new needs that emerged as the intervention progressed. The practitioners provided a toolkit of educational activities to employees and facilitated the exchange of information among the VHA sites. Throughout the process, employee feedback was obtained to learn which intervention tools appeared to work and which did not.

At one site, "managers and employees worked to eliminate seemingly small slights like glaring, interruptions, and treating people as if they were 'invisible'—slights that had escalated into big problems in the past."[56] Pre-intervention and post-intervention surveys revealed that employee-rated perceptions of workplace civility increased at the VHA sites that implemented the CREW intervention. Employees also demonstrated that they were aware of the importance of workplace civility and understood the connection between civil behavior and carrying out the VHA mission to provide excellent health services to veterans.[57]

## COMMUNITY-BASED INITIATIVES

Mona Haydar was looking to buy some frozen yogurt at a busy airport. A stranger came up to her while she stood in line and in a menacing fashion, whispered, "You killed my people." Haydar lost her breath during the gut-wrenching incident because she knew that it was her *hijab* that caused him to whisper such uncivil words. Haydar thought to herself, "If you knew me, you wouldn't say that," and she subsequently launched the "Ask a Muslim" program in Cambridge, Massachusetts. Every week Haydar sets up signs outside of the Cambridge Public Library and invites passersby to have free donuts and coffee and to her ask her questions about her Muslim beliefs and traditions. The experience has been overwhelmingly positive, both for those who engage her in discussions of Islam and for Muslims in the community who feel inspired and supported. Haydar now has more than five thousand followers on social media and is similarly encouraged by the residents of Cambridge. Haydar says, "It's about dialogue and humanizing each other. I'm a Muslim, but first, I'm human."[58]

Mona Haydar's "Ask a Muslim" personal initiative is similar to other programs sponsored by nonprofit organizations and communities. Such initiatives include the Random Acts of Kindness foundation's programs, which are based on the idea that "Kindness starts with one." The nonprofit organization provides classroom lessons about kindness, responsibility, and respect. The foundation encourages people to become "RAKtivists," kindness ambassadors who exemplify civil behavior. RAKtivists include students who hold the door open for a teacher with her/his hands full and commuters who offer their seat to a senior citizen. In addition to classroom lessons, the Random Acts of Kindness foundation sponsors RAK Week in February (a celebration of kindness); World Kindness Day in November; and RAK Friday in November, a day that encourages doing a random act of kindness rather than shopping on Black Friday.[59]

In addition to adopting initiatives developed by nonprofit organizations, cities also create civility initiatives and programs. Anaheim, California, sponsors the "Anaheim's Hi Neighbor" program, which encourages neighbors to get to know each other and to form neighborhood crime watches.[60] Albuquerque, New Mexico, has a new "ABQKindness" campaign, the purpose of which is to track and celebrate acts of kindness by using an app to submit descriptions of kind acts.[61]

A number of initiatives are based on P. M. Forni's book, *Choosing Civility*. "Speak Your Peace" is a civility initiative created by the Duluth Superior Area Community Foundation. The initiative aims to "improve communication by reminding ourselves of the basic principles of respect."[62] Speak Your Peace is based on nine core principles for practicing civility which are included in *Choosing Civility*: "pay attention, listen closely, be inclusive, don't gossip, show respect, be agreeable, apologize sincerely, give constructive comments, and accept responsibility."[63] The initiative not only targets politicians and includes the goal of increasing civic participation, but also aims to reach neighborhood organizations, religious groups, and even parents on the sidelines of youth athletic competitions.

The "Oshkosh Civility Project" is a community-based initiative based on Speak Your Peace. The initiative includes training sessions, downloadable materials such as posters and PowerPoint presentations, and an invitation to sign the Oshkosh civility pledge that centers on the nine core principles.[64] The Howard County Library in Maryland leads an ongoing community-wide initiative centered on fifteen of *Choosing Civility*'s principles and seeks to position Howard County as a model of civility.[65] The initiative includes events such as "Conversations in Come-UNITY," during which community members meet to discuss the nation's color divide. Similar to Mona Haydar's "Ask a Muslim" personal initiative, another event sponsored by Howard County's program is the "Human Library: Don't Judge a Book by its Cover." This international initiative is designed to provide a positive climate for conversations that challenge stereotypes and prejudice. The Human Library is described as a "place where real people are on loan to readers and a place where difficult questions are expected, appreciated, and answered."[66]

## SELF-HELP

Father Joshua J. Whitfield is the parochial vicar and director of faith formation at St. Rita Catholic Church in Dallas. He is also a lover of baseball. Whitfield writes that "the great thing about baseball is that it allows for conversation." Whitfield contends that baseball is a more "human" sport than football because its rhythms are amenable to thinking and speaking. He claims that "between innings, batters, and even pitches, the mind may relax and reflect; the soul may speak unhurried, calmly." Father Whitfield attended a Rangers–Blue Jays game in October 2016 during which he began a conversation with a fellow baseball fan. They chatted about various topics before their talk turned to politics. Whitfield, who describes himself as the offspring of old Texas Democrats, discovered that his conversation partner was a Republican. He explains that "given the tone of cultural and political discourse today, all the Facebook anger and the poison of cable news, one would think we were in for a fight . . . [and] would have found proof of each other's idiocy or immorality." However, that wasn't the case. Whitfield writes:

> We were politically very different but very genuinely polite. More so, even, we were downright friendly. I listened to him and him to me. We weren't just waiting for the other to shut up. We heard each other, we reflected, we spoke in turn gently. And I found myself hopeful. Not for the game or the election, of course—disasters, each of them—but for the country, for we the people.[67]

Whitfield's comments illustrate the idea of "conversational civility" in that communication, no matter where it occurs, can be viewed as a way to potentially solve problems and focus on hope rather than cynicism. This idea is also found in Whitfield's suggestion that on Opening Day, we either invite a "cold-hearted Republican" or a "dirty liberal" to come with us to a baseball game, "buy a beer, watch, start talking—about anything, it doesn't really matter. Just talk."[68]

Father Whitfield's suggestion to enjoy baseball and converse civilly with a fellow fan is one way that we can promote civility at the individual level. It's important that we, as individuals, do our part to promote civility, because "all of the civility policies, programs, and initiatives in the world cannot cause people to change unless they are first willing to alter their behavior and attempt to see the world through a different lens."[69] It is therefore up to us to put into action the themes included in this book.

Specifically, we can attempt to communicate on the basis of respect, restraint, and responsibility; realize that our judgment of uncivil behavior may be based on norms for appropriate behavior that are different rather inferior than to ours; and try to understand and empathize with others' beliefs, attitudes, values, and lived experiences. Although this may appear to be an overwhelming and perhaps unrealistic task, we can begin with one simple act of civility each day. We may want to begin with easy behaviors, such as slowing or briefly stopping our car to allow another car into our lane. We may also want to make it a point to compliment or thank someone for being a caring, thoughtful, or kind individual. We can additionally train ourselves to count to three before responding to comments that are disrespectful, unrestrained, and focused on the self to the detriment of others. We can also practice "conversational civility" and the goal on which it is based—that is, to keep a conversation going with the hope that we can find solutions to problems that we share.

Although it may be difficult, if not impossible, to change others, we have the ability to change ourselves. Communicating with civility and replying in a civil manner, even in response to uncivil messages, is one way to promote everyday civility. Because in the end, "breaking the cycle of incivility takes people who are willing to choose civility when incivility is the easy default. . . . In so many circumstances, it takes just one person to buck the status quo of incivility, inspiring others to do the same. To pay it forward."[70]

## SUMMARY AND CONCLUSION

There are a number of ways to promote everyday civil communication. One way that we can promote civility is to better design and manage physical spaces, especially when they become crowded. Signage which can make clear the norms associated with a particular area can also be used to promote civil behavior in public places. Legislation and the implementation of civility policies are also used to encourage civil behavior. In addition, civility courses and training programs make a difference when presented to students of all ages. Programs and lessons about civility have been created for elementary and secondary students, and these programs are adopted by public schools and school districts, in addition to private schools. Similarly, civility can be taught at universities by means of stand-alone courses and by integrating civility education into core courses in which all students must enroll. Universities are also home to institutes that not only research civility but also offer outreach activities to students and members of the community. Furthermore, organizations can implement interventions to promote civil behavior when faced with challenges and employee incivility. Nonprofit and community-based initiatives also teach and encourage civil communication. However, promoting everyday civility should begin with us because "one person can positively change the course of an interaction from a path of polarized positions, to one of understanding and respecting each other as complex human beings."[71]

**Box 9-1**
**Strategies for Change: Promoting Everyday Civility**

- Communicating with civility and replying in a civil manner, even in response to uncivil messages, can promote everyday civility.
- We can attempt to communicate on the basis of respect, restraint, and responsibility.
- We should realize that our judgment of uncivil behavior may be based on norms for appropriate behavior that are different rather than inferior to ours.
- We should try to understand and empathize with others' beliefs, attitudes, values, and lived experiences.
- We can begin with one simple act of civility each day. We may want to begin with easy behaviors, such as slowing or briefly stopping our car to allow another car into our lane. We may also want to make it a point to compliment or thank someone for being a caring, thoughtful, or kind individual.
- We can train ourselves to count to three before responding to comments that are disrespectful, unrestrained, and focused on the self to the detriment of others.
- We can practice "conversational civility" and the goal on which it is based; that is, to keep a conversation going with the hope that we can find solutions to problems that we share.

# Notes

## 1. INTRODUCTION TO
## EVERYDAY INCIVILITY

1. Steve Farkas et al., *Aggravating Circumstances: A Status Report on Rudeness in America* (New York: Pew Charitable Trusts, 2002), http://research.policyarchive.org/5628.pdf (accessed December 20, 2016): 11.

2. Julia Dahl, "Threat or Disrespect? Florida Loud Music Florida Loud Shooting Trial Begins," *CBS News*, February 6, 2014, http://www.cbsnews.com/news/threat-or-disrespect-florida-loud-music-shoting-trial-begins-for-michael-dunn (accessed December 20, 2016); see also Derek Kinner, "Man Guilty in Shooting over Music," *Dallas Morning News*, February 16, 2014, 22A.

3. Piers M. Forni, "Is Civility Dead? From an Expert in the Field," *Costco Connection*, February 17, 2010, 16–17.

4. Benet Davetian, *Civility: A Cultural History* (Toronto, CA: University of Toronto Press, 2009), 5.

5. L. Sandy Maisel, "The Negative Consequences of Uncivil Political Discourse," *PS: Political Science & Ethics* 45, no. 3 (2012) 405–11. See also Cherie J. Strachan and Michael R. Wolf, "Introduction to Political Incivility," *PS: Political Science & Ethics* 45, no. 3 (2012): 401–03.

6. Thomas W. Benson, "The Rhetoric of Civility: Power, Authenticity, and Democracy," *Journal of Contemporary Rhetoric* 1, no. 1 (2011): 27.

7. Susan Herbst, *Rude Democracy: Civility and Incivility in American Politics* (Philadelphia, PA: Temple University Press, 2010).

8. Jack Marshall, "Ethics and Civility 101: Rep. Joe ('You Lie!') Wilson has NOT been vindicated," *Ethics Alarms* (blog), November 11, 2013, http://ethicsalarms.com/2013/11/10/ethics-and-civility-101-rep-joe-you-lie-wilson-has-not-been-vindated/ (accessed December 20, 2016).

9. Shelley D. Lane and Helen McCourt, "Uncivil Communication in Everyday Life: A Response to Benson's 'The Rhetoric of Civility,' " *Journal of Contemporary Rhetoric* 3, no. 1–2 (2013): 25.

10. Claire Z. Cardona, " 'Lives Matter; We are All Americans:' Dallas Protesters, Counterprotesters Come Together with Police," *Dallas Morning News*, July 10, 2016, www.dallasnews.com/news/crime/headlines/20160710-lives-matter-we-are-all-americans-dallas-protesters-counterprotesters-come-together-with-police.ece (accessed July 10, 2016).

11. Forni, "Is Civility Dead? From an Expert in the Field"; see also Sara Hacala, *Saving Civility: 52 Ways to Tame Rude, Crude, and Attitude for a Polite Planet* (Woodstock, VT: Skylights Paths Publishing, 2011).

12. "Civility in America: A Nationwide Study," *Weber Shandwick*. June 10, 2010, www.webershandwick.com/resources/ws/flash/WS_Civility_Study_Social_Media_Exec_Summary_6_10.pdf.

13. "Civility in America 2011." *Weber Shandwick*. June 20, 2011, www.webershandwick.com/resources/ws/flash/CivilityinAmerica2011.pdf (accessed December 20, 2016).

14. "Civility in America 2012." *Weber Shandwick*. June 15, 2012, www.webershandwick.com/uploads/news/files/2012_Civility_ExecutiveSummary.pdf (accessed December 20, 2016).

15. "Civility in America 2013." *Weber Shandwick*. July 30, 2013, www.webershandwick.com/uploads/news/files/Civility_in_America_2013_Exec_Summary.pdf (accessed December 20, 2016).

16. "Civility in America 2014." *Weber Shandwick*. July 2015, http://www.webershandwick.com/uploads/news/files/civility-in-america-2014.pdf (accessed December 20, 2016).

17. "Weber Shandwick—Press Release," *Weber-Shandwick*. January 28, 2016, http://www.webershandwick.com/news/article/nearly-all-likely-voters-say-candidates-civility-will-affect-their-vote (accessed December 20, 2016).

18. "Weber Shandwick—Press Release," *Weber-Shandwick*. January 23, 2017, http://www.webershandwick.com/news/article/poll-finds-americans-united-in-seeing-an-uncivil-nation-divided-about-cause (accessed February 1, 2017).

19. Adam J. Cox, "The Case for Boredom," *New Atlantis* 27 (2010): 122.

20. "Civility in America 2013," *Weber Shandwick*, 2.

21. Richard Boyd, "The Value of Civility?," *Urban Studies* 43, no. 5/6 (2006): 863–78.

22. Chris Mayo, "The Binds that Tie: Civility and Social Difference," *Educational Theory* 52, no. 2 (2002): 171.

23. Jim Leach, foreword to *Civility in Politics and Education*, ed. Deborah S. Mower and Wade L. Robison (New York, NY: Routledge, 2010), ix.

24. Stephen L. Carter, *Civility: Manners, Morals and the Etiquette of Democracy* (New York, NY: Harper Perennial, 1998).

25. Philip Smith, Timothy L. Phillips, and Ryan D. King, *Incivility: The Rude Stranger in Everyday Life* (New York: Cambridge University Press, 2010), 1.

26. ABC, "What Would You Do?" http://abc.go.com/shows/what-would-you-do (accessed December 20, 2016).

27. Bob Henault, "Interracial Engagement Meets Parental Disapproval: What Would You Do?," *ABCnews*, April 22, 2011, http://abcnews.go.com/WhatWouldYouDo/parents-disapprove-interracial-couple-married/story?id=13409130 (accessed May 29, 2015).

28. Matt Ward, "'Mean Girls' Bully Teen on Facebook: What Would You Do?," *ABCnews*, March 10, 2011, http://abcnews.go.com/WhatWouldYouDo/girls-bully-teen-facebook/story?id=13094996 (accessed May 29, 2015).

29. Eric Hanan, "Calorie Police Patrol Supermarkets Aisles," *ABCnews*, November 12, 2010, http://abcnews.go.com/WhatWouldYouDo/overweight-mom-criticized-buying-junk-food/story?id=12111162 (accessed May 29, 2015).

30. Ward, "'Mean Girls' Bully Teen on Facebook: What Would You Do?"; see also Hanan, "Calorie Police Patrol Supermarkets Aisles."

31. Sophia Dembling, "Surrounded by Rudeness," *Dallas Morning News*, March 22, 2010, p. 15a; see also Pier M. Forni, *The Civility Solution: What to Do When People Are Rude* (New York: St. Martin's Griffin, 2008).

32. Rod L. Troester and Cathy Sargent Mester, *Civility in Business and Professional Communication* (New York: Peter Lang, 2007).

33. Emrys Westacott, *The Virtues of Our Vices: A Modest Defense of Gossip, Rudeness, and Other Bad Habits* (Princeton, NJ: Princeton University Press, 2011).

34. Abbott L. Ferris, "Studying and Measuring Civility: A Framework, Trends, and Scale," *Sociological Inquiry* 72, no. 3 (2002): 376–92.

35. "Comics and Puzzles," *Dallas Morning News*, May 29, 2015, 1E.

36. "Comics and Puzzles."

37. Westacott, *The Virtues of Our Vices.*

38. Ira Berkow, "What Is Baseball's Meaning and Its Effect on America," *New York Times*, May 31, 1981, http://www.nytimes.com /1981/05/31/sports/what-is-baseball-s-meaning-and-its-effect-on-america.html?pagewanted=all (accessed December 19, 2016).

39. "Phillies' Papelbon Grabs Crotch toward Booing Fans," *New York Post*, Associated Press, September 15, 2014, http://nypost.com/2014/09/15/phillies-papelbon-grabs-crotch-toward-booing-fans/ (accessed December 18, 2016).

40. Jack Marshall, "Crotch-Grabbing Ethics: A Pitcher and an Umpire Make a Dunce/Hero Pair, and Baseball Teaches the NFL about Values," *Ethics Alarms*, September 17, 2014, https://ethicsalarms.com/2014/09/17/crotch-grabbing-ethics-a-pitcher-and-an-umpire-make-a-duncehero-pair-and-baseball-teaches-the-nfl-about-values/ (accessed December 18, 2016).

41. Marshall, "Crotch-Grabbing Ethics"; see also Jean M. Twenge and W. Keith Campbell, *The Narcissism Epidemic: Living in the Age of Entitlement* (New York: Free Press, 2009).

42. Smith et al., *Incivility: The Rude Stranger in Everyday Life.*

43. W. Barnett Pearce and Kimberly A. Pearce, "Taking a Communication Perspective on Dialogue," in *Dialogue: Theorizing Difference in Communication*, eds. Richard Anderson, Leslie A. Baxter, and Kenneth N. Cissna (Thousand Oaks, CA: Sage), 41.

44. Pearce and Pearce, "Taking a Communication Perspective on Dialogue," 42.

45. Destiny Herndon-DeLaRosa, "Seeing Pro-Lifers in a New Light," *Dallas Morning News*, January 2, 2010.

46. Brian H. Spitzberg and William R. Cupach, *Interpersonal Communication Competence* (Thousand Oaks, CA: Sage, 1984).

47. Susan B. Shiminoff, *Communication Rules: Theory and Research* (Thousand Oaks, CA: Sage, 1980).

48. Davetian, *Civility: A Cultural History.*

49. Spitzberg and Cupach, *Interpersonal Communication Competence*, 116.

50. Spitzberg and Cupach, *Interpersonal Communication Competence*, 101.

51. Andrew Calabrese, "Liberalism's Disease: Civility above Justice," *European Journal of Communication* 30, no. 5 (2015): 539–53.

52. Froma Harrop, "The Casualization of America," *Dallas Morning News*, February 12, 2010, www.dallasnews.com/opinion/latest-columns/20100211-Froma-Harrop-The-casualization-of-8181.ece (accessed February 17, 2010).

53. "White House Fans Flip-Flop Kerfuffle," Associated Press, *nbcnews*, July 22, 2005, http://www.nbcnews.com/id/8670164/ns/us_news/t/white-house-footwear-fans-flip-flop-kerfuffle/#.U2Vw-1f578s (accessed May 3, 2014).

54. "White House Fans Flip-Flop Kerfuffle." See also Richard Frye, "Millennials Overtake Baby Boomers as America's Largest Generation," *Pew Research Center*, April 25, 2016, http://www.pewresearch.org/fact-tank/2016/04/25/millennials-overtake-baby-boomers/ (accessed May 1, 2017).

55. E. Georgoudi and R. L. Rousnow, "Notes Toward a Contextualist Understanding of Social Psychology," *Personality and Social Psychology Bulletin* 11 (1985): 76–88.

56. Brian H. Spitzberg, "Interpersonal Communication Competence," in *Essays on Human Communication*, ed. Thomas Hurt and Brian H. Spitzberg (Boston, MA: Ginn, 1984): 31–39.

57. Craig Rood, "Rhetorics of Civility: Theory, Pedagogy, and Practice in Speaking and Writing," *Rhetoric Review* 32, no. 3 (2013): 334.

58. Shelley D. Lane and Helen McCourt, "Uncivil Communication in Everyday Life: A Response to Benson's 'The Rhetoric of Civility,' " *Journal of Contemporary Rhetoric* 3, no. 1–2 (2013).

59. Westacott, *The Virtues of Our Vices.*

60. Westacott, *The Virtues of Our Vices.*

61. Shelley D. Lane, *Interpersonal Communication: Competence and Contexts* (Boston, MA: Pearson, 2010).

62. Smith et al., *Incivility: The Rude Stranger in Everyday Life.*

63. Smith et al., *Incivility: The Rude Stranger in Everyday Life*, 1.

64. Westacott, *The Virtues of our Vices*; see also Hacala, *Saving Civility.*

65. Hacala, *Saving Civility*, 47.

66. Hacala, *Saving Civility*, 51.
67. "Kansas Teen's Tweet of Dissent Goes Viral," *iCLIMERBLOG*, November 28, 2011, http://blog.iclimber.com/kansas-teens-tweet-of-dissent-goes-viral/ (accessed January 16, 2012).
68. Huma Kahn, "Tweeting Kansas Teen Gets Apology from Gov. Brownbeck, Her Following Soars." *ABCnews*, November 11, 2011, http://abcnews.go.com/blogs/politics/2011/11/tweeting-kansas-teen-wont-apologize-to-gov-her-following-soars/ (accessed January 16, 2012).
69. Ruth Marcus, "Emma Sullivan's Potty-Mouthed Tweet Has a Lesson for All of Us," *Washington Post*, November 29, 2011, https://www.washingtonpost.com/opinions/emma-sullivans-potty-mouthed-tweet-has-a-lesson-for-all-of-us/2011/11/29/gIQAG6CEAO_story.html?utm_term=.b11b324b51bc (accessed January 16, 2012).
70. Westacott, *The Virtues of Our Vices*, 63.
71. Timothy C. Shiell, "Debunking Three Myths about Civility," in *Civility in Politics and Education*, ed. Deborah S. Mower and Wade L. Robinson (New York: Routledge, 2012): 4–22.
72. Nicole Billante and Peter Saunders, *Six Questions about Civility* (St. Leonards, Australia: The Centre for Independent Studies Ltd., 2002).
73. Billante and Saunders, *Six Questions about Civility*; see also Mark Caldwell, *A Short History of Rudeness: Manners, Morals and Misbehavior in Modern America* (New York: Picador, 1999).
74. Billante and Saunders, *Six Questions about Civility*, 21–22.
75. Caldwell, *A Short History of Rudeness*.
76. "Socrates quotes," *Thinkexist.com*, http://thinkexist.com/quotation/children_today_are_tyrants-they_contradict_their/149587.html (accessed September 24, 2015).
77. Hua Hus, "The Civility Wars," *New Yorker*, December 1, 2014, http://www.newyorker.com/culture/cultural-comment/civility-wars (accessed September 28, 2015).
78. Billante and Saunders, *Six Questions about Civility*, 23.
79. Ronald C. Arnett and Pat Arneson, *Dialogic Civility in a Cynical Age: Community, Hope and Interpersonal Relationships* (New York: SUNY Press, 1999), 26.
80. Dorothy Nevill, quoted in Priya Iyengar, "What, Where, When, Why, and How: Know the Specifics of Your Communication," *Indian Journal of Management* 5, no. 2 (2012): 22.

# 2. CHARACTERIZING EVERYDAY INCIVILITY

1. Kathleen Parker, "Word of the Year: Courage," *Dallas Morning News*, January 3, 2014.
2. David L. Hudson Jr., "Remembering Justice Potter Stewart," First Amendment Center, 2012, http://www.firstamendmentcenter.org/remembering-justice-potter-stewart (accessed June 13, 2014).
3. Barak Orbach, "On Hubris, Civility, and Incivility," *Arizona Law Review* 54, no. 443 (2012): 444–56.
4. Timothy C. Shiell, "Debunking Three Myths about Civility," in *Civility in Politics and Education*, ed. Deborah S. Mower and Wade L. Robison (New York: Routledge, 2012), 4–22.
5. Cynthia M. Clark and Joan Carnosso, "Civility: A Concept Analysis," *Journal of Theory and Construction and Testing* 12, No. 2 (2008): 11–15.
6. Nicole Billante and Peter Saunders, *Six Questions about Civility* (St. Leonards, Australia: The Centre for Independent Studies Limited, 2002).
7. Richard Sinopoli, "Thick-Skinned Liberalism: Redefining Civility," *American Political Science Review* 89 (1995): 612–20.
8. Billante and Saunders, *Six Questions about Civility*, 17–18.
9. Kirsten Gillibrand, *Off the Sidelines: Raise Your Voice, Change the World* (New York: Ballantine Books, 2014), 128.
10. Gillibrand, *Off the Sidelines*.
11. Jack Marshall, "Sen. Gillibrand and the Pigs," *Ethics Alarms*, August 31, 2014, http://ethicsalarms.com/2014/08/31/sen-gillibrand-and-the-pig/ (accessed December 23, 2016).

12. Robin Abcarian, "Should Sen. Kirsten Gillibrand Out the Man Who Called Her 'Porky'?," *Los Angeles Times*, August 28, 2014, http://www.latimes.com/local/abcarian/la-mera-kirsten-gillibrand-porky-20140828-column.html (accessed December 23, 2016).

13. Beverly Davenport Sypher, "Reclaiming Civil Discourse in the Workplace," *Southern Communication Journal* 69, no. 3 (2004): 257–69.

14. Zapoto Marini, "The Thin Line between Civility and Incivility: Fostering Reflection and Self-Awareness to Create a Civil Learning Community," in *Collected Essays on Learning and Teaching* (Vol. 2), ed. Alan Wright, Margaret Wilson, and Dawn MacIsaac (Ontario, Canada: Centre for Teaching and Learning, University of Windsor, 2009), http://apps.medialab.uwindsor.ca/ct1/CELT/vol2/CELT10.pdf (accessed December 23, 2016).

15. Marini, "The Thin Line between Civility and Incivility," 62.

16. Marini, "The Thin Line between Civility and Incivility," 62.

17. Cindy Hunt and Zopito Marini, "Incivility in the Practice Environment: A Perspective from Clinical Nursing Teachers," *Nurse Education in Practice* 12, no. 6 (2012): 366–70.

18. Cynthia M. Clark, *Creating and Sustaining Civility in Nursing Education* (Indianapolis, IN: Sigma Theta Tau International, 2013).

19. Rod L. Troester and Cathy Sargent Mester, *Civility in Business and Professional Communication* (New York: Peter Lang, 2007).

20. Sypher, "Reclaiming Civil Discourse in the Workplace," 257–69.

21. Clark, *Creating and Sustaining Civility in Nursing Education.*

22. Troester and Mester, *Civility in Business and Professional Communication.*

23. Carol Bishop Mills and Amy Muckleroy Carwile, "The Good, the Bad, and the Borderline: Separating Teasing from Bullying," *Communication Education* 58, no. 2 (2009): 276–301.

24. James W. Moore and A. Pope, "The Intentionality Bias and Schizotypy," *The Quarterly Journal of Experimental Psychology* (May 6, 2014): 1–7; see also Evelyn Rossett, "It's No Accident: Our Bias for Intentional Explanations," *Cognition* 108 (2008): 771–80.

25. Bertram F. Malle, *How the Mind Explains Behavior: Folk Explanations, Meaning, and Social Interaction* (Boston, MA: Massachusetts Institute of Technology, 2004), 88.

26. Clark, *Creating and Sustaining Civility in Nursing Education*, 14.

27. Hunt and Marini, "Incivility in the Practice Environment," 366–70; see also Marini, "The Thin Line between Civility and Incivility; Sypher, "Reclaiming Civil Discourse in the Workplace," 257–69.

28. C. Nathan DeWall and Brad J. Bushman, "Social Acceptance and Rejection: The Sweet and the Bitter," *Current Directions in Psychological Science* 20, no. 4 (2011): 256–60; see also Kristen Weir, "The Pain of Social Rejection," *American Psychological Association*, April. 2012, http://www.apa.org/monitor/2012/04/rjection.aspx (accessed July 21, 2014).

29. Sypher, "Reclaiming Civil Discourse in the Workplace," 260.

30. Noam Cohen, "Hashtag Calls for Compassion," *Dallas Morning News*, December 16, 2014, 2A.

31. Kent M. Weeks, *Doing Civility: Breaking the Cycle of Incivility on the Campus* (New York: Morgan James Publishing, 2014); see also Philip Smith, Timothy L. Phillips, and Ryan D. King, *Incivility: The Rude Stranger in Everyday Life* (New York: Cambridge University Press, 2010).

32. Benet Davetian, *Civility: A Cultural History* (Toronto, CN: University of Toronto Press, 2009); see also Megan Laverty, "Communication and Civility," in *Civility in Politics and Education*, ed. Deborah S. Mower and Wade L. Robison (New York: Routledge, 2012), 65–69; Barak Orbach, "On Hubris, Civility, and Incivility," *Arizona Law Review* 54, no. 43 (2012): 444–56; Ronald C. Arnett, Janie Harden Fritz, and Leeann M. Bell, *Communication Ethics Literacy: Dialogue and Difference* (Los Angeles, CA: Sage, 2009).

33. Troester and Mester, *Civility in Business and Professional Communication*; see also Billante and Saunders, *Six Questions about Civility*; K. M. Williamson, "Civility Proxies and Social Tolerance in American Marketplaces," *Sociological Inquiry* 72, no. 3 (2002); 486–99; and Ronald C. Arnett, "Dialogic Civility as Pragmatic Ethical Practice: An Interpersonal Metaphor for the Public Domain," *Communication Theory* 11, no. 3 (2001): 315–38.

34. Abbot L. Ferriss and Dennis L. Peck, "Guest Editors' Introduction," *Sociological Inquiry* 72, no. 3 (2002): 354–57; see also Edward Shils, "Civility and Civil Society," in *Civility*

*and Citizenship in a Liberal Democratic Society*, ed. Edward C. Banfield (New York: Paragon Press, 1992).

35. Ferriss and Peck, "Guest Editors' Introduction," 354–57; see also Andrew Terjesen, "Civility and Magnanimity," in *Civility in Politics and Education*, ed. Deborah S. Mower and Wade L. Robison (New York: Routledge, 2012), 99–116.

36. Edward Shils, *The Virtue of Civility* (Indianapolis, IN: Liberty Fund, 1997), 322.

37. Shils, *The Virtue of Civility*, 322.

38. Cheshire Calhoun, "The Virtue of Civility," *Philosophy and Public Affairs* 29, no. 3 (2002): 251–75.

39. Calhoun, "The Virtue of Civility," 259.

40. Billante and Saunders, *Six Questions about Civility*.

41. Billante and Saunders, *Six Questions about Civility*, 11.

42. Marilyn Price-Mitchell, "Teaching Civility in an F-Word Society," *Psychology Today*, June 23, 2012, https://www.psychologytoday.com/blog/the-moment-youth/201206/teaching-civility-in-f-word-society (accessed September 24, 2015).

43. Cynthia M. Clark and Joan Carnosso, "Civility: A Concept Analysis," *Journal of Theory and Construction and Testing* 12, No. 2 (2008): 11–15.

44. Larry Lage, "Armando Galarraga Perfect Game LOST by Blown Umpire Call," *Huffington Post*, June 30, 2014, http://www.huffingtonpost.com/2010/06/02/armando-galarraga-perfect_n_598626.html (accessed December 23, 2016).

45. Ben Walker, "Selig Won't Overturn Call That Cost Perfect Game," *MSNBC*, June 3, 2010, http://nbcsports.msnbc.com/id/37479309/ns/sports-baseball/ (accessed December 23, 2016).

46. Jonathan McFadden, "Police: Man Assaulted at Tega Cay Taco Bell for Failing to Say 'Excuse Me' after Belching," *Charlotte Observer*, March 17, 2014, http://www.charlotteobserver.com/2014/03/17/4772836/police-man-assaulted-at-tega-cay.html#.U6Gj07FwUjq (accessed December 23, 2016).

47. Michael Hyde, "The Ontological Workings of Dialogue and Acknowledgment," in *Dialogue: Theorizing Difference in Communication*, ed. Robert Anderson, Leslie A. Baxter, and Kenneth N. Cissna (Thousand Oaks: CA: Sage, 2004), 57–73.

48. Mark Caldwell, *A Short History of Rudeness: Manners, Morals, and Misbehavior in Modern America* (New York, NY: Picador, 1999).

49. Stephen L. Carter, *Civility: Manners, Morals, and the Etiquette of Democracy* (New York: Harper Perennial, 1998); see also Shils, *The Virtue of Civility*.

50. Caldwell, *A Short History of Rudeness*.

51. Cheshire Calhoun, "The Virtue of Civility," *Philosophy and Public Affairs* 29, no. 3 (2002): 251–75.

52. George Bernard Shaw, *Pygmalion* (1912; repr., London, England: Prestwick House, Inc., 2005), 56.

53. Caldwell, *A Short History of Rudeness:* 26–27

54. David Zax, "Choosing Civility in a Rude Culture," *Smithsonian Magazine*, December 1, 2008, http://www.smithsonianmag.com/arts-culture/Choosing-Civility-in-a-Rude-Culture.html?c=y&page=1 (accessed December 23, 2016).

55. Richard Boyd, "The Value of Civility?" *Urban Studies* 43, no. 5 (2006): 863–78.

56. Emrys Westicott, *The Virtues of Our Vices: A Modest Defense of Gossip, Rudeness, and Other Bad Habits* (Princeton, NJ: Princeton University Press, 2011).

57. Jim Leach, "Foreword," in *Civility in Politics and Education*, ed. Deborah S. Mower and Wade L. Robison (New York: Routledge, 2012), ix–xiv; see also Troester and Mester, *Civility in Business and Professional Communication*.

58. James Ragland, "They Make Their Cases and Mind Their Manners," *Dallas Morning News*, September 12, 2009.

59. Ragland, "They Make Their Cases and Mind Their Manners."

60. Ragland, "They Make Their Cases and Mind Their Manners."

61. Troester and Mester, *Civility in Business and Professional Communication*.

62. Shils, *The Virtue of Civility*, 38.

63. Donna Hicks, *Dignity: Its Essential Role in Resolving Conflict* (New Haven, CT: Yale University Press, 2011), 4–5.

64. Calhoun, "The Virtue of Civility," 251–75; see also Carter, *Civility: Manners, Morals, and the Etiquette of Democracy.*

65. Laverty, "Communication and Civility," in *Civility in Politics and Education.*

66. Pier M. Forni, *Choosing Civility: The Twenty-Five Rules of Considerate Conduct* (New York: St. Martin's Griffin, 2002), 13.

67. Emrys Westacott, *The Virtue of Our Vices: A Modest Defense of Gossip, Rudeness, and Other Bad Habits* (Princeton, NJ: Princeton University Press, 2011), 228.

68. Westacott, *The Virtue of Our Vices*; see also Shelley D. Lane and Helen McCourt, "Uncivil Communication in Everyday Life: A Response to Benson's 'The Rhetoric of Civility,' " *Journal of Contemporary Rhetoric* 3, no. 1/2 (2013): 17–29.

69. Westacott, *The Virtue of Our Vices*, 222.

70. Forni, *Choosing Civility.*

71. Michael Josephson, "Commentary 854.4—Listening: A Vital Dimension of Respect," *What Will Matter?* November 13, 2013, http://whatwillmatter.com/2013/13/11/commentary-803-2-listening-a-vital-dimension-of-respect/ (accessed December 23, 2016).

72. Carter, *Civility: Manners, Morals, and the Etiquette of Democracy.*

73. Pier M. Forni, "The Case for Formality," *Spectra*, 37, no. 3 (2011), 10.

74. Forni, "The Case for Formality," 8–10.

75. Carter, *Civility: Manners, Morals, and the Etiquette of Democracy*, 57.

76. Forni, "The Case for Formality," 8–10.

77. Billante and Saunders, *Six Questions about Civility.*

78. Troester and Mester, *Civility in Business and Professional Communication*, 8.

79. Andrew Terjesen, "Civility and Magnanimity," in *Civility in Politics and Education*, ed. Deborah S. Mower and Wade L. Robison (New York: Routledge, 2012), 99–116.

80. David Zahniser, Emily Alpert Reyes, and Hailey Branson-Potts, "Garcetti Drops the F-Bomb at Kings Celebration—And There's Fallout," *Los Angeles Times*, June 17, 2014, www.latimes.com/local/cityhall/la-me-garcetti-f-word-20140617-story.html (accessed December 23, 2016).

81. Lauren Rabb, "Mayor Eric Garcetti Employs F-Bomb to Mark L.A. Kings Victory," *Los Angeles Times*, June 26, 2014, www.latimes.com/local/lanow/la-me-In-garcetti-stanley-cup-swear-20140616-story.html (accessed December 23, 2016).

82. Zahniser et al., "Garcetti Drops the F-Bomb at Kings Celebration."

83. Rabb, "Mayor Eric Garcetti Employs F-Bomb to Mark L.A. Kings Victory."

84. John Rogers, "LA Mayor's F-Bomb Blows Up Worries about Bad Words," *ABCnews*, June 17, 2014, http://abcnews.go,com/Weird/wireStory/major-drops-bomb-declaring-big-day-la24175254 (accessed December 23, 2016).

85. Zahniser et al., "Garcetti Drops the F-Bomb at Kings Celebration."

86. Jack Marshall, "#$!@&! Ethics Dunce and Incompetent Elected Official of the Month: L.A. Mayor Eric Garcetti," *Ethics Alarms*, June 17, 2014, http://ethicsalarms.com/2014/06/17/ethics-dunce-and-incompetent-elected-official-of-the-month-l-a-mayor-eric-garcetti/ (accessed December 23, 2016).

87. Zahniser et al., "Garcetti Drops the F-Bomb at Kings Celebration."

88. Billante and Saunders, *Six Questions about Civility*; see also Lane and McCourt, "Uncivil Communication in Everyday Life," 17–29; Stephen L. Carter, "Just Be Nice," *Yale Alumni Magazine*, May 1998, www.yalealumnimagazine.com/issues/98_05/Stephen_Carter.html (accessed December 23, 2016).

89. Forni, *Choosing Civility*, 23.

90. Mark Kingwell, *A Civil Tongue: Justice, Dialogue, and the Politics of Pluralism* (University Park, PA: Penn State University Press, 1995).

91. Janie M. Harden Fritz, *Professional Civility: Communicative Virtue at Work* (New York, NY: Peter Lang, 2013).

92. Janie M. Harden Fritz, "Civility in the Workplace," *Spectra* 47, no. 3 (2011): 11–15.

93. Forni, *Choosing Civility*, 22.

94. Vincent Ryan Ruggiero, "Bad Attitude: Confronting Views That Hinder Students' Learning," *American Educator* 21 (Summer 2000): 1–10.

95. Forni, *Choosing Civility*, 168.

96. Roy F. Baumeister, Todd F. Heatheron, and Dianne M. Tice, *Losing Control: How and Why People Fail at Self-Regulation* (Waltham, MA: Academic Press, 1994).

97. Roy F. Baumeister, "The Lowdown on High-Esteem: Thinking You're Hot Stuff Isn't the Promised Cure-All," *Los Angeles Times*, January 25, 2005, www.latimes.com/news/opinion/commentary/la-oe-baumeister25jan,0,1298447.story?coll=la-news-comment.opinions/ (accessed December 23, 2016).

98. Carter, *Civility: Manners, Morals, and the Etiquette of Democracy*.

99. Carter, *Civility: Manners, Morals, and the Etiquette of Democracy*.

100. Abbott L. Ferriss, "Studying and Measuring Civility: A Framework, Trends, and Scale," *Sociological Inquiry* 72, no. 4 (2002): 376–92.

101. Amber DeBono, Dikla Shmueli, and Mark Muraven, "Rude and Inappropriate: The Role of Self-Control in Following Social Norms," *Personality and Social Psychology Bulletin* 37, no. 1 (2011) 136–56.

102. Forni, *Choosing Civility*.

103. Forni, *Choosing Civility*, 22.

104. Cheshire Calhoun, *Moral Aims: Essays on the Importance of Getting It Right and Practicing Morality with Others* (Oxford, UK: Oxford University Press, 2015), 160.

105. Calhoun, *Moral Aims*, 160.

106. Jack Marshall, "Ethics Quiz (Inadvertent Offense Division): The Transsexual Vote. *Ethics Alarms*, July 2, 2014, http://ethicsalarms.com/2014/07/02ethics-quiz-iinadvertent-offense-division-the-transsexual-vote/ (accessed December 28, 2016).

107. Marshall, "Ethics Quiz (Inadvertent Offense Division."

108. Marshall, "Ethics Quiz (Inadvertent Offense Division."

109. Herbert G. Grice, "Logic and Conversation," in *Syntax and Semantics, Volume 3: Speech Acts*, ed. Peter Cole and Jerry L. Morgan (New York: Academic Press, 1975), 41–58; see also Shelley D. Lane, Ruth Anna Abigail, and John Casey Gooch, *Communication in a Civil Society* (Boston, MA: Pearson Education, 2014); Stephanie J. Coopman and James Lull, *Public Speaking: The Evolving Art*, 3rd ed. (Boston, MA: Cengage Learning, 2014).

110. Shils, *The Virtue of Civility*; see also Forni, *Choosing Civility*; Leonard Pitts Jr., "Our Coarseness Undercuts the Social Covenant," *Dallas Morning News* (Dallas, TX), May 8, 2012, 21A.

111. Pitts Jr., "Our Coarseness Undercuts the Social Covenant," 21A.

112. Richard Boyd, "The Value of Civility?" *Urban Studies* 43, no. 5 (2006): 863–68.

113. Thomas W. Benson, "The Rhetoric of Civility: Power, Authenticity, and Democracy," *Journal of Contemporary Rhetoric* 1, no. 1 (2011): 22–30; see also Lane and McCourt, "Uncivil Communication in Everyday Life," 17–29.

114. Carter, *Civility: Manners, Morals, and the Etiquette of Democracy*; see also Corey L. M. Keyes, "Social Civility in the United States," *Sociological Inquiry* 72, no. 3 (2002): 393–408; Dennis L. Peck, "Civility: A Contemporary Context for a Meaningful Historical Concept, *Sociological Inquiry* 72, no. 3 (2002): 358–75.

115. Keyes, "Social Civility in the United States," 393–408.

116. Peck, "Civility: A Contemporary Context for a Meaningful Historical Concept," 358–75.

117. Carter, *Civility: Manners, Morals, and the Etiquette of Democracy*, 56.

118. Pitts Jr., "Our Coarseness Undercuts the Social Covenant," 21A.

119. Pitts Jr., "Our Coarseness Undercuts the Social Covenant," 23A.

120. Carter, *Civility: Manners, Morals, and the Etiquette of Democracy*; see also Forni, *Choosing Civility*.

121. Carter, *Civility: Manners, Morals, and the Etiquette of Democracy*.

122. James A. Jaksa and Michael S. Pritchard, *Communication Ethics: Methods of Analysis*, 2nd ed. (Belmont, CA: Wadsworth, 1996), 3.

## 3. INFLUENCES ON EVERYDAY INCIVILITY

1. Nicole Billante and Peter Saunders, "Six Questions about Civility," *CIS Occasional Paper* 82 (St. Leonards, Australia: The Centre for Independent Studies, 2002): 10.

2. Donal Carbaugh, *Cultures in Conversation* (Mahwah, NJ: Lawrence Erlbaum, 2005), 15–16.

3. Carbaugh, *Cultures in Conversation*, 16–17

4. Gary Althen with Janet Bennett, *American Ways: A Cultural Guide to the United States*, 3rd ed. (Boston, MA: Intercultural Press, 2011), 12.

5. Edward C. Stewart and Milton J. Bennett, *American Cultural Patterns*, revised edition (1991; repr., Yarmouth, ME: Intercultural Press, 2011), 91.

6. Benet Davetian, *Civility: A Cultural History* (Toronto, CN: University of Toronto Press, 2009), 446.

7. hoK leahciM, "30 People Reveal Their Embarrassing Moments Because of a Cultural Misunderstanding," *Thought Catalogue*, April 30, 2014, http://thoughtcatalog.com/hok-leahcim/2014/04/30-people-reveal-their-embarrassing-moments-because-of-a-cultural-misunderstanding/ (accessed December 28, 2016).

8. Edwin R. McDaniel, "Japanese Nonverbal Communication: A Reflection of Cultural Themes," in *Intercultural Communication: A Reader*, ed. Larry A. Samovar, Richard E. Porter, Edwin R. McDaniel, and Carolyn Sexton Roy, 14th ed. (Boston, MA: Cengage Learning, 2014), 242–50.

9. Craig Storti, *Figuring Foreigners Out: A Practical Guide* (Yarmouth, ME: Intercultural Press, 1999).

10. Peter A. Andersen, "Cues of Culture: The Basis of Intercultural Differences in Nonverbal Communication," in *Intercultural Communication: A Reader*, ed. Larry A. Samovar and Richard E. Porter, 8th ed. (Belmont, CA: Wadsworth), 224.

11. Judith Martin and Thomas K. Nakayama, *Intercultural Communication in Contexts*, 6th ed. (Boston, MA: McGraw-Hill, 2012).

12. Stewart and Bennett, *American Cultural Patterns*, x.

13. Edward T. Hall, *Beyond Culture* (New York: Anchor Books, 1976).

14. P. M. Forni, *Choosing Civility* (New York: St. Martin's Griffin, 2002), 169.

15. Eun-Yun Kim, *The Yin and Yang of American Culture: A Paradox* (Boston, MA: Intercultural Press, 2001).

16. Donal Carbaugh, *Talking American: Cultural Discourses on "Donahue"* (Norwood, NJ: Ablex, 1988).

17. Myron W. Lustig and Jolene Koester, *Intercultural Competence*, 7th ed. (London, UK: Pearson, 2013).

18. Edwin R. McDaniel, "Japanese Nonverbal Communication: A Reflection of Cultural Themes," in *Intercultural Communication: A Reader*, ed. Larry A. Samovar, Richard E. Porter, Edwin R. McDaniel, and Carolyn Sexton Roy, 14th edition (Boston, MA: Cengage Learning, 2014), 242–50.

19. McDaniel, "Japanese Nonverbal Communication," 10.

20. McDaniel, "Japanese Nonverbal Communication," 242–50.

21. Deborah Tannen, " 'Don't Just Sit There—Interrupt!' Pacing and Pausing in Conversational Style," *American Speech* 75, no. 4 (2000): 393–95.

22. Tannen, " 'Don't Just Sit There—Interrupt!,' " 394.

23. Tannen, " 'Don't Just Sit There—Interrupt!,' " 395.

24. Richard Brislin, *Understanding Culture's Influence on Behavior* (Orlando, FL: Harcourt Brace, 2003); see also Lustig and Koester, *Intercultural Competence*, 218; Deborah Tannen, "The Pragmatics of Cross-Cultural Communication," *Applied Linguistics* 5, no. 3 (1984):189–95.

25. Deborah Tannen, *Conversational Style: Analyzing Talk among Friends* (New York: Oxford University Press, 2005); see also Tannen, "The Pragmatics of Cross-Cultural Communication," 189–95; Deborah Tannen, "Cross-Cultural Communication," in *Handbook of Discourse Analysis: Vol. 4*, ed. Teun A. Van Duk (London, UK: Academic Press, 1985), 203–15.

26. Mark L. Knapp, Judith A. Hall, and Terrence G. Horgan, *Nonverbal Communication in Human Interaction,* 8th ed. (Boston, MA: Wadsworth Cengage Learning, 2014).

27. Dianne Hofner Saphiere, Barbara Kappler Mikk, and Basma Ibrahim Devries, *Communication Highwire: Leveraging the Power of Diverse Communication Styles* (Yarmouth, ME: Nicholas Brealey, 2005), 7.

28. Saphiere et al., *Communication Highwire*, 8.

29. Jeffrey Walsh, "Cross Cultural Faux Pas Stories," ed. Lisa B. Marshall , *Lisabmarshall.com,* 2012–2013, www.lisabmarshall.com/2008/10/15cross-cultural-faux-pas-stories/ (accessed January 5, 2016).

30. Walsh, "Cross Cultural Faux Pas Stories."

31. Richard D. Lewis, *When Cultures Collide: Leading across Cultures*, 3rd ed. (Boston, MA: Nicholas Brealey, 2006), xvii.

32. David G. Savage, "Penn Debates Meaning of Water Buffalo," *Los Angeles Times*, May 10, 1993, http://articles.latimes.com/print/1993-05-10/news/mn-33609_1_water-buffalo (accessed December 29, 2016); see also Mary R. Lefkowitz, *History Lesson: A Race Odyssey* (Boston, MA: Yale University Press, 2003), 23–24.

33. Polly Platt, *French or Foe?*, 2nd ed. (UK: Culture Crossings, 1994).

34. Martin and Nakayama, *Intercultural Communication in Contexts*, 227; see also Lustig and Koester, *Intercultural Competence*.

35. Lustig and Koester, *Intercultural Competence*, 166–67.

36. John Kifner, "What's A-OK, in the U.S.A. is Lewd and Worthless Beyond," *New York Times*, August 18, 1996, http://www.nytimes.com/1996/08/18/weekinreview/what-s-a-ok-in-the-usa-is-lewd-and-worthless-beyond.html (accessed January 31, 2016).

37. Mary R. Lefkowitz, *History Lesson: A Race Odyssey* (Boston, MA: Yale University Press, 2003).

38. Lefkowitz, *History Lesson*.

39. Holley S. Hodgins and Richard Koestner, "The Origins of Nonverbal Sensitivity," *Personality and Social Psychology Bulletin* 19 (1993): 466–73; see also Anna-Marie Dew and Colleen Ward, "The Effects of Ethnicity and Culturally Congruent and Incongruent Nonverbal Behaviors on Interpersonal Attraction," *Journal of Applied Social Psychology* 23 (1993): 1376–89.

40. Peter A. Andersen, *Nonverbal Communication: Forms and Functions*, 2nd ed. (Long Grove, IL: Waveland Press, 2008).

41. Nina-Jo Moore, Mark Hickson III, and Don W. Stacks, *Nonverbal Communication: Studies and Applications*, 6th ed. (New York: Oxford University Press, 2014).

42. Andersen, *Nonverbal Communication: Forms and Functions*, 80–81.

43. Martin and Nakayama, *Intercultural Communication in Contexts.*

44. Stewart and Bennett, *American Cultural Patterns.*

45. Carbaugh, *Cultures in Conversation*, 39–40.

46. Carbaugh, *Cultures in Conversation*, 42–43.

47. Raymonde Carroll, *Cultural Misunderstandings: The French-American Experience*, trans. Carol Volk (Chicago: University of Chicago Press, 1988), 30.

48. Carroll, *Cultural Misunderstandings*; see also Platt, *French or Foe?*

49. Lewis, *When Cultures Collide*, 157.

50. Martin and Nakayama, *Intercultural Communication in Contexts*, 280.

51. Lustig and Koester, *Intercultural Competence*, 216–17.

52. Vijai N. Giri, "Culture and Communication Style," *The Review of Communication* 6, no. 1–2 (2006), 124–30.

53. E. Wu, "Name Change May be Sign of the Times," *Dallas Morning News*, July 22, 2004, 7B.

54. Mark P. Orbe, *Constructing Co-Cultural Theory: An Explication of Culture, Power and Communication* (Thousand Oaks, CA: Sage, 1998); see also Tannen, " 'Don't Just Sit There—Interrupt!,' " 393–95.

55. Tannen, *Conversational Style*; see also Deborah Tannen, "New York Style: It's Not What You Say, It's the Way that You Say It," *Do You Speak American*, American Varieties, 2005, http://www.pbs.org/speak/seatosea/americanvarieties/newyorkcity/ (accessed March 1,

2005); Deborah Tannen, "Talking New York: It's Not Just the Accent that Makes Us Different," *Do You Speak American*, American Varieties, 2005, http://www.pbs.org/speak/seatosea/ americanvarieties/newyorkcity/accent/ (accessed March 1, 2005).

56. Stewart and Bennett, *American Cultural Patterns*; see also Gary Althen and Janet Bennett, *American Ways: A Cultural Guide to the United States of America,* 3rd ed. (Yarmouth, ME: Intercultural Press, 2011).

57. Althen and Bennett, *American Ways: A Cultural Guide to the United States of America,* 30.

58. Alison R. Lanier and Jef C. Davis, *Living in the U.S.A,* 6th ed. (Boston, MA: Intercultural Press, 2004).

59. Shirley N. Weber, "The Need to Be: The Socio-Cultural Significance of Black Language" in *Voices: A Selection of Multicultural Readings,* ed. Kathleen.S. Verderber (Belmont, CA: Wadsworth, 1995), 30–36; see also Thomas Kochman, *Black and White Styles in Conflict* (Chicago, IL: University of Chicago Press, 1981).

60. Stella Ting-Toomey, "Intercultural Conflict Styles: A Face-Negotiation Theory," in *Theories of Intercultural Communication,* ed. Young Yun Kim and William B. Gudykunst (Thousand Oaks, CA: Sage, 1988), 213–35; see also Norma Carr-Ruffino, *Managing Diversity,* 9th ed. (Boston, MA: Pearson Learning Solutions, 2012); Fern L. Johnson, *Speaking Culturally: Language Diversity in the United States* (Thousand Oaks, CA: Sage, 2000), 239.

61. Donald W. Klopf and James McCroskey, *Intercultural Communication Encounters* (Boston, MA: Pearson, 2006); see also Johnson, *Speaking Culturally.*

62. Jack Marshall, "Sexism, Feminists, and the Scientist's Shirt," *Ethics Alarms* (blog), November 14, 2014, http://ethicsalarms.com/2014/11/14/sexism-feminists-and-the-scientists-shirt/ (accessed December 29, 2016); see also Lisa Respers France, "Philae Researcher Criticized for Shirt Covered in Scantily Clad Women," *CNN*, November 14, 2014, http://www.cnn.com/2014/11/13/living/matt-taylor-shirt-philae-rosetta-project/ (accessed December 29, 2016).

63. France, "Philae Researcher Criticized for Shirt Covered in Scantily Clad Women."

64. Deborah Tannen, *The Argument Culture: Stopping America's War of Words* (New York: Ballantine Books, 1998).

65. Em Griffin, Andrew Ledbetter, and Glenn Sparks, *A First Look at Communication Theory,* 9th ed. (New York: McGraw Hill, 2015), 432.

66. Deborah Tannen, *Gender and Discourse* (New York, NY: Oxford University Press, 1996), 180.

67. Deborah Tannen, *You Just Don't Understand: Women and Men in Conversation* (London, UK: Virago, 1991), 51.

68. Tannen, *You Just Don't Understand.*

69. Julia T. Wood, "She Says / He Says: Communication, Caring, and Conflict in Heterosexual Relationships," in *Gendered Relationships,* ed. Julia T. Wood (New York: McGraw-Hill, 1995), 149–62; see also Tannen, *You Just Don't Understand.*

70. Deborah Borisoff, "Gender Issues and Listening," in *Listening in Everyday Life: A Personal and Professional Approach,* ed. Deborah Borisoff and Michael Purdy (Lanham, MD: University Press of America, 1991), 59–85.

71. Daniel N. Maltz and Ruth B. Borker, "A Cultural Approach to Male-Female Miscommunication," in *Language and Social Identity,* ed. John Gumperz (New York: Cambridge University Press, 1982), 196–216.

72. Griffin et al., *A First Look at Communication Theory,* 436.

73. Rosalind Barnett and Caryl Rivers. "Men Are from Earth, and So Are Women. It's Faulty Research That Sets Them Apart," *Chronicle of Higher Education,* 51, no. 2 (2004): B11.

74. Ben Widdicombe, "Millennials in Charge," *Dallas Morning News*, March 27, 2016, 2D; see also Bruce Horovitz, "After Gen X, Millennials, What Should Next Generation Be?" *USATODAY.com*, May 4, 2012, http://usatoday30.usatoday.com/money/advertising/story/2012-05-03/naming-the-next-generation/54737518/1 (accessed July 3, 2016).

75. Sara Hacala, *Saving Civility: 52 Ways to Tame Rude, Crude, and Attitude for a Polite Planet* (Woodstock, VT: Skylights Paths Publishing, 2001), 26; see also Scott Keeter and Paul Taylor, "The Millennials," *Pew Research Center*, December 11, 2009, http://pewresearch.org/pubs/1427/millennials-profile (accessed December 17, 2009).

76. Scott Keeter and Paul Taylor, "The Millennials," *Pew Research Center*, December 11, 2009, http://pewresearch.org/pubs/1427/millennials-profile (accessed December 17, 2009).

77. Shelley D. Lane and Tara Lewis, "Exploring the Twitterverse: Connecting with Millennials in the Digital Age," *Texas Speech Communication Journal Online*, August 2010, http://www.etsca.com/tscjonline/0810-twitterverse/ (accessed December 29, 2016); see also Shelley D. Lane and Tara N. Lewis, "The 'Digital Divide,' Social Media, and Education-Related Outcomes," *The Online Journal of New Horizons in Education* 3, no. 2 (2013): 39–50.

78. Eric Hoover, "The Millennial Muddle," *The Chronicle of Higher Education*, October 11, 2009, http://chronicle.com/article/The-Millennial-Muddle-How-/48772/ (accessed December 17, 2009).

79. Neil Howe and William Strauss, *Millennials Rising: The Next Great Generation* (New York: Vintage Books, 2000); see also "Millennials: Breaking the Myths," *Nielson*, January 27, 2014, http://www.nielsen.com/us/en/insights/reports/2014/millennials-breaking-the-myths.html (accessed December 29, 2016).

80. Jean M. Twenge, *Generation Me: Why Today's Young Americans are More Confident, Assertive, Entitled—and More Miserable than Ever Before* (New York: Free Press, 2006); see also Regina Luttrell and Karen McGrath, *The Millennial Mindset: Unraveling Fact from Fiction* (Lanham, MD: Rowman & Littlefield, 2016).

81. Corey Seemiller and Meghan Grace, *Generation Z Goes to College* (San Francisco, CA: Jossey-Bass, 2016), 6. See also George Beall, "8 Key Differences between Gen Z and Millennials," *The Huffington Post*, November 5, 2016, http://www.huffingtonpost.com/george-beall/8-key-differences-betwee_b_12814200.html (accessed November 30, 2016); Ryan Scott, "Get Ready for Generation Z," *Forbes*, November 28, 2016, https://www.forbes.com/sites/causeintegration/2016/11/28/get-ready-for-generation-z/#7eae0ff22048 (accessed November 30, 2016); and Phillip Tanzillo, "Generation Z: Understanding these iGeneration Screenagers, Transformational Learning and Leadership Strategies," July 22, 2016, http://www.philliptanzilo.com/generation-z-understanding-igeneration-screenagers/ (accessed May 3, 2017).

82. Caelainn Barr, "Who Are Generation Z? The Latest Data on Today's Teens," *The Guardian*, December 10, 2016, https://www.theguardian.com/lifeandstyle/2016/dec/10/generation-z-latest-data-teens (accessed December 11, 2016).

83. Beall, "8 Key Differences."

84. Stephen Abram, "Millennials: Deal with Them! Part II," *School Library Media Activities Monthly* 24, no. 2 (2007): 55–58.

85. Luttrell and McGrath, *The Millennial Mindset*, 22.

86. Mallory Schlossberg, "Teen Generation Z is being called 'Millennials on Steroids,' and that could be Terrifying for Retailers," *Business Insider*, February 11, 2016, http://www.businessinsider.com/millennials-vs-gen-z-2016-2 (accessed November 30, 2016).

87. Don Tapscott, "The Eight Net Gen Norms," in *The Digital Divide*, ed. Mark Bauerlein (New York: Jeremy P. Tarcher / Penguin, 2011); see also "Millennials: Breaking the Myths."

88. "Is Online Privacy Over? Findings from the USC Annenberg Center for the Digital Future Show Millennials Embrace a New Online Reality," *USC Annenberg Center for the Digital Future*, April 22, 2013, http://annenberg.usc.edu/news/around-usc-annenberg/online-privacy-over-findings-usc-annenberg-center-digital-future-show (accessed January 15, 2015).

89. Janna Quitney Anderson and Lee Rainie, *Millennials Will Make Online Sharing in Networks a Lifelong Habit* (Washington, DC: Pew Internet and American Life Project, 2010), 17–18.

90. "The Generation AFTER Millennials Will Change How You Use Technology," *Gen Z Technology Usage Infographic*, The Center for Generational Kinetics, 2016, http://genhq.com/igen-genz-technology-trends-infographic (accessed May 4, 2017).

91. Anderson and Rainie, *Millennials Will Make Online Sharing in Networks a Lifelong Habit*, 12.

92. "Center for the Digital Future Survey Finds Generation Gap in Cell Phone Etiquette," *USC Annenberg Center for the Digital Future*, February 11, 2013, http://annenberg.usc.edu/news/around-usc-annenberg/center-digital-future-survey-finds-generation-gap-cell-phone-etiquette (accessed July 28, 2016).

93. "The Generation AFTER Millennials Will Change How You Use Technology."
94. Tapscott, "The Eight Net Gen Norms," 152.
95. Jonathan D. Glater, "To: Professor@University.edu Subject: Why It's All About Me," February 21, 2006, *New York Times*, http://www.nytimes.com/2006/02/21/education/21professors.html?pagewanted+all (accessed January 28, 2014).
96. Glater, "To: Professor@University.edu Subject"; see also Brigitta R. Brunner, Bradford L. Yates, and Jennifer Wood Adams, "Mass Communication and Journalism Faculty and Their Electronic Communication with College Students: A Nationwide Examination," *Internet and Higher Education* 11 (2008): 106–11; Keri K. Stephens, Marian L. Houser, and Renee L. Cowan, "R U Able to Meat Me: The Impact of Students' Overly Casual Email Messages to Instructors," *Communication Education* 58, no. 3 (2009) 303–26.
97. "2012 Professionalism on Campus," *Center for Professional Excellence*, January 2013, 17.
98. Stephens et al., "R U Able to Meat Me," 303–26; see also Paul T. Corrigan and Cameron Hunt McNabb, "Re: Your Recent Email to Your Professor," *Inside Higher Ed*, April 16, 2015, https://www.insidehighered.com/views/2015/04/16/advice-students-so-they-dont-sound-silly-emails-essay (accessed April 16, 2015).

# 4. THE GOOD, THE BAD, AND
# THE VIRTUE OF CIVILITY

1. Nicole Billante and Peter Saunders, "Six Questions about Civility," *CIS Occasional Paper* 82 (St. Leonards, Australia: The Centre for Independent Studies, 2002): 20.
2. Mark Thiessen, "TV Reporter Goes to Pot, Quits with 4-Letter Sign-Off," *Dallas Morning News*, September 23, 2014, 5A.
3. Rebecca Aguilar, "Charlo Greene's Controversial On-Air Exit Hurt Us," *Digitocracy*. September 24, 2014, http://alldigitocracy.org/charlo-greenes-controversial-on-air-exit-hurt-us/ (accessed December 30, 2016).
4. Mark Caldwell, *A Short History of Rudeness: Manners, Morals and Misbehavior in Modern America* (New York: Picador, 1999); see also Stephen L. Carter, *Civility: Manners, Morals, and the Etiquette of Democracy* (New York: Harper Perennial, 1998); Edward Shils, *The Virtue of Civility* (Indianapolis, IN: Liberty Fund, 1997).
5. Scott Farwell, Joshua Menton, and Kristen Holland, "Students Rapped for Thug Day Attire," *Dallas Morning News*, October 28, 2005, 1B.
6. Farwell et al., "Students Rapped for Thug Day Attire."
7. Jacquielynn Floyd, " 'Thug Day' More Rude than Racist," *Dallas Morning News*, November 1, 2005, 5B.
8. Floyd, " 'Thug Day' More Rude than Racist."
9. David Zax, "Choosing Civility in a Rude Culture," *Smithsonian Magazine*, December 1, 2008, http://www.smithsonianmag.com/arts-culture/choosing-civility-in-a-rude-culture-97997109/ (accessed December 30, 2016).
10. Richard Boyd, "The Value of Civility?," *Urban Studies* 43, no. 5 (2006): 863–78.
11. Janie M. Harden Fritz, "Civility in the Workplace," *Spectra* 47, no. 3 (2011): 11–15.
12. Christine Pearson and Christine Porath, *The Cost of Bad Behavior: How Incivility Is Damaging Your Business and What to Do about It* (New York: Portfolio, 2009).
13. Brianna Barker Caza and Lilia M. Cortina, "From Insult to Injury: Explaining the Impact of Incivility," *Basic and Applied Social Psychology* 29, no. 4 (2007): 335–50.
14. Kent M. Weeks, *Doing Civility: Breaking the Cycle of Incivility on the Campus* (New York: Morgan James, 2014).
15. Harlan Lebo, *The Digital Future Report: Surveying the Digital Future, Year Eleven* (Los Angeles, CA: USC Annenberg School Center for the Digital Future, 2013).

16. Robert S. Tokunaga, "Following You Home from School: A Critical Review and Synthesis of Research on Cyberbullyng Victimization," *Computers in Human Behavior* 26 (2010): 277–87.

17. Rusty Wright, "Civil Discourse? Radio Version—Bridgebuilding: From Foot Fights to Finding Common Ground," *Probe Ministries*, 2007, https://www.probe.org/civil-discourse-radio-version/ (accessed December 30, 2016).

18. Boyd, "The Value of Civility?," 873.

19. Boyd, "The Value of Civility?," 870.

20. Boyd, "The Value of Civility?," 865.

21. Cheshire Calhoun, "The Virtue of Civility," *Philosophy and Public Affairs* 29, no. 3 (2000): 266.

22. Chris Mayo, "The Binds that Tie: Civility and Social Difference," *Educational Theory* 52, no. 1 (2002): 169–86.

23. Nicole Billante and Peter Saunders, *Six Questions about Civility* (St. Leonards, AU: The Centre for Independent Studies Limited, 2002).

24. Megan J. Laverty, "Communication and Civility," in *Civility in Politics and Education* (New York: Routledge, 2012).

25. Janie M. Harden Fritz, *Professional Civility: Communicative Virtue at Work* (New York: Peter Lang, 2013).

26. Ryan T. Anderson, "New York Times Reporter: 'Some People Are Deserving of Incivility,' " *Daily Signal*, July 31, 2014, http://dailysignal.com/2014/07/31/new-york-times-reporter-people-deserving-incivility/ (accessed December 30, 2016).

27. Anderson, "New York Times Reporter."

28. Anderson, "New York Times Reporter."

29. Anderson, "New York Times Reporter."

30. Natalie Angier, "Almost before We Spoke, We Swore," *New York Times*, September 20, 2005, http://www.nytimes.com/2005/09/20/science/almost-before-we-spoke-we-swore.html?_r=0 (accessed December 30, 2016).

31. Emrys Westacott, *The Virtues of Our Vices: A Modest Defense of Gossip, Rudeness, and Other Bad Habits* (Princeton, NJ: Princeton University Press, 2011).

32. David Yamada, "Can Workplace Incivility Ever Be Healthy?" *Minding the Workplace: The New Workplace Institute Blog*, October 26, 2011, https://newworkplace.wordpress.com/2011/10/26/can-workplace-incivility-ever-be-healthy/ (accessed December 30, 2016).

33. Yamada, "Can Workplace Incivility Ever Be Healthy?"

34. Shils, *The Virtue of Civility*, 97.

35. Chris Trueman, "The Suffragettes," *History Learning Site*, 2012, http://www.historylearningsite.co.uk/the-role-of-british-women-in-the-twentieth-century/suffragettes/ (accessed December 30, 2016).

36. Rebecca Myers, "General History of Women's Suffrage in Britain," *The Independent*, May 28, 2013, www.independent.co.uk/news/uk/hone-news/general-history-of-womens-suffrage-in-britain-8631733.html (accessed December 30, 2016).

37. Myers, "General History of Women's Suffrage in Britain."

38. Myers, "General History of Women's Suffrage in Britain."

39. Tracy Chevalier, "The Women's Suffrage Movement," *Tchevalier.com*, 2014, www.tchevalier.com/fallingangels/bckgrnd/suffrage/ (accessed December 30, 2016).

40. Trueman, "The Suffragettes."

41. "The Influence of Suffragettes," *Positive Power and Influence*, 2013, https://positivepowerandinfluence.co.uk/thought-leadership/the-influence-of-suffragettes/ (accessed December 30, 2016).

42. "The Influence of Suffragettes."

43. Chevalier, "The Women's Suffrage Movement."

44. Sandy L. Maisel, "The Negative Consequences of Uncivil Political Discourse," *PS: Political Science & Politics* 45, no. 3 (2012): 405–11.

45. Todd J. Gillman, "Texan Explains His 'Baby Killer' Shout," *Dallas Morning News*, March 23, 2010, 7A.

46. Gillman, "Texan Explains His 'Baby Killer' Shout."

47. Laverty, "Communication and Civility."

48. Mayo, "The Binds that Tie: Civility and Social Difference," 169–86.

49. Billante and Saunders, *Six Questions about Civility*, 26.

50. Barak Orbak, "On Hubris, Civility, and Incivility," *Arizona Law Review* 54, no. 433 (2012): 444–56.

51. Lawrence Cohen and Anthony DeBenedet, "Penn State Cover-Up: Groupthink in Action," *Time*, January 7, 2012, http://ideas.time.com/2012/07/17/penn-state-cover-up-groupthink-in-action/ (accessed December 30, 2016); see also Varun Dutt, "How to Avoid Groupthink Complications in Entrepreneurship," *Financial Chronicle*, November 15, 2012, http://www.pressreader.com/india/financial-chronicle/20121115/282200828197093 (accessed December 30, 2016); Carol Tavris and Elliott Aaronson, *Mistakes Were Made, But Not by Me: Why We Justify Foolish Beliefs, Bad Decisions, and Hurtful Acts* (Orlando, FL: Harcourt Publishers, 2008).

52. Mayo, "The Binds That Tie: Civility and Social Difference," 169–86; see also Philip Smith, Timothy L. Phillips, and Ryan D. King, *Incivility: The Rude Stranger in Everyday Life* (London, UK: Cambridge University Press, 2010).

53. Smith et al., *Incivility: The Rude Stranger in Everyday Life*, 160.

54. Eleanor Sadler, "Boy, 11, Respectful in His Civility Lesson," *Dallas Morning News*, March 1, 2003, 7B.

55. Sadler, "Boy, 11, Respectful in His Civility Lesson," 7B.

56. Sadler, "Boy, 11, Respectful in His Civility Lesson," 7B.

57. Sadler, "Boy, 11, Respectful in His Civility Lesson," 7B.

58. "Virtue," *Oxford Dictionaries: Language Matters*, 2015, http://www.oxforddictionaries.com/us/definition/american_english/virtue (accessed December 30, 2016).

59. James Schmidt, "Is Civility a Virtue?" in *Civility*, ed. Leroy S. Roumer (Notre Dame, IN: University of Notre Dame Press, 2000), 17–39.

60. "Ethics and Compliance Glossary," *ECI—Ethics and Compliance Initiative*, Ethics Resource Center, 2016, https://www.ethics.org/resources/free-toolkit/toolkit-glossary (accessed December 30, 2016).

61. "Ethics and Compliance Glossary," *ECI—Ethics and Compliance Initiative*.

62. "Definitions of Values," *ECI—Ethics and Compliance Initiative*, Ethics Resource Center, 2016, https://www.ethics.org/resources/free-toolkit/definition-values (accessed December 30, 2016).

63. Lawrence Cahoone, "Civic Meetings, Cultural Meanings," in *Civility*, ed. Leroy S. Rouner (Notre Dame, IN: University of Notre Dame Press, 2000), 40–64.

64. Robert B. Pippin, "The Ethical Status of Civility," in *Civility*, ed. Leroy S. Rouner (Notre Dame, IN: Notre Dame University Press, 2000), 103–17; see also Daniel O. Dahlsrom, "Response to Robert B. Pippin," in *Civility*, ed. Leroy S. Rouner (Notre Dame, IN: University of Notre Dame Press, 2000), 118–25.

65. Janie M. Harden Fritz, "Civility in the Workplace," *Spectra* 47, no. 3 (2011): 11.

66. Billante and Saunders, *Six Questions about Civility*, 31.

67. Shils, *The Virtue of Civility*, 4.

68. Boyd, "The Value of Civility?," 863–78.

69. Abbott L. Ferriss and Dennis L. Peck, "Guest Editors' Introduction," *Sociological Inquiry* 72, no. 3 (2002): 355.

70. Carter, *Civility: Manners, Morals, and the Etiquette of Democracy*.

71. Carter, *Civility: Manners, Morals, and the Etiquette of Democracy*.

72. Nicole Billante and Peter Saunders, "Why Civility Matters," *Policy* 18, no. 3 (2002): 34.

73. Harold Barrett, *Rhetoric and Civility: Human Development, Narcissism, and the Good Audience* (New York: State University of New York Press, 1991), 147.

74. Pippin, "The Ethical Status of Civility," 106.

75. Pippin, "The Ethical Status of Civility," 116.

76. Pippin, "The Ethical Status of Civility," 110.

77. Calhoun, "The Virtue of Civility."

78. Calhoun, "The Virtue of Civility," 255.

79. Laverty, "Communication and Civility."

80. Janie M. Harden Fritz, *Professional Civility: Communicative Virtue at Work* (New York: Peter Lang, 2013), x; see also Caldwell, *A Short History of Rudeness*, 241.

81. Andrew Terjesen, "Civility and Magnanimity," in *Civility in Politics and Education*, ed. Deborah S. Mower and Wade L. Robison (New York: Routledge), 99–116.

82. Ronald C. Arnett, Janie Harden Fritz, and Leeann M. Bell, *Communication Ethics Literacy: Dialogue and Difference* (Los Angeles, CA: Sage, 2009), 1–2.

83. Ronald C. Arnett and Pat Arneson, *Dialogic Civility in a Cynical Age: Community, Hope and Interpersonal Relationships* (New York: State University of New York Press, 1999), 52.

84. Colleen Flaherty, "Panel Criticizes ASA's Israel Boycott at Association's Annual Meeting," *Inside Higher Ed*, November 7, 2014, https://www.insidehighered.com/news/2014/11/07/panel-criticizes-asas-israel-boycott-associations-annual-meeting (accessed December 30, 2016).

85. Liz Sly, "Progress Scant in Peace Talks," *Dallas Morning News*, February 1, 2014, 12A.

86. Alan Wolfe, "Are We Losing Our Virtue? The Case of Civility," in *Civility*, ed. Leroy S. Rouner (Notre Dame, IN: University of Notre Dame Press, 2000), 126–41.

87. Wolfe, "Are We Losing Our Virtue?"

88. Matthew Hansen, "Hansen: Telling a Woman to Smile May Seem Like an Innocent Request, but There's a Darker Undertone," *Omaha World-Herald*, January 3, 2017, http://www.omaha.com/columnists/hansen/hansen-telling-a-woman-to-smile-may-seem-like-an/article_06daf2f9-7cc3-53b9-b9ba-f5534a5d6223.html (accessed January 18, 2017).

89. Matthew Hansen, "Hansen: Stories of Women Being Told by Random Men to Smile Provoked Strong Reactions—and Some Denial," *Omaha World-Herald*, January 8, 2017, http://www.omaha.com/columnists/hansen/hansen-stories-of-women-being-told-by-random-men-to/article_e3665cc7-ed65-598e-a298-3e230f909d4a.html (accessed January 18, 2017).

90. Mark Kingwell, *A Civil Tongue: Justice, Dialogue, and the Politics of Pluralism* (University Park, PA: Penn State University Press, 1995), 238.

91. Michael Hyde, "The Ontological Workings of Dialogue and Acknowledgement," in *Dialogue: Theorizing Difference in Communication*, ed. Robert Anderson, Leslie A. Baxter, and Kenneth N. Cissna (Thousand Oaks, CA: Sage, 2009), 57–73.

92. Leonard Hawes, "The Dialogues of Conversation: Power, Control, Vulnerability," *Communication Theory* 9, no. 3 (1999): 231.

93. Julia Wood, foreword to *Dialogic Civility in a Cynical Age: Community, Hope, and Interpersonal Relationships*, ed. Ronald C. Arnett and Pat Arneson (New York: State University of New York Press, 1999), xii.

94. George Will, "The Rise of the Right Not to Be Offended," *Dallas Morning News*, December 26, 2014, 25A.

95. Adam Liptak, "Supreme Court Says Texas Can Reject Confederate Flag License Plates," *New York Times*, June 18, 2015, http://www.nytimes.com/2015/06/19/us/supreme-court-says-texas-can-reject-confederate-flag-license-plates.html (accessed December 30, 2016).

96. Will, "The Rise of the Right Not to be Offended," 25A.

97. Mark Fitzpatrick, "Get a Bumper Sticker [Letter to the Editor]," *Dallas Morning News*, January 1, 2015, 18A.

98. Arnett et al., *Communication Ethics Literacy*.

99. Arnett and Arneson, *Dialogic Civility in a Cynical Age*, 76.

100. Benjamin J. Broome, "Dialogue Theories," in *Encyclopedia of Communication Theory*, eds. Stephen W. Littlejohn and Karen A. Foss (Los Angeles, CA: Sage, 2009) 301–06.

101. W. Barnett Pearce and Kimberly A. Pearce, "Taking a Communication Perspective on Dialogue," in *Dialogue: Theorizing Difference in Communication Studies*, eds. Richard Anderson, Leslie A. Baxter, and Kenneth N. Cissna (Thousand Oaks, CA: Sage, 2004), 76.

102. Shelley D. Lane, "Dialogic Civility: A Narrative to Live By," *Texas Speech Communication Journal* 29, no. 2 (2005): 174–83.

103. Matt Sedensky, "Teens Urged to Feast on Elders' Views," *Dallas Morning News*, November 24, 2016, 4A.

104. Sedensky, "Teens Urged to Feast on Elders' Views."

105. Sedensky, "Teens Urged to Feast on Elders' Views."

106. Arnett and Arneson, *Dialogic Civility in a Cynical Age.*

107. Arnett and Arneson, *Dialogic Civility in a Cynical Age.*

108. Carter, *Civility: Manners, Morals, and the Etiquette of Democracy*, 67.

109. Arnett and Arneson, *Dialogic Civility in a Cynical Age.*

110. Julia Wood, foreword to *Theorizing Difference in Communication Studies*, ed. Rob Anderson, Leslie A. Baxter, and Kenneth N. Cissna (Thousand Oaks, CA: Sage, 2003), xiv.

111. Miguel Solis, "Eyes on Improvement: DISD Must Focus on Unity, Best Interests of Students," *Dallas Morning News*, January 8, 2015, 13A.

112. Solis, "Eyes on Improvement."

113. Solis, "Eyes on Improvement."

114. Solis, "Eyes on Improvement."

115. Wood, foreword to *Theorizing Difference in Communication Studies*, xiv.

116. Ronald C. Arnett, "Dialogic Civility as Pragmatic Ethical Praxis," *Communication Theory* 11, no. 3 (2001): 315–38; see also Ron Anderson, Leslie A. Baxter, and Kenneth N. Cissna, "Texts and Contexts of Dialogue," in *Dialogue: Theorizing Difference in Communication Studies* (Los Angeles, CA: Sage, 2004), 1–17.

117. Arnett and Arneson, *Dialogic Civility in a Cynical Age*, 26.

# 5. POWER AND EVERYDAY INCIVILITY

1. Priyianka V. Doshy and Jia Wang, "Workplace Incivility: What Do Targets Say?," *American Journal of Management* 14, no. 1–2 (2014): 38.

2. Katie Leslie and Jordan Rudner, "Clinton, Trump and Gender Politics," September 25, 2016, *Dallas Morning News*, 1A and 24A.

3. Rosalind C. Barnett and Caryl Rivers, "Will Hillary's Speaking Style Derail Her? Women's Speech Is Judged Differently than Men's," *Psychology Today*, February 10, 1016, https://www.psychologytoday.com/blog/womans-place/201602/will-hillarys-speaking-style-derail-her (accessed September 17, 2016); see also Carol Kinsey Goman, "Is Your Communication Style Dictated by Your Gender?," *Forbes*, March 31, 2016, http://www.forbes.com/sites/carolkinseygoman/2016/03/31/is-your-communication-style-dictated-by-your-gender/2/#50dc72dd302d (accessed September 17, 2016).

4. Leslie and Rudner, "Clinton, Trump and Gender Politics," 1A and 24A.

5. Jessica Bennett, "Hillary Clinton Will Not be Manterrupted," *New York Times*, September 27, 2016, http://www.nytimes.com/2016/09/28/opinion/campaign-stops/hillary-clinton-will-not-be-manterrupted.html?_r=0 (accessed September 27, 2016).

6. "Trump's Demeanor Reminds Many Women of Everyday Sexism," *Dallas Morning News*, September 28, 2016, 1A and 5a.

7. Bernard E. Harcourt, "The Politics of Incivility," *Arizona Law Review* 54, no. 2 (2012): 4.

8. Lorraine G. Kisselburgh and Mohan J. Dutta, "The Construction of Civility in Multicultural Organizations," in *Deconstructive Organizational Communication: Processes, Consequences, and Constructive Ways of Organizing*, ed. Pamela Lutgen-Sandvik and Beverly Davenport Sypher (New York: Routledge, 2009), 121–42; see also Jasmine Ingham, "Sexual Orientation, Gender Expectations and Patriarchy in the United States," *Cjournal*, May 26, 2014, http://www.cjournal.info/2013/05/26/sexual-orientation-gender-expectations-and-patriarchy-in-the-united-states/ (accessed September 17, 2016).

9. Kisselburgh and Dutta, "The Construction of Civility in Multicultural Organizations," 9.

10. Deborah Tannen, *Gender and Discourse* (New York: Oxford University Press, 1996), 21.

11. Tannen, *Gender and Discourse*, 32.

12. Deborah Tannen, *Talking from 9 to 5: How Women's and Men's Conversational Styles Affect Who Gets Heard, Who Gets Credit, and What Gets Done at Work* (New York: William Morrow and Company, 1994), 78–79.

13. Tannen, *Talking from 9 to 5.*

14. Haru Yamada, *Different Games, Different Rules: Why Americans and Japanese Misunderstand Each Other* (New York: Oxford University Press, 2002).

15. Tannen, *Gender and Discourse*, 102.

16. Katie McDonough, "Lean Back, Eric Schmidt! How Interrupting Men and Unconscious Bias are Killing Women's Careers," *Salon*, March 17, 2015, http://www.salon.com/2015/03/17/lean_back_eric_schmidt_how_interrupting_men_unconscious_bias_in_tech_are_killing_womens_career_prospects/ (accessed November 3, 2016).

17. Alice Robb, "Why Men are Prone to Interrupting Women," *New York Times*, March 19, 2015, http://nytlive.nytimes.com/womenintheworld/2015/03/19/google-chief-blasted-for-repeatedly-interrupting-female-government-official/ (accessed November 12, 2016).

18. Adrienne B. Hancock and Benjamin A. Rubin, "Influence of Communication Partner's Gender on Language," *Journal of Language and Social Psychology* 34, no.1 (2015), 50, 56.

19. Emma Gray, "Donald Trump Couldn't Stop Interrupting Hillary Clinton on Debate Night," *Huffington Post*, September 26, 2016, http://www.huffingtonpost.com/entry/donald-trump-couldn't-stio-interrupting-hillary-clinton-on-debate-night_us_57e9ca11e4b020a52d2a0e26 (accessed September 26, 2016).

20. Tannen, *Gender and Discourse*, 34.

21. Tannen, *Gender and Discourse*, 35.

22. Deborah Tannen, " 'Don't Just Sit There—Interrupt!' Pacing and Pausing in Conversational Style," in *American Speech* 75, no. 2 (2000): 393.

23. Tannen, *Talking from 9 to 5*, 233.

24. Tannen, *Gender and Discourse*, 27; see also Deborah Tannen, *You Just Don't Understand: Women and Men in Conversation* (London, UK: Virago, 1991).

25. Gray, "Donald Trump Couldn't Stop Interrupting Hillary Clinton on Debate Night"; see also Soraya Chemaly, "10 Words Every Girl Should Learn," *Alternet*, July 5, 2014, http://alternet.org/gender/10-words-every-girl-should-learn (accessed May 13, 2015).

26. Gray, "Donald Trump Couldn't Stop Interrupting Hillary Clinton on Debate Night."

27. Bennett, "Hillary Clinton Will Not Be Manterrupted"; see also Juliet Eilperin, "Did You Hear What I Heard about Meetings?," *Dallas Morning News*, October 27, 2016, 15A.

28. McDonough, "Lean Back, Eric Schmidt!"

29. Peter Applebome, "Dallas Death: Shootings by Police Stoking Anger," *New York Times*, May 26, 1987, http://www.nytimes.com/1987/05/26/us/dallas-death-shootings-by-police-stoking-anger.html (accessed September 22, 2016).

30. Cecil Sharp, "The Briefcase Blacks," *D Magazine*, May 1989, www.dmagazine.com/publications/d-magazine/1989/may/the-briefcase-blacks/ (accessed September 22, 2016).

31. Dennis Holder, "Power Profile: Diane Ragsdale, a Firebrand, a Shouter, and a Gentle Woman Who Reads Poetry and Wants to be More Serene," *D Magazine*, October 1990, http://www.dmagazine.com/publications/d-magazine/1990/october/position/ (accessed September 22, 2016).

32. Sharp, "The Briefcase Blacks."

33. Sharp, "The Briefcase Blacks."

34. Sharp, "The Briefcase Blacks."

35. Stephen J. Aguilar, "Why It's Better to Talk about 'Advantage' Rather than 'Privilege,' " *Inside Higher Ed*, November 15, 2016, www.insidehighered.com/views/2016/11/15/why-its-better-talk-about-advantage-rather-privilege-essay?width=775&height=500&iframe=true (accessed November 15, 2016).

36. Thomas K. Nakayama and Robert L. Krizek, "Whiteness as Strategic Rhetoric," in *Whiteness*, ed. Thomas K. Nakayama and Judith N. Martin (Thousand Oaks, CA: Sage, 1999), 87–106; see also Francis E. Kendall, *Understanding White Privilege: Creating Pathways to Authentic Relationships across Race* (New York: Routledge, 2006).

37. Marc Ramirez, "Calling for Action in Unison: Community Unites, Opens Up at Forum in Wake of Ambush," *Dallas Morning News*, September 18, 2016, 1B, 3B.

38. Ramirez, "Calling for Action in Unison"; see also Judith Shapiro, "Our History, Our Selves," *Inside Higher Ed*, September 23, 2016, https://www.insidehighered.com/views/2016/

09/23/cultivating-sociological-imagination-colleges-and-universities-essay (accessed September 23, 2016).

39. Nakayama and Krizek "Whiteness as Strategic Rhetoric," 87–106.

40. Christine Emba, "What Is White Privilege?" *Washington Post*, January 16, 2016, https://www.washingtonpost.com/blogs/post-partisan/wp/2016/01/16/white-privilege-explained/?utm_term=.e256522c6624 (accessed January 27, 2016).

41. Lori Lakin Hutcherson, "What I Told My White Friend When He Asked for My Black Opinion on White Privilege," *Everyday Feminism*, August 25, 2016, http://everydayfeminism.com/2016/08/told-white-friend-black-opinion/ (accessed October 7, 2016).

42. Emba, "What Is White Privilege?"

43. Emba, "What is White Privilege?"

44. Derald Wing Sue, *Microaggressions in Everyday Life: Race, Gender, and Sexual Orientation* (New York: John Wiley & Sons, 2010).

45. Nakayama and Krizek "Whiteness as Strategic Rhetoric," 87–106.

46. Amy Adams, "Barres Examines Gender, Science Debate and Offers a Novel Critique," *Stanford News*, July 26, 2006, http://news.stanford.edu/news/2006/july26/med-gender-072606.html (accessed October 15, 2016); see also Shankar Vedantam, "Male Scientist Writes of Life as Female Scientist," *Washington Post*, July 14, 2006, http://www.washingtonpost.com/wp-dyn/content/article/2006/07/12/AR2006071201883.html (accessed October 15, 2016).

47. Vedantam, "Male Scientist Writes of Life as Female Scientist."

48. Vedantam, "Male Scientist Writes of Life as Female Scientist."

49. Jessica Nordell, "Why Aren't Women Advancing at Work: Ask a Transgender Person," *New Republic*, August 27, 2014, https://newrepublic.com/article/119239/transgender-people-can-explain-why-women-don't-advance-work (accessed October 15, 2016).

50. Kristen Schilt, *Just One of the Guys? Transgender Men and the Persistence of Gender Inequality* (Chicago, IL: University of Chicago Press, 2011).

51. Shankar Vedantam, "Male Scientist Writes of Life as Female Scientist,"

52. Schilt, *Just One of the Guys?*

53. Ingham, "Sexual Orientation, Gender Expectations and Patriarchy in the United States."

54. Shannon B. Wanless et al., "Gender Differences in Behavioral Regulation in Four Societies: The United States, Taiwan, South Korea, and China," *Early Childhood Research Quarterly* 28, no. 3 (2013): 621–33.

55. Jasmine Ingham, "Sexual Orientation, Gender Expectations and Patriarchy in the United States," *Cjournal*, May 26, 2014, http://www.cjournal.info/2013/05/26/sexual-orientation-gender-expectations-and-patriarchy-in-the-united-states/ (accessed September 17, 2016); see also Amy Allen, *The Power of Feminist Theory* (Boulder, CO: Westview Press, 1999).

56. Ingham, "Sexual Orientation, Gender Expectations and Patriarchy in the United States."

57. Nakayama and Krizek "Whiteness as Strategic Rhetoric," 87–106.

58. Rebecca Solnit, *Men Explain Things to Me* (Chicago, IL: Haymarket Books, 2014), 7.

59. Sean Blanda, "The 'Other Side' Is not Dumb," *Medium Corporation*, January 7, 2016, https://medium.com/@SeanBlanda/the-other-side-is-not-dumb-2670c1294063#.ecmgqpwip (accessed November 27, 2016).

60. Blanda, "The 'Other Side' Is not Dumb."

61. Christine M. Flowers, "I Refuse to Legitimize Fears Fueled by Partisan Rhetoric," *Dallas Morning News*, December 4, 2016, 6P.

62. Jack Marshall, "Yes, That Was a Microaggression," *Ethics Alarms*, July 3, 2016, https://ethicsalarms.com/2016/07/03/yes-that-was-a-microaggression/ (accessed July 3, 2016).

63. Sue, *Microaggressions in Everyday Life*, 5.

64. "Microaggressions: Power, Privilege, and Everyday Life," www.microaggressions.com (accessed July 23, 2015); see also "Students Take a Stand on 'Microaggression,' Too," *Dallas Morning News*, November 13, 2015, 1A.

65. Sue, *Microaggressions in Everyday Life*.

66. Sue, *Microaggressions in Everyday Life*.

67. Sue, *Microaggressions in Everyday Life*; see also Bradley Campbell and Jason Manning, "Microaggression and Changing Moral Cultures," *Chronicle of Higher Education*, July 9,

2015, http://www.chronicle.com/article/MicroaggressionChanging/231395/ (accessed July 23, 2015).

68. Sue, *Microaggressions in Everyday Life*, 128–29.

69. Shahram Heshmat, "What Is Confirmation Bias?" *Psychology Today*, April 23, 2015, https://www.psychologytoday.com/blog/science-choice/201504/what-is-confirmation-bias (accessed October 29, 2016).

70. Marshall, "Yes, That Was a Microaggression."

71. Sue, *Microaggressions in Everyday Life.*

72. Sue, *Microaggressions in Everyday Life*,; see also Kerry Ann Rockquemore, "Allies and Microaggressions," *Inside Higher Ed*, April 13, 2016, https://www.insidehighered.com/advice/2016/04/13/how-be-ally-someone-experiencing-microaggressions-essay (accessed October 29, 2016); Kevin L. Nadal, "A Guide to Responding to Microaggressions," *CUNY Forum* 2.1 (2014): 71–76, http://advancingjustice-la.org/sites/default/files/ELAMICRO%20A_Guide_to_Responding_to_Microaggressions.pdf (accessed October 29, 2016).

73. Solnit, *Men Explain Things to Me*, 12–13.

74. Solnit, *Men Explain Things to Me*, 12–13.

75. Benjamin Hart, "RIP 'Mansplaining': The Internet Ruined One of Our Most Useful Terms," *Salon*, October 20, 2014, http://www.salon.com/2014/10/20/rip_mansplaining_how_the_internet_killed_one_of_our_most_useful_words/ (accessed July 3, 2016).

76. "Rebecca Solnit: Men Explain Things to Me," *GUERNICA: A Magazine of Arts & Politics*, August 12, 2012, www.guernicamag.com/rebecca-solnit-men-explain-things-to-me/ (accessed July 3, 2016).

77. R. Nithya, "Breaking Down the Problem with Mansplaining (and Other Forms of Privileged Explaining)," *Everyday Feminism*, December 28, 2014, http://everydayfeminism.com/2014/12/the-problem-with-privilege-explaining/ (accessed July 6, 2016).

78. Rex Huppke, "The Harm of Mansplaining at Work," *Chicago Tribune*, May 13, 2016, http://www.chicagotribune.com/business/careers/ijustworkhere/ct-huppke-work-advice-mansplaining-0515-biz-20160512-column.html (accessed August 24, 2016).

79. Roxanne Earley, "10 Women Reveal What It's Like to Experience 'Mansplaining,' " *Thought Catalog*, April 27, 2015, http://thoughtcatalog.com/Roxanne-early/2015/04/10-women-reveal-what-its-like-to-experience-mansplaining/ (accessed August 24, 2016).

80. Kirsten Powers, "Illiberal Feminism is Running Amok," *Daily Beast*, May 12, 2015, www.thedailybeast.com/articles/2015/05/12/illiberal-feminism-is-running-amok.html (accessed August 24, 2016).

81. Annie-Rose Strasser, "Viewpoint: Why We Need to Stop 'Mansplaining,' " *ThinkProgress*, March 3, 2013, https://thinkprogress.org/viewpoint-why-we-need-to-stop-mansplaining-773e26d533a0#.wfuzq6yaj (accessed August 24, 2016).

82. Earley, "10 Women Reveal What It's Like to Experience 'Mansplaining.'"

83. Erin McCann, "A 'Mansplaining' Hotline? Yes, Actually, Sweden Has One," *New York Times*, November 16, 2016, www.nytimes.com/2016/11/17/world/europe/mansplaining-hotline-swedish-union.html?_r=0 (accessed November 16, 2016); see also Charlotte English, "Swedish Women Get Hotline to Report Mansplaining," *Guardian*, November 16, 2016, www.independent.co.uk/news/sweden-mansplaining-hotline-woman-get-to-report-patronising-male-colleagues-a7418491.html (accessed November 16, 2016).

84. Laura Bates, "Mansplaining: How Not to Talk to Female NASA Astronauts," *Guardian*, September 13, 2016, https://www.theguardian.com/lifeandstyle/womens-blog/2016/sep/13/mansplaining-how-not-talk-female-nasa-astronauts (accessed August 24, 2016).

85. Nithya, "Breaking Down the Problem with Mansplaining."

86. Huppke, "The Harm of Mansplaining at Work."

87. Bates, "Mansplaining: How Not to Talk to Female NASA Astronauts."

88. Idrees M. Kahloon, "The Placemat Problem," *Harvard Crimson*, December 15, 2015, www.thecrimson.com/article/2015/12/16/harvard-placemats-social-justice/ (accessed November 12, 2016).

89. The Crimson Staff, "No Masterstroke: Changing the House Title Does Nothing," *Harvard Crimson*, December 12, 2015, www.thecrimson.com/article/2015/12/2/staff-house-master-change/ (accessed November 12, 2016).

90. Kahloon, "The Placemat Problem."

91. Kahloon, "The Placemat Problem."

92. Jack Marshall, "The Social Justice Talking Points Placemat: Harvard Finally Snaps," *Ethics Alarms*, December 17, 2015, http://ethicsalarms.com/2015/12/17/the-social-justice-talking-points-placemat-harvard-finally-snaps/ (accessed November 12, 2016); see also Jack Marshall, "Oh Fine, I Already Burned My Diploma: Harvard Apologizes for the 'Holiday Placemats for Social Justice,' " *Ethics Alarms*, December 18, 2015, https://ethicsalarms.com/2015/12/18/oh-fine-and-i-already-burned-my-diploma-harvard-apologizes-for-the-holiday-placemats-for-social-justice/ (accessed November 12, 2016).

93. Morgan Chalfant, "Harvard Apologizes for 'Social Justice' Placemats After Outrage," *Washington Free Beacon*, December 17, 2015, http://freebeacon.com/issues/harvard-apologizes-for-social-justice-placemats-after-outrage/ (accessed November 12, 2016).

94. Jonathan Zimmerman, "An Examination of Two Kinds of Political Correctness," *Inside Higher Ed*, June 16, 2016, https://www.insidehighered.com/views/2016/06/16/examination-two-kinds-political-correctness-essay (accessed June 20, 2016).

95. Jacquielynn Floyd, "Political Correctness Both an Insult and a Lament," *Dallas Morning News*, October 18, 2016, 1B, 8B.

96. Emily Norton, "Is PC Destroying U.S.? No: And Saying So Demonizes the Idea of Tolerance," *Dallas Morning News*, October 9, 2015, 21A.

97. Zimmerman, "An Examination of Two Kinds of Political Correctness."

98. Floyd, "Political Correctness Both an Insult and a Lament," 8B.

99. David Brooks, "Terrorism Not Outgrowth of Spiritual Quest," *Dallas Morning News*, June 21, 2016, 13A.

100. Haig A. Bosmajian, *The Language of Oppression* (Lanham, MD: University Press of America, 1983).

101. Bosmajian, *The Language of Oppression*, 44.

102. Paul Butler, "A Mix of Colors: Country's Swirling Demographics Put New Twist on Meaning of 'Minority,' " *Dallas Morning News*, June 3, 2001, 1J, 6J.

103. Paul Pringle, "California Looks to Find Identity in Changing Face." *Dallas Morning News*, December 24, 2000, 1A.

104. Solnit, *Men Explain Things to Me*, 129.

105. Bosmajian, *The Language of Oppression*, 139.

# 6. EVERYDAY INCIVILITY AT WORK

1. Henry Rollins Quotes, *BrainyQuote*, https://www.brainyquote.com/quotes/quotes/h/henryrolli616774.html (accessed December 23, 2016).

2. John Biggs, "Product Guy Tries to Cancel Comcast Service, Hilarity Ensues," *Tech-Crunch*, July 15, 2014, https://techcrunch.com/2014/07/15/tech-blogger-tries-to-cancel-comcast-service-hilarity-ensues/ (accessed August 31, 2014); see also Laura Stampler, "Recording of Man's Attempt to Cancel Comcast Will Drive You Insane," *Time*, July 14, 2014, http://time.com/2985964/comcast-cancel-ryan-block/ (accessed August 31, 2014); Meg Marco, "Comcast Demands an Explanation Before Agreeing to Cancel Your Account," *Consumerist*, July 14, 2014, https://consumerist.com/2014/07/14/comcast-demands-an-explanation-before-agreeing-to-cancel-your-account/ (accessed August 31, 2014).

3. Dave Lieber, "Quality Assurance for Me," *Dallas Morning News*, August 31, 2014, 1B, 5B.

4. Stampler, "Recording of Man's Attempt to Cancel Comcast Will Drive You Insane."

5. Charles Duhigg, "What Google Learned from its Quest to Build the Perfect Team," *New York Times Magazine*, February 25, 2016, http://www.nytimes.com/2016/02/28/magazine/what-google-learned-from-its-quest-to-build-the-perfect-team.html?_r=0 (accessed July 27, 2016).

6. Aamna Mohdin, "After Years of Intensive Analysis, Google Discovers that the Key to Good Teamwork Is Being Nice," *Quartz*, February 26, 2016, http://qz.com/625870/after-years-

of-intensive-analysis-google-discovers-the-key-to-good-teamwork-is-being-nice/ (accessed July 27, 2016); see also David Yamada, "Psychological Safety and the Successful Workplace," *Minding the Workplace*, July 26, 2016, https://newworkplace.wordpress.com/2016/07/26/psychological-safety-and-the-successful-workplace/ (accessed July 27, 2016).

7. Lynne M. Andersson and Christine M. Pearson, "Tit for Tat? The Spiraling Effect of Incivility in the Workplace," *Academy of Management Review* 24, no. 3 (1999): 547.

8. Edwin Hartman, *Organizational Ethics and the Good Life* (New York: Oxford University Press, 1996); see also Shelley D. Lane, Ruth Anna Abigail, and John Casey Gooch, *Communication in a Civil Society* (Boston, MA: Pearson Education, 2014); Pamela R. Johnson and Julie Indvik, "Rudeness at Work: Impulse over Restraint," *Public Personnel Management* 30, no. 4 (2001): 457–65.

9. Lilia M. Cortina and Vicki J. Magley, "Patterns and Profiles of Response to Workplace Incivility," *Journal of Occupational Health Psychology* 14, no. 3 (2009): 272–88.

10. Andersson and Pearson, "Tit for Tat? The Spiraling Effect of Incivility in the Workplace," 456.

11. David Yamada, "Distinguishing Workplace Incivility and Abrasiveness from Bullying and Mobbing," *Minding the Workplace*, June 23, 2015, https://newworkplace.wordpress.com/2015/06/23/distinguishing-workplace-incivility-and-abrasiveness-from-bullying-and-mobbing/ (accessed June 25, 2015).

12. Andersson and Pearson, "Tit for Tat? The Spiraling Effect of Incivility in the Workplace"; see also Cortina and Magley, "Patterns and Profiles of Response to Workplace Incivility," 272–88.

13. Christine Pearson and Christine Porath, *The Cost of Bad Behavior: How Incivility is Damaging Your Business and What to Do About It* (New York: Portfolio, 2009); see also Christine Porath and Christine Pearson, "The Price of Incivility," *Harvard Business Review* 91, no. 1–2 (2013): 115–21.

14. Weber Shandwick and Powell Tate, *Civility in America: Corporate Reputation Edition* (2013), https://www.webershandwick.com/uploads/news/files/Civility-in-Business-Exec-Summary.pdf (accessed December 9, 2016).

15. Pauline Schiulpzand, Irene E. De Pater, and Amir Erez, "Workplace Incivility: A Review of the Literature and Agenda for Future Research," *Journal of Organizational Behavior*, 37 (2016): S57–S88; see also Christine M. Pearson, Lynn M. Andersson, and Christine L. Porath, "Assessing and Attacking Workplace Incivility," *Organizational Dynamics*, 29, no. 2 (2000): 123–37.

16. Lilia M. Cortina et al., "Selective Incivility as Modern Discrimination in Organizations: Evidence and Impact," *Journal of Management* 39 (2013): 1579–1605; see also Pearson et al., "Assessing and Attacking Workplace Incivility," 123–37.

17. Sandy Lim and Alexia Lee, "Work and Nonwork Outcomes of Workplace Incivility: Does Family Support Help?" *Journal of Occupational Health Psychology*, 16 no. 1 (2011): 95–111.

18. Jack Marshall, "Once Again, We are Reminded that Beauty is Only Skin Deep. Do ESPN Viewers Care? Should They?" *Ethics Alarms*, April 17, 2015, https://ethicsalarms.com/2015/04/17/once-again-we-are-reminded-that-beauty-is-only-skin-deep-do-espn-viewers-care-should-they/ (accessed April 17, 2015).

19. Clinton Yates, "ESPN Suspends Reporter Britt McHenry following Incident with Towing Company Employee," *Washington Post*, April 16, 2015, https://www.washingtonpost.com/news/dc-sports-bog/wp/2015/04/16/espn-reporter-britt-mchenry-apologizes-for-incident-with-parking-lot-attendant/?utm_term=.415573bd9c68 (accessed April 17, 2016).

20. David Yamada, "The Bullying Consumer: Is There a Little Bit of Britt McHenry in Most of Us?" *Minding the Workplace*, April 17, 2015, https://newworkplace.wordpress.com/2015/04/17/the-bullying-consumer-is-there-a-little-bit-of-britt-mchenry-in-most-of-us/ (accessed April 17, 2015).

21. Pearson and Porath, *The Cost of Bad Behavior*, xvii.

22. Johnson and Indvik, "Rudeness at Work: Impulse over Restraint," 449.

23. Christine Porath, "No Time to be Nice at Work," *New York Times*, June 19, 2015, http://www.nytimes.com/2015/06/21/opinion/sunday/is-your-boss-mean.html (accessed June 20, 2015).

24. Sandra L. Robinson and Kira Schabram, "Invisible at Work: Workplace Ostracism as Aggression," in *Research and Theory on Workplace Aggression*, eds. Nathan A. Bowling and M. Sandy Hershcovis (New York, NY: Cambridge University Press, 2017), 221–244.

25. Robinson and Schabram, "Invisible at Work," 229.

26. Wu Liu, Shu-Cheng Steve Chi, Ray Friedman, and Ming-Hong Tsai, "Explaining Incivility n the Workplace: The Effects of Personality and Culture," *Negotiation and Conflict Management Research* 2, no.2 (2009): 164–184.

27. Laura Severance, Lan Bui-Wrzosinska, Michele J. Gelfand, Sarah Lyons, Andrzej Nowak, Wojciech Borkowski, Nazar Soomro, Naureen Soomro, Anat Rafaeili, Dorit Efrat Treister, Chun-Chi Lin, and Susume Yamaguchi, "The Psychological Structure of Aggression Across Cultures," *Journal of Organizational Behavior* 34 (2013), 835–865. DOI: 10.1002/job.1873.

28. Lauren Zurbrugg and Kathi N. Miner, "Gender, Sexual Orientation, and Workplace Incivility: Who Is Most Targeted and Who Is Most Harmed?" *Frontiers in Psychology* 7, Article 565 (May 2016), 8. DOI: 10.3389/fpsychg.2016.00565. https://www.ncbi.nlm.nih.gov/pmc/articles/PMC4851979/pdf/fpsyg-07-00565.pdf (accessed May 10, 2017).

29. Brad Stone, "The Children of Cyberspace: Old Fogies by Their 20s," *New York Times* (January 9, 2010), http://www.nytimes.com/2010/01/10/weekinreview/10stone.html (accessed January 11, 2010).

30. Doug White and Polly White, "What to Expect from Gen-X and Millennial Employees," *Entrepreneur*, December 23, 2014, https://www.entrepreneur.com/article/240556 (accessed January 25, 2010).

31. "Millennials at Work: Reshaping the Workplace," *PwC—PricewaterhouseCoopers*, 2011, https://www.pwc.com/gx/en/managing-tomorrows-people/future-of-work/assets/reshaping-the-workplace.pdf (accessed May 10, 2017).

32. Stone, "The Children of Cyberspace."

33. "Millennials at Work."

34. Andersson and Pearson, "Tit for Tat? The Spiraling Effect of Incivility in the Workplace"; see also Christopher C. Rosen, Joel Koopman, Allison S. Gabriel, and Russell E. Johnson, "Who Strikes Back? A Daily Investigation of When and Why Incivility Begets Incivility," *Journal of Applied Psychology* (2016):1–15.

35. Andersson and Pearson, "Tit for Tat? The Spiraling Effect of Incivility in the Workplace."

36. Trevor Foulk, Andrew Woolum, and Amir Erez, "Catching Rudeness Is like Catching a Cold: The Contagion Effect of Low-Intensity Negative Behaviors," *Journal of Applied Psychology*, (2015): 4.

37. David McCormack, "She's Nuts for Good Service! Furious Airline Exec's Daughter Turned Jet Back to Gate at JFK Because She Was Served Macadamias in a Bag, Not a Dish," *Daily Mail*, December 8, 2014, http://www.dailymail.co.uk/news/article-2866329/Nut-rage-Daughter-Korean-Air-s-chief-executive-threw-tantrum-JKF-demanded-plane-return-gate-served-nuts-bag-not-dish.html (accessed December 14, 2014); see also Ju-min Park, "Korean Air Executive Apologizes after Nuts Incident Sparks National Outrage," *Reuters*, December 12, 2014, http://www.reuters.com/article/us-kal-probe-idUSKBN0JQ0AO20141212 (accessed December 14, 2014).

38. McCormack, "She's Nuts for Good Service."

39. Maureen B. Costello, "The Trump Effect: The Impact of the Presidential Campaign on our Nation's Schools," *Southern Poverty Law Center*, November 28, 2016, https://www.splcenter.org/sites/default/files/splc_the_trump_effect.pdf (accessed December 13, 2016).

40. Pier M. Forni, *The Civility Solution: What to Do When People Are Rude* (New York: St. Martin's Griffin, 2008); see also Steve Farkas, Jean Johnson, Ann Duffett, and Kathleen Collins, *Aggravating Circumstances: A Status Report on Rudeness in America* (New York: Public Agenda, 2002).

41. Stephan Rechtschaffen, *Time-Shifting: Creating More Time to Enjoy Your Life* (New York: Doubleday, 1996).

42. Michael Gross, "Got a Minute? Survey Finds a Nation in a Hurry," AP/Ipsos Poll, May 31, 2006, http://www.ipsos-na.com/news/pressrelease.cfm?id=3096 (accessed June 7, 2006); see also "Fed Up? We're Not Gonna Wait," *Dallas Morning News*, May 29, 2006, 7A.

43. Stephen L. Carter, *Civility: Manners, Morals, and the Etiquette of Democracy* (New York: Harper Perennial, 1998).

44. Beverly Davenport Sypher, "Reclaiming Civil Discourse in the Workplace," *Southern Communication Journal* 69, no. 3 (Spring 2004), 264.

45. Sypher, "Reclaiming Civil Discourse in the Workplace."

46. Pearson and Porath, *The Cost of Bad Behavior*.

47. Johnson and Indvik, "Rudeness at Work: Impulse over Restraint," 461.

48. Sypher, "Reclaiming Civil Discourse in the Workplace," 265.

49. Pearson et al., "Assessing and Attacking Workplace Incivility," 129.

50. David Yamada, "Slow Retaliation: When Workplace Payback is Subtle, Nuanced, and Drawn Out," *Minding the Workplace*, March 28, 2016, https://newworkplace.wordpress.com/2016/03/28/slow-retaliation-when-workplace-payback-is-subtle-nuanced-and-drawn-out/ (accessed December 19, 2016).

51. Dennis Romero, "*Cat on a Hot Tin Roof* Production Canceled After Homophobic Fracas," *LA Weekly*, June 2, 2014, http://www.laweekly.com/news/cat-on-a-hot-tin-roof-production-canceled-after-homophobic-fracas-4762882 (accessed June 4, 2014).

52. Pearson and Porath, *The Cost of Bad Behavior*.

53. Pearson and Porath, *The Cost of Bad* Behavior, 55.

54. Porath, "No Time to be Nice at Work."

55. Pearson et al., "Assessing and Attacking Workplace Incivility"; see also Christine M. Pearson, Lynn M Andersson, and Judith W. Wegner, "When Workers Flout Convention: A Study of Workplace Incivility," *Human Relations* 54, no. 11 (2001): 1387–1419; Rod L. Troester and Cathy Sargent Mester, *Civility in Business and Professional Communication* (New York: Peter Lang, 2007); Janie M. Harden Fritz, *Professional Civility: Communicative Virtue at Work* (New York: Peter Lang, 2013).

56. Sandy Lim et al., "Emotional Mechanisms Linking Incivility at Work to Aggression and Withdrawal at Home: An Experience-Sampling Study," *Journal of Management* (2016): 1–21.

57. David Yamada, "Bullying, Incivility, and Conflict Resolution at Work," *Minding the Workplace*, June 29, 2010, https://newworkplace.wordpress.com/2010/06/29/bullying-incivility-and-conflict-resolution-at-work/ (accessed June 4, 2017).

58. David Yamada, "Can Workplace Incivility Ever Be Healthy?" *Minding the Workplace*, October 26, 2011, https://newworkplace.wordpress.com/2011/10/26/can-workplace-incivility-ever-be-healthy/ (accessed August 9, 2014).

59. Harvey A. Hornstein, "Boss Abuse and Subordinate Payback," *Journal of Applied Behavioral Science* 52, no. 2 (2016): 231–39.

60. Cortina and Magley, "Patterns and Profiles of Response to Workplace Incivility."

61. Cortina and Magley, "Patterns and Profiles of Response to Workplace Incivility."

62. Lim and Lee, "Work and Nonwork Outcomes of Workplace Incivility."

63. Hornstein, "Boss Abuse and Subordinate Payback," 231–39.

64. Hornstein, "Boss Abuse and Subordinate Payback," 231–39.

65. "Amazon Doing What It Must for the Good of Valhalla," *Imgur*, August 26, 2014, http://imgur.com/IDFkz82 (accessed January 8, 2017).

66. "Amazon Doing What It Must for the Good of Valhalla."

67. August Mariah Bruce, "Team Leadership at Amazon's Customer Service," Penn State—Leadership (PSYCH 485 blog), October 26, 2014, https://sites.psu.edu/leadership/2014/10/26/team-leadership-at-amazon-customer-service/ (accessed January 8, 2017).

68. Bruce, "Team Leadership at Amazon's Customer Service."

69. Bruce, "Team Leadership at Amazon's Customer Service."

70. Johnson and Indvik, "Rudeness at Work: Impulse over Restraint," 457–65.

71. Cortina and Magley, "Patterns and Profiles of Response to Workplace Incivility," 286.

72. Pearson and Porath, *The Cost of Bad Behavior*, 141–50.

73. Pearson et al., "Assessing and Attacking Workplace Incivility"; see also Pearson and Porath, *The Cost of Bad Behavior*.

## 7. EVERYDAY INCIVILITY ONLINE

1. Steve Farkas et al., *Aggravating Circumstances: A Status Report on Rudeness in America* (New York: Pew Charitable Trusts, 2002), http://www.policyarchive.org/handle/10207/5628 (accessed December 20, 2016), 22.

2. Jon Ronson, "How One Stupid Tweet Blew Up Justine Sacco's Life," *New York Times*, February 12, 2015, www.nytimes.com/2015/02/15/magazine/how-one-stupid-tweet-ruined-justine-saccos-life.html (accessed March 11, 2015).

3. Ronson, "How One Stupid Tweet Blew Up Justine Sacco's Life."

4. Ronson, "How One Stupid Tweet Blew Up Justine Sacco's Life."

5. Jon Ronson, *So You've Been Publicly Shamed* (London, UK: Picador, 2015), 67.

6. Ronson, "How One Stupid Tweet Blew Up Justine Sacco's Life."

7. William McKenzie, "The Internet Is Forcing us to Rethink Ethics," *Dallas Morning News*, June 21, 2011, 13A.

8. McKenzie, "The Internet Is Forcing us to Rethink Ethics."

9. Gary W. Giumetti et al., "Cyber Incivility @ Work: The New Age of Interpersonal Deviance," *Cyberpsychology, Behavior, and Social Networking*, 15, no. 3 (2012): 148.

10. Jacquielynn Floyd, "Body-Shaming Fail Turned into a Viral Win for 'Ordinary' Women," *Dallas Morning News*, July 27, 2016, 1B, 8B.

11. "Flaming," *Urban Dictionary*, March 12, 2004, http://www.urbandictionary.com/define.php?term=flaming (accessed December 26, 2016).

12. Joel Stein, "How Trolls Are Ruining the Internet," *Time*, September 28, 2016, http://time.com/4457110/internet-trolls/ (accessed December 26, 2016).

13. Stein, "How Trolls Are Ruining the Internet."

14. Stein, "How Trolls Are Ruining the Internet."

15. Missy Diaz, " 'Sexting' Can Be Criminal for Unknowing Teens," *Dallas Morning News*, August 2, 2009, 10A; see also Melissa Henderson, "IT HAPPENED TO ME: I Caught My Boyfriend Posting Revenge Porn of his Ex-Girlfriend," *XO Jane*, July 20, 2016, http://www.xojane.com/it-happened-to-me/my-boyfriend-posted-revenge-porn-of-his-ex-girlfriend (accessed December 26, 2016).

16. Asam Ahmad, "A Note on Call-Out Culture," *Briarpatch Magazine: Fiercely Independent*, March 2, 2015, http://briarpatchmagazine.com/articles/view/a-note-on-call-out-culture (accessed December 26, 2016).

17. Harlan Lebow, "The 2016 Digital Future Report, Surveying the Digital Future—Year Fourteen," *USC Annenberg School Center for the Digital Future*, June 2016, http://www.digitalcenter.org/wp-content/uploads/2013/06/2016-Digital-Future-Report.pdf (accessed December 15, 2016).

18. Aaron Smith, "6 New Facts about Facebook," *Pew Research Center*, February 3, 2014, www.pewresearch.org/fact-tank/2014/02/03/6-new-facts-about-facebook (accessed February 3, 2014).

19. Maeve Duggan, "Online Harassment: Summary of Findings," *Pew Research Internet Project*, October 22, 2014, www.pewinternet.org/2014/10/22/online-harassment/ (accessed October 22, 2014).

20. Maeve Duggan, "Online Harassment Part 1: Experiencing Online Harassment," *Pew Research Internet Project*, October 22, 2014, www.pewinternet.org/2014/10/22/part-1-experiencing-online-harassment (accessed October 22, 2014).

21. Duggan, "Online Harassment Part 1: Experiencing Online Harassment."

22. Maeve Duggan, "Online Harassment Part 5: Witnessing Harassment Online," *PEW Research Internet Project*, October 22, 2014, www.pewinternet.org/2014/10/22/part-5-witnessing-harassment-online (accessed October 22, 2014).

23. "39% of American Public Tuning Out of Social Networks Due to Incivility, According to New Weber Shandwick Survey," *PR Newswire*, June 23, 2010, http://www.prnewswire.com/news-releases/39-of-american-public-tuning-out-of-social-networks-due-to-incivility-according-to-new-weber-shandwick-survey-96971629.html (accessed June 24, 2010).

24. "39% of American Public Tuning Out of Social Networks Due to Incivility."

25. David Smiley, "Officers Fired Over Racial Chat," *Dallas Morning News*, December 30, 2016, 8A.

26. Duggan, "Online Harassment Part 1: Experiencing Online Harassment."

27. Giumetti et al., "Cyber Incivility @ Work," 148.

28. Ryan C. Martin et al., "Anger on the Internet: The Perceived Value of Rant Sites," *Cyberpsychology, Behavior, and Social Networking* 16, no. 2 (2013): 119–22.

29. Ashley A. Anderson et al., " 'The 'Nasty Effect': Online Incivility and Risk Perceptions of Emerging Technologies," *Journal of Computer-Mediated Communication* 19, no. 3 (2014): 373–87.

30. Stein, "How Trolls Are Ruining the Internet."

31. Abby Haglage, "What to Answer: Your Phone or Your Wife?" *Daily Beast*, March 19, 2014, www.thedailybeast.com/articles/2014/03/19/what-to-answer-your-phone-or-your-wife.html (accessed December 16, 2016); see also "Digital Divisiveness: Electronic Displays of Insensitivity (EDIs) Take Toll on Relationships," *VitalSmarts*, March 19, 2014, https://www.vitalsmarts.com/press/2014/03/digital-divisiveness-electronic-displays-of-insensitivity-edis-take-toll-on-relationships/ (accessed December 31, 2016).

32. Jack Marshall (March 12, 2015), "Unethical App: Yik Yak," *Ethics Alarms*, https://ethicsalarms.com/2015/03/12/unethical-app-yik-yak/ (accessed December 28, 2016).

33. Jonathan Mahler, "Yik Yak App Has Colleges Talking about Preventing Abuse of Anonymity," *Dallas Morning News*, March 8, 2015, http://www.dallasnews.com/news/news/2015/03/08/yik-yak-app-has-colleges-talking-about-preventing-abuse-of-anonymity (accessed March 9, 2015).

34. Joanna Weiss, "A Bright Spot in the Social Media Sludge?" *Dallas Morning News*, May 19, 2014, 13A.

35. Sean Decatur, "Respectful Difference," *Inside Higher Ed*, October 6, 2014, https://www.insidehighered.com/views/2014/10/06/essay-how-one-college-responded-anonymous-offensive-postings-yik-yak (accessed April 17, 2015).

36. Emily Sakamoto and Victoria Ungvarsky, "Trending Now: Respect," *Kenyon Collegian*, October 2, 2014, http://digital.kenyon.edu/collegian/169 (accessed December 7, 2015).

37. Sarah Bence, "Respectful Difference across Campus: What This Means to Her Campus Kenyon," *Kenyon: Her Campus*, October 5, 2014, http://www.hercampus.com/school/kenyon/respectful-difference-across-campus-what-means-her-campus-kenyon (accessed December 7, 2015).

38. Brooks Buffington and Tyler Droll, "Thank You, Yakkers," *Yik Yak Blog*, April 28, 2017, http://blog.yikyak.com/blog/thank-you-yakkers (accessed May 4, 2017).

39. Carl Straumsheim, "Students Lose Interest in Yik Yak, a Relief for Administrators," *Inside Higher Ed*, December 19, 2016, https://www.insidehighered.com/news/2016/12/19/students-lose-interest-yik-yak-relief-administrators (accessed December 28, 2016).

40. Jeffrey Zaslow, "Surviving the Age of Humiliation," *Wall Street Journal*, May 5, 2010, http://www.wsj.com/articles/SB10001424052748703612804575222580214035638 (accessed December 16, 2016).

41. Kim Ode, "Ticked Off on Twitter, Yowling on Yelp: As a Culture, Why Are We So Darn Mad?" *StarTribune*, March 11, 2016, www.startribune.com/ticked-off-on-twitter-yowling-on-yelp-as-a-culture-why-are-we-so-sarn-mad/371727961/ (accessed March 15, 2016).

42. Ode, "Ticked Off on Twitter, Yowling on Yelp."

43. Marilyn Price-Mitchell, "Teaching Civility in an F-Word Society," *Psychology Today*, June 23, 2012, www.psychologytoday.com/blog/the-moment-youth/201206/teaching-civility-in-f-word-society (accessed September 24, 2015).

44. Janice Denegri-Knott, "Consumers Behaving Badly," *Journal of Consumer Behavior* 5, no. 1 (2006): 82–94.

45. Neil Selwyn, "A Safe Haven for Misbehaving? An Investigation of Online Misbehavior among University Students," *Social Science Computer Review* 26, no. 4 (2008): 462.

46. Stein, "How Trolls are Ruining the Internet."

47. Price-Mitchell, "Teaching Civility in an F-Word Society"; see also Richard Baird, "Anonymity: Familiarity's Ugly Cousin and the Bane of Civility," *Collapse of Civility*, October 7, 2009, https://collapseofcivility.com/2009/10/07/anonymity-familiaritys-ugly-cousin-and-civilitys-bane/ (accessed April 28, 2014).

48. Rebecca A. Clay, "That's Just Rude: Psychologists Are Finding that Boorish Behavior Can Have a Lasting Effect on Well-Being," *Monitor on Psychology*, November 2013, http://www.apa.org/monitor/2013/11/rude.aspx (accessed November 16, 2013).

49. Mich E. Kabay, "Anonymity and Pseudonymity in Cyberspace: Deindividuation, Incivility and Lawlessness Versus Freedom and Privacy" (paper presented at the annual conference of the European Institute for Computer Anti-Virus Research (EICAR), Munich, Germany, 1998); see also Neil Selwyn, "A Safe Haven for Misbehaving? An Investigation of Online Misbehavior among University Students," *Social Science Computer Review* 26, no. 4 (2008).

50. Barbara A. Ritter, "Say That to My Face: Factors Inherent to the Online Environment that Increase the Likelihood of Harassing and Prejudicial Behavior," in *Misbehavior Online in Higher Education: Cutting Edge Technologies in Higher Education, vol. 5* (UK: Emerald Group Publishing, 2012), ed. Laura A. Wankel and Charles Wankel, 25–42.

51. "Why We React on Social Media," *UT Dallas Magazine* 7, no. 1 (2016): 5.

52. Scott Rosenberg, "Newspaper Comments: Forget Anonymity! The Problem Is Management," *Wordyard*, April 13, 2014, www.wordyard.com/2010/04/13/newspaper-comments-forget-anonymity-the-problem-is-management/ (accessed July 2, 2015).

53. Jack Marshall, "Ethics Hero: Former Red Sox Pitcher Curt Shilling," *Ethics Alarms*, March 4, 2015, http://ethicsalarms.com/2015/03/04/ethics-hero-former-red-sox-pitcher-curt-schilling/ (accessed March 4, 2015).

54. Jimmy Wales, foreword in *Civility in the Digital Age* by Andrea Weckerle (Boston, MA: Pearson, 2013): xi.

55. Barbara Ortutay and Michael Kunzelman, "Anti-Hate Drive Grows Stronger," *Dallas Morning News*, February 8, 2017, 2D.

56. Stein, "How Trolls are Ruining the Internet."

57. Maeve Duggan, "Online Harassment: Introduction," *PEW Research Internet Project*, October 22, 2014, http://www.pewinternet.org/2014/10/22/introduction-17/ (accessed October 22, 2014); see also L. Gordon Crovitz, "Information Age: Is Internet Civility an Oxymoron?" *Wall Street Journal*, April 19, 2010, http://www.wsj.com/articles/SB10001424052748704246804575190632247184538 (accessed May 8, 2010).

58. Giumetti et al., "Cyber Incivility @ Work."

59. Alex Williams, "The Emily Posts of the Digital Age," *New York Times*, March 29, 2013, http://www.nytimes.com/2013/03/31/fashion/etiquette-returns-for-the-digital-generation.html (accessed April 12, 2013).

60. Ode, "Ticked Off on Twitter, Yowling on Yelp."

61. Rex Huppke, "Companies Can Help Tackle Internet Trolls," *Dallas Morning News*, February 21, 2016, 2D.

62. Andrew F. Wood, *Communicating with Millennials: Closing the Loop with the Always-On-But-Never-There Generation* (paper presented at the 97th meeting of the National Communication Association, New Orleans, LA, 2011).

63. Wood, *Communicating with Millennials*.

64. Wood, *Communicating with Millennials*.

65. Lebow, "The 2016 Digital Future Report, Surveying the Digital Future—Year Fourteen."

66. Aaron Smith, "The Best (and Worst) of Mobile Connectivity," *Pew Internet and American Life Project*, November 30, 2012, http://www.pewinternet.org/files/old-media/Files/Reports/2012/PIP_Best_Worst_Mobile_113012.pdf (accessed December 16, 2016), 19.

67. Smith, "The Best (and Worst) of Mobile Connectivity."

68. Alex Williams, "The Emily Posts of the Digital Age," *New York Times*, March 29, 2013, http://www.nytimes.com/2013/03/31/fashion/etiquette-returns-for-the-digital-generation.html (accessed April 12, 2013).

69. Terry Maxon, "Hang-Ups in the Air," *Dallas Morning News*, March 24, 2014, 1D, 4D.

70. Paul Brady, "Can You Text on a Plane? A Guide to In-Flight Phone Use," *Conde Nast Traveler*, May 25, 2016, http://www.cntraveler.com/stories/2014-06-16/everything-you-need-to-know-about-using-a-cell-phone-on-a-plane (accessed December 31, 2016).

71. Elisa Batista, "Hush-Hush Hooray, Says NYC," *Wired News*, August 17, 2002, http://archive.wired.com/techbiz/media/news/2002/08/54608?currentPage=all (accessed January 7, 2017); see also Amy Wu, "Cell Phones: All the Rage," *Wired News,* January 4, 2000, http://archive.wired.com/culture/lifestyle/news/2000/01/33291?currentPage=all (accessed January 7, 2016).

72. Wu, "Cell Phones: All the Rage."

73. Veronica V. Galvan, Rosa S. Vessal, and Matthew T. Golley, "The Effects of Cell Phone Conversations on the Attention and Memory of Bystanders," *PLOS One*, March 13, 2013, http://journals.plos.org/plosone/article?id=10.1371/journal.pone.0058579 (accessed December 31, 2016); see also Andrew Monk, Jenni Carroll, Sarah Parker, and Mark Blythe, "Why Are Mobile Phones Annoying?" *Behaviour and Information Technology* 23 (January–February 2004): 33–41; Andrew Monk, Evi, Fellas, and Eleanor Ley, "Hearing Only One Side of Normal and Mobile Phone Conversations," *Behaviour and Information Technology* 23 (September–October 2004): 301–05.

74. Jakob Nielsen, "Why Mobile Phones Are Annoying," *Jakob Nielsen's Alertbox*, April 12, 2004, https://www.nngroup.com/articles/why-mobile-phones-are-annoying/ (accessed April 2, 2005).

75. "Digital Divisiveness: Electronic Displays of Insensitivity (EDIs) Take Toll on Relationships."

76. "Digital Divisiveness: Electronic Displays of Insensitivity (EDIs) Take Toll on Relationships."

77. Robert Shuter and Sumana Chattopadhyay, "Emerging Interpersonal Norms of Text Messaging in India and the United States," *Journal of Intercultural Communication Research* 39, no. 2 (2010): 143.

78. Melvin C. Washington, Ephraim A. Okoro, and Peter W. Cardon, "Perceptions of Civility for Mobile Phone Use in Formal and Informal Meetings," *Business and Professional Communication Quarterly* 77, no. 1 (2014): 52–64.

79. "New Survey Shows Americans Believe Civility Is on the Decline," *Associated Press-NORC Center for Public Affairs Research,* April 15, 2016, http://www.apnorc.org/PDFs/Rudeness/APNORC%20Rude%20Behavior%20Report%20%20PRESS%20RELEASE.pdf (accessed December 13, 2016).

80. "The Generation AFTER Millennials Will Change How You Use Technology," *Gen Z technology Usage Trends Infographic*, The Center for Generational Kinetics, 2016, http://genhq.com/igen-genz-technology-trends-infographic (accessed May 4, 2017).

81. Corey Seemiller and Meghan Grace, *Generation Z Goes to College* (San Francisco, CA: Jossey-Bass, 2016), 57.

82. Jack Marshall, "Ethics Quiz: The Vigilante Cell Phone Police," *Ethics Alarms*, June 1, 2013, http://ethicsalarms.com/2013/06/01/ethics-quiz-the-vigilante-cell-phone-police/ (accessed June 3, 2013).

83. Marshall, "Ethics Quiz: The Vigilante Cell Phone Police."

84. "Digital Divisiveness: Electronic Displays of Insensitivity (EDIs) Take Toll on Relationships."

85. Jamie McKenzie, "Mobile Etiquette," *Phoneybusiness.com*, 2006; see also "Etiquette: It Is Very Simple, Just Follow It!" *Phone Manners and Etiquette*, 2004, http://www.nophones.com/manners/etiquette.html (accessed April 10, 2016).

86. "Digital Divisiveness: Electronic Displays of Insensitivity (EDIs) Take Toll on Relationships."

87. "Digital Divisiveness: Electronic Displays of Insensitivity (EDIs) Take Toll on Relationships."

88. "Digital Divisiveness: Electronic Displays of Insensitivity (EDIs) Take Toll on Relationships."

## 8. EVERYDAY INCIVILITY AT HOME

1. C. S. Lewis, *The Four Loves*, http://www.goodreads.com/quotes/tag/civility (accessed January 7, 2017).

2. Tom Walker and Heather Saul, "Rachel Canning: Judge Rules Parents Don't Have to Pay College Fees of Daughter Who Tried to Sue Them," *INDEPENDENT*, March 5, 2014, http://www.independent.co.uk/news/world/americas/new-jersey-judge-rules-against-teenager-rachel-canning-suing-for-college-tuition-9170615.html (accessed January 5, 2017).

3. Carol Kuruvilla, "Rachel Canning, 'Spoiled' New Jersey Teen, Goes Home to Parents," *New York Daily News*, March 13, 2014, http://www.nydailynews.com/news/national/rachel-canning-spoiled-n-teen-home-parents-article-1.1719110 (accessed January 5, 2017).

4. Kuruvilla, "Rachel Canning, 'Spoiled' New Jersey Teen, Goes Home to Parents"; see also Ben Horowitz, "Mom's Call Brings Rachel Canning Home, but Lawyer Seeks Guardian for Teen," *NJ.com*, March 13, 2014, http://www.nj.com/news/index.ssf/2014/03/a_mothers_call_brings_rachel_canning_home_but_lawyer_seeks_guardian_for_teen_who_sued_parents.html (accessed January 5, 2017).

5. Kuruvilla, "Rachel Canning, 'Spoiled' New Jersey Teen, Goes Home to Parents"; see also Joel Christie, "Parent-Suing Cheerleader who Claimed 'Ex-Boyfriend Choked her During Domestic Violence Incident' Reaches Agreement to Drop Restraining Orders," *Daily Mail*, August 6, 2014, http://www.dailymail.co.uk/news/article-2718182/Parent-suing-cheerleader-claimed-boyfriend-choked-domestic-violence-incident-makes-agreement-drop-restraining-orders.html (accessed January 5, 2017).

6. Carol Kuruvilla, "Rachel Canning, 'Spoiled' New Jersey Teen, Goes Home to Parents," *New York Daily News*, March 13, 2014, http://www.nydailynews.com/news/national/rachel-canning-spoiled-n-teen-home-parents-article-1.1719110 (accessed January 5, 2017).

7. Ben Horowitz, "NJ Teen Rachel Canning Agrees to Dismiss Lawsuit Against Her Parents," *NJ.com*, March 18, 2014, http://www.nj.com/morris/index.ssf/2014/03/case_ends_as_nj_teen_agrees_to_dismiss_lawsuit_against_her_parents.html (accessed January 5, 2017).

8. Kuruvilla, "Rachel Canning, 'Spoiled' New Jersey Teen, Goes Home to Parents."

9. Janet Yerby, Nancy Buerkel-Rothfuss, and Arthur P. Bochner, *Understanding Family Communication*, 2nd ed. (Boston, MA: Allyn & Bacon, 1990).

10. Gabriele Kembuan, "What Are Some Family Norms and Values?" *Quora*, July 31, 2016, https://www.quora.com/What-are-some-family-norms-and-values (accessed January 4, 2017).

11. Virginia Satir, "The Rules You Live By," *Making Connections: Readings in Relational Communication*, 3rd edition, ed. Kathleen M. Galvin and Pamela J. Cooper (New York: Oxford University Press, CA: Roxbury, 2003), 199–205.

12. Elizabeth Stone, *Black Sheep and Kissing Cousins: How Our Family Stories Shape Us* (New York: Transaction Publishers, 2004).

13. Harlan Cohen, "Grandma Roasts Chestnuts and Loved Ones," *Harlan Cohen—Blog*, December 12, 2016, http://www.harlancohen.com/grandma-roasts-chestnuts-and-loved-ones/ (accessed January 5, 2017).

14. Cohen, "Grandma Roasts Chestnuts and Loved Ones."

15. Shelley D. Lane, *Interpersonal Communication: Competence and Contexts*, 2nd ed. (Boston, MA: Allyn & Bacon, 2010): 232.

16. Kenneth N. Leone Cissna and Evelyn Sieberg, "Patterns of Interactional Confirmation and Disconfirmation," *Rigor and Imagination: Essays from the Legacy of Gregory Bateson,* ed. Carol Wilder and John H. Weakland (New York: Praeger, 1981), 153–282.

17. Deborah Y. Cohn, "Thanks, I Guess: What Consumers Complain about When They Complain about Gifts," *Journal of Consumer Satisfaction, Dissatisfaction, and Complaining Behavior*, 29 (2016): 77-89.

18. Cohn, "Thanks, I Guess: What Consumers Complain About."

19. Cohn, "Thanks, I Guess: What Consumers Complain About."

20. Cohn, "Thanks, I Guess: What Consumers Complain About."

21. Deborah Tannen, *You're Wearing That? Understanding Mothers and Daughters in Conversation* (New York: Random House, 2006): 21–22.

22. Tannen, *You're Wearing That?*; see also Deborah Tannen, *I Only Say This Because I Love You: How the Way We Talk Can Make or Break Family Relationships Throughout Our Lives* (New York: Ballantine Books, 2001), xvii.

23. Paul Watzlawick, Janet Beavin, and Dan Jackson, *Pragmatics of Human Communication: A Study of Interpersonal Patterns, Pathologies, and Paradoxes,* (New York: Norton, 1967).

24. Deborah Tannen, *You Just Don't Understand: Women and Men in Conversation* (New York: Harper Paperbacks, 2001).

25. Tannen, *You Just Don't Understand: Women and Men in Conversation.*

26. Larry Fitzmaurice, "Jack White and Karen Elson Divorce, Throw Party," *Pitchfork*, June 10, 2011, http://pitchfork.com/news/42798-jack-white-and-karen-elson-divorce-throw-party/ (accessed January 7, 2017).

27. Matthew Perpetua, "Jack White and Karen Elson 'Celebrating' Separation with Divorce Party," *RollingStone*, June 10, 2011, http://www.rollingstone.com/music/news/jack-white-and-karen-elson-celebrating-separation-with-divorce-party-20110610 (accessed January 7, 2017).

28. Jane Greer, "Jack White: Is There a Good Divorce?" *Huffington Post*, June 16, 2011, http://www.huffingtonpost.com/dr-jane-greer/jack-white-is-there-a-goo_b_878405.html (accessed July 17, 2011).

29. John M. Gottman, *Why Marriages Succeed or Fail* (New York: Simon & Schuster, 1994), 29.

30. Gottman, *Why Marriages Succeed or Fail.*

31. Gottman, *Why Marriages Succeed or Fail.*

32. Emily Esfahani Smith, "Marital Love," *Atlantic*, June 12, 2014, www.theatlantic.com/health/archive/2014/06/happily-ever-after/372573/ (accessed December 29, 2016).

33. Gottman, *Why Marriages Succeed or Fail.*

34. Gottman, *Why Marriages Succeed or Fail*, 94.

35. Gottman, *Why Marriages Succeed or Fail*, 72.

36. Smith, "Marital Love."

37. Carrie Doehring, "Civility in the Family," *Civility*, ed. Leroy S. Rouner (Notre Dame, Indiana: University of Notre Dame Press, 2000): 168–84.

38. Smith, "Marital Love."

39. Gottman, *Why Marriages Succeed or Fail*; see also John Gottman and Nan Silver, *The Seven Principles for Making Marriage Work* (New York: Crown Publishers, 1999); John Gottman, *What Predicts Divorce?* (Mahwah, NJ: Lawrence Erlbaum, 1994).

40. Gottman, *What Predicts Divorce?*

41. Gottman, *Why Marriages Succeed or Fail*, 62.

42. Patricia Evans, *The Verbally Abusive Relationship* (Avon, MA: Adams Media, 2009), Kindle Locations 1859–69.

43. Suzette H. Elgin, *The Gentle Art of Verbal Self-Defense* (Upper Saddle River, NJ: Prentice-Hall, 1980).

44. Evans, *The Verbally Abusive Relationship*; see also Berit Brogaard, "Why You Can't Reason with a Verbally Abusive Partner," *Psychology Today*, April 20, 2015, https://www.psychologytoday.com/blog/the-mysteries-love/201504/why-you-can-t-reason-verbally-abusive-partner (accessed January 4, 2017).

45. Linda L. Marshall, "Physical and Psychological Abuse," *The Dark Side of Interpersonal Communication*, ed. William R. Cupach and Brian H. Spitzberg (Mahwah, NJ: Lawrence Erlbaum, 1994), 281–311.

46. Albert Ellis and Marcia Grad Powers, *The Secret of Overcoming Verbal Abuse* (Los Angeles, CA: Wilshire Book Co., 2000).

47. Marshall, "Physical and Psychological Abuse."

48. Shelley D. Lane and Gustavo A. Yep, *Verbally Abusive Communication in Intimate and Nonintimate Relationships: A Review and Critique* (presented at the Speech Communication Association convention, Chicago, IL, 1994); see also Ellis and Powers, *The Secret of Overcoming Verbal Abuse*, 29.

49. Larry Venable, "Let the Kids Play: It's Their Dream, Not Yours," *Dallas Morning News*, November 4, 2016, 15A.

50. Martin Gross, "AP/Ipsos Poll: The Decline of American Civilization, or at Least Its Manners," *Ipsos*, October 14, 2005, http://www.ipsos-na.com/news/pressrelease.cfm?id=2827 (accessed October 14, 2005); see also "American Manners Poll: The Associated Press/Ipsos Poll on Public Attitudes about Rudeness," *USATODAY.com.* October 14, 2005, http://www.usatoday.com/news/nation/2005-10-14-rudeness-poll-method_x.htm (accessed January 28, 2006).

51. Sven Wahlroos, *Family Communication* (Boston, MA: Macmillan, 1983).

52. Laura Stafford and Marianne Dainton, "The Dark Side of 'Normal' Family Interaction," in *The Dark Side of Interpersonal Communication*, ed. William R. Cupach and Brian R. Spitzberg (Mahwah, NJ: Lawrence Erlbaum, 1994), 259–80.

53. Brant R. Burleson, Jesse G. Delia, and James L. Applegate, "The Socialization of Person-Centered Communication: Parents' Contributions to Their Children's Social-Cognitive and Communication Skills," in *Explaining Family Interactions*, ed. Mary Ann Fitzpatrick and Anita L. Vangelisti (CA: Sage, 1995), 34–76.

54. Lane, *Interpersonal Communication: Competence and Contexts.*

55. National Center for Education Statistics, Institute of Education Sciences, U.W. Department of Education, "1.5 Million Homeschooled Students in the United States in 2007," *nces.ed.gov,* December 2008, http://nces.ed.gov/pubs2009/2009030.pdf (accessed August 21, 2010); see also "American Manners Poll: The Associated Press/Ipsos Poll on Public Attitudes about Rudeness."

56. Stephen L. Carter, *Civility: Manners, Morals, and the Etiquette of Democracy* (New York: Harper Perennial, 1998).

57. Leonard Sax, *The Collapse of Parenting: How We Hurt Our Kids When We Treat Them Like Grown-Ups* (New York: Basic Books, 2015); see also Leonard Sax, "Parenting in the Age of Awfulness," *Wall Street Journal*, December 17, 2015, www.wsj.com/articles/parenting-in-the-age-of-awfulness (accessed December 28, 2016).

58. Sax, *The Collapse of Parenting.*

59. Jane Greer and Edward Myers, *Adult Sibling Rivalry: Understanding the Legacy of Childhood* (New York: Crown Publishers, 1992), 9.

60. Greer and Myers, *Adult Sibling Rivalry.*

61. Tannen, *I Only Say This Because I Love You*, 268.

62. Deborah Tannen, *Conversational Style: Analyzing Talk among Friends* (New York: Oxford University Press, 2005).

63. Frances M. Malpezzi and William M. Clements, *Italian American Folklore* (Little Rock, AR: August House Publishers, 1992), 74; see also Joseph J. Bonocore, *Raised Italian-American: Stories, Values, and Traditions from the Neighborhood* (Lincoln, NE: iUniverse, 2005) 106.

64. Tannen, *I Only Say This Because I Love You*, 301.

65. Tannen, *I Only Say This Because I Love You*, 280.

66. Anne Katherine, *Boundaries: Where You and I Begin* (New York: A Fireside Book, 1991).

67. Anne Katherine, *Where to Draw the Line: How to Set Healthy Boundaries Every Day* (New York: Fireside, 2000).

# 9. PROMOTING EVERYDAY CIVILITY

1. Britt-Mari Sykes, *Questioning Psychological Health and Well-Being* (Macon, GA: Mercer University Press, 2010), 45.

2. Brendan Meyer, "Dallas Running Pals Don't Shy Away from Differing Politics," *Dallas Morning News*, November 8, 2016, 1A, 8A.

3. Jack Marshall, "Ethics Musings While Sitting in Line at the Gas Station," *Ethics Alarms*, January 22, 2016, https://ethicsalarms.com/2016/01/21/ethics-musings-while-sitting-in-line-at-the-gas-station/ (accessed January 22, 2016).

4. Philip Smith, Timothy L. Phillip, and Ryan D. King, *Incivility: The Rude Stranger in Everyday Life* (New York: Cambridge University Press, 2010).

5. Smith et al., *Incivility: The Rude Stranger in Everyday Life*.

6. Smith et al., *Incivility: The Rude Stranger in Everyday Life*.

7. Jessica Gelt, "When Diners' Eyes Feast on their Cellphones," *Los Angeles Times*, January 26, 2012, http://articles.latimes.com/2012/jan/26/food/la-fo-0126-table-texting-20120126 (accessed January 13, 2017).

8. Emma C Fitzsimmons, "A Scourge is Spreading. M.T.A.'s Cure? Dude, Close Your Legs," *New York Times*, December 20, 2014, https://www.nytimes.com/2014/12/21/nyregion/MTA-targets-manspreading-on-new-york-city-subways.html?_r=0 (accessed December 20, 2014).

9. Rachel Holliday Smith, "Manspreading Through the Ages: MTA Explains How 'Transit Etiquette' Evolved," *This Is New York*, April 3, 2016, https://www.dnainfo.com/new-york/20160401/midtown/manspreading-through-ages-mta-explains-how-transit-etiquette-evolved (accessed April 15, 2016).

10. Teresa Jusino, "How One Man is Fighting the Good Fight Against 'Manspreading' in South Korea," *Mary Sue*, April 15, 2016, https://www.themarysue.com/stop-the-spread/ (accessed April 15, 2016).

11. Kristin M. Hall, "Gay Couple Asked to Reverse Shirt at Dollywood," *Yahoo! News*, July 27, 2011, https://www.yahoo.com/news/gay-couple-asked-reverse-shirt-dollywood-200120079.html (accessed July 28, 2011); see also Jeremy Kinser, "Did Dollywood Discriminate Against a Lesbian Couple?" *Advocate*, July 20, 2011, http://www.advocate.com/news/daily-news/2011/07/20/did-dollywood-discriminate-against-lesbian-couple (accessed August 31, 2011).

12. Hall, "Gay Couple Asked to Reverse Shirt at Dollywood"; see also Alex Murashko, "Dolly Parton's Dollywood Charged with Gay Discrimination," *Christian Post*, July 23, 2011, http://www.christianpost.com/news/dolly-partons-dollywood-charged-with-gay-discrimination-52751/ (accessed August 31, 2011).

13. "Being Annoying Now Illegal in Brighton," *Portland Mercury*, December 22, 2008, http://www.portlandmercury.com/BlogtownPDX/archives/2008/12/22/being_annoying_now_illegal_in (accessed January 13, 2017).

14. Amy Wu, "Cell Phones: All the Rage," *Wired News*, January 4, 2000, http://archive.wired.com/culture/lifestyle/news/2000/01/33291?currentPage=all (accessed July 9, 2005); see also Dan Briody, "Opinion: Table for Two, Cell Phone or Noncell Phone?" *CNN.com*, November 30, 1999, http://edition.cnn.com/TECH/computing/9911/30/nocellzone.idg/index.html (accessed January 13, 2017); and "Louisiana Law Goes Too Far," *SunSentinel*, June 26, 1999, http://articles.sun-sentinel.com/1999-06-26/news/9906250810_1_civility-louisiana-legislature-ma-am (accessed December 22, 2008).

15. Josh Sanburn, "What the @!#$? Cursing in Public in This Massachusetts Town Will Cost You $20.00," *Time*, June 13, 2012, http://business.time.com/2012/06/13/what-the-cursing-in-public-in-this-massachusetts-town-will-cost-you-20/ (accessed January 8, 2017).

16. "Massachusetts Town OKs $20 Fines for Swearing in Public," *USA Today*, June 12, 2012, http://usatoday30.usatoday.com/news/nation/story/2012-06-12/middleborough-swearing-fine/55542416/1 (accessed November 14, 2012).

17. "Beijing to Fine Subway Riders for 'Uncivilized Behavior,' " *China Daily*, February 20, 2014, http://www.chinadaily.com.cn/beijing/2014-02/20/content_17293883.htm (accessed March 7, 2014).

18. Henry Chu, "Distasteful Posts Draw Punishment, Debate," *Dallas Morning News*, November 18, 2012, 37A.

19. "Recommendations for Communities Developed through the National Summit on Raising Community Standards in Children's Sports," *National Alliance for Youth Sports*, n.d., http:/

/www.nays.org/cmscontent/file/nays_community_recommendations.pdf (accessed January 10, 2017).

20. John Gehring, "More Schools Calling Foul on Unsportsmanlike Behavior," *Education Week*, October 17, 2001, http://www.edweek.org/ew/articles/2001/10/17/07parents.h21.html (accessed January 10, 2017).

21. Robert I. Sutton, *The No Asshole Rule: Building a Civilized Workplace and Surviving One That Isn't* (New York: Grand Central Publishing, 2007), 56–58.

22. Deborah Fleck, "High School's Anti-Bullying Rally Puts Spotlight on Students' Good Deed," *Dallas Morning News*, September 24, 2014, 1B, 9B; see also Ben Russell, "Grand Prairie Homecoming Queen Shares Her Crown," *NBCDFW.com*, September 16, 2014, http://www.nbcdfw.com/news/local/Grand-Prairie-Homecoming-Queen-Shares-Her-Crown-275390651.html (accessed September 16, 2014).

23. Harry Brighouse, "Civility, Citizenship, and the Limits of Schooling," in *Civility in Politics and Education,* ed. Deborah S. Mower and Wade L. Robison (New York: Routledge, 2012).

24. Brighouse, "Civility, Citizenship, and the Limits of Schooling," 204.

25. Paul Gaffney, "Competition in the Classroom: An Ideal for Civility," in *Civility in Politics and Education,* ed. Deborah S. Mower and Wade L. Robison (New York: Routledge, 2012).

26. "Character Counts!," *Character Counts*, 2017, https://charactercounts.org/ (accessed January 10, 2017).

27. "The Golden Rule: Do Unto Otters," *Character.org*, 2017, http://character.org/lessons/lesson-plans/elementary/plattin-primary-school-2/ (accessed January 10, 2017).

28. "Words Hurt!" *Character.org*, 2017, http://character.org/lessons/lesson-plans/middle/brentwood-middle-school/ (accessed January 10, 2017).

29. "Me and We: A Mix It Up Activity," *Character.org*, 2017, http://character.org/lessons/lesson-plans/middle/rosa-international-middle-school/ (accessed January 10, 2017).

30. "Conflict Resolution Skills Training," *Character.org*, 2017, http://character.org/lessons/lesson-plans/high/hinsdale-central-high-school/ (accessed January 10, 2017).

31. Jeffry Weiss, "School Stresses Civility with R Time Program," *Dallas Morning News*, November 25, 2011, 1B, 3B.

32. Kathleen McCleary, "Operation Good Citizen," *Parade Magazine*, August 2, 2015, 6–8.

33. "Awards and Achievements," *Premier Charter School*, 2017, http://www.premiercharterschool.org/?PageName=bc&n=172247 (accessed January 10, 2017).

34. Timothy C. Shiell, "Debunking Three Myths about Civility," in *Civility in Politics and Education*, ed. Deborah S. Mower and Wade L. Robison (New York: Routledge, 2012), 4.

35. Stephen Sales, "Teaching Civility in the Age of Jerry Springer," *Teaching Ethics* 10, no. 2 (Spring 2010), 1.

36. Shiell, "Debunking Three Myths about Civility."

37. Shiell, "Debunking Three Myths about Civility," 17.

38. Susan Herbst, "Change through Debate," *Inside Higher Ed*, October 9, 2009, https://www.insidehighered.com/views/2009/10/05/change-through-debate (accessed February 23, 2010).

39. Robert J. Connelly, "Introducing a Culture of Civility in First-Year College Classes," *JGE: The Journal of General Education* 58, no. 1 (2009): 47–64.

40. "Archive: The Civility Project," *UC Davis Humanities Institute*, June 20, 2013, http://dhi.ucdavis.edu/archive/civilities (accessed January 8, 2014).

41. "DHI'S Civility Project," *UC Davis Humanities Institute*, February 15, 2012, http://dhi.ucdavis.edu/featured-stories/dhis-civility-project (accessed January 8, 2014).

42. "Sample Center Carries the Message of Civility," *Penn State Erie—The Behrend College*, July 18, 20015, http://news.psu.edu/story/212100/2005/02/09/sample-center-carries-message-civility (accessed January 13, 2017); see also "Janet Neff Sample Center for Manners and Civility," *Penn State Erie—The Behrend College*, February 17, 2009, https://psbehrend.psu.edu/school-of-humanities-social-sciences/research-outreach-1/janet-neff-sample-center-for-manners-and-civility (accessed August 8, 2009).

43. "About," *National Institute for Civil Discourse*, 2017, http://nicd.arizona.edu/about (accessed January 10, 2017).

44. Carolyn J. Lukensmeyer, "Post-Election: Your Civility Survival Guide for Thanksgiving," *National Institute for Civil Discourse*, November 21, 2016, https://medium.com/@CarolynLukensmeyer/post-election-your-civility-survival-guide-for-thanksgiving-cec70609dcce#.skoq24ma2 (accessed January 10, 2017).

45. Christine Porath, "Civility," in *The Oxford Handbook of Positive Organizational Scholarship*, ed. Kim S. Cameron and Gretchen M. Spreitzer (New York: Oxford University Press, 2012), 443; see also Christine Pearson and Christine Porath, *The Cost of Bad Behavior: How Incivility Is Damaging Your Business and What to Do about It* (New York: Portfolio, 2009), 139.

46. Pearson and Porath, *The Cost of Bad Behavior*, 125.

47. Pearson and Porath, *The Cost of Bad Behavior*, 126–27.

48. "World's Most Admired Companies," *Fortune*, 2016, http://fortune.com/worlds-most-admired-companies/ (accessed January 9, 2017).

49. Pearson and Porath, *The Cost of Bad Behavior*, 131.

50. Pearson and Porath, *The Cost of Bad Behavior*, 133.

51. Cheryl Dumont et al., "Horizontal Violence Survey Report," *Nursing 2012* 42, no. 1 (2012): 44–49.

52. Kathie Lasater et al., "Reducing Incivility in the Workplace: Results of a Three-Part Educational Intervention," *Journal of Continuing Education in Nursing* 46, no. 1 (2015): 15–24.

53. Lasater et al., "Reducing Incivility in the Workplace: Results of a Three-Part Educational Intervention," 22.

54. Katherine Osatuke et al., "Civility, Respect, Engagement in the Workforce (CREW)," *Journal of Applied Behavioral Science* 45, no. 3 (September 2009), 184–410.

55. Sutton, *The No Asshole Rule*, 76.

56. Sutton, *The No Asshole Rule*, 77.

57. Osatuke et al., "Civility, Respect, Engagement in the Workforce (CREW)," 184–410.

58. "Pride and Prejudice," *People*, April 4, 2016, 58.

59. "We Are Random Acts of Kindness," *Random Acts of Kindness*, 2017, https://www.randomactsofkindness.org/ (accessed January 9. 2017); see also "What is a RAKtivist?" *Random Acts of Kindness*, 2017, https://www.randomactsofkindness.org/become-a-raktivist (accessed January 8, 2017).

60. "Hi Neighbor," *Anaheim*, 2017, http://www.anaheim.net/1441/Hi-Neighbor (accessed January 9, 2017).

61. "Mayor Launches Youth-Driven Kindness Initiative," *City of Albuquerque*, 2017, https://www.cabq.gov/mayor/news/mayor-launches-youth-driven-kindness-initiative (accessed January 9, 2017).

62. "Speak Your Peace: The Civility Project," *Duluth Superior Area Community Foundation*, n.d., http://www.dsaspeakyourpeace.org/index.html (accessed January 9, 2017).

63. Pier M. Forni, *Choosing Civility* (New York: St. Martin's Griffin, 2002); see also Kim Biedermann, "The Oshkosh Civility Project," *Oshkosh Civility Project: A Community-Based Initiative*, April 1, 2014, http://www.oshkoshcivilityproject.org/ (accessed January 9, 2017).

64. Biedermann, "The Oshkosh Civility Project."

65. "choose2Bkind," *Choose Civility: Howard County, MD*, 2017, http://choosecivility.org (accessed January 9, 2017).

66. "Choose Civility Events and Activities," *Choose Civility, Howard County, MD*, 2017, http://choosecivility.org/events-programs/ (accessed January 9, 2017).

67. Joshua J. Whitfield, "We Lost the Game, but Civility Won," *Dallas Morning News*, October 14, 2016, 15A.

68. Whitfield, "We Lost the Game, but Civility Won."

69. Kent. M. Weeks, *Doing Civility: Breaking the Cycle of Incivility on the Campus* (New York: Morgan James, 2014), 127.

70. Weeks, *Doing Civility: Breaking the Cycle of Incivility on the Campus*, 127.

71. Deborah L. Flick, *From Debate to Dialogue: Using the Understanding Process to Transform Our Conversations* (Boulder, CO: Orchid Publications, 1998), 43.

# Index

University of California–Davis Humanities
  Institute, 193
University of Southern California, 70

value(s): civility as, debates on, 84, 86;
  cynicism due to diversity of, 91;
  definition, 84; personal beliefs and
  diversity of, 86–87, 88, 89–90
Venezuela, 58
verbal abuse, covert, 174–176
Veterans Health Administration (VHA),
  197–198
violence, 3, 33, 122
virtue(s): civility as, debates on, 83–87, 85;
  cynicism due to diversity of, 91;
  definition, 83; personal beliefs and
  diversity of, 86–87, 88, 89–90
vocal qualities, 59

Weber Shandwick polls, 6–7, 122
West, Joe, 10
*What Would You Do?* (television show), 8
whistleblowers, 130
White, Jack, 170
White House, 13, 15
white privilege, 101–102, 106, 114
Whitfield, Joshua J., 199–200
Will, George, 89–90
Williams, David, 83
Williams, Judith, 98
Williamson, Kevin, 156
Wilson, Joe, 5
Win, Chris, 81
womansplaining, 109
Women's Social and Political Union
  (WSPU), 80–81
women's suffrage movement, 80–81, 83
Wood, Andrew F., 152

Woods, Matthew, 189
"Words Hurt" (education curriculum), 192
workplace, 120–121, 121, 130, 190. *See
  also* workplace incivility
workplace incivility: benefits of, 80, 131;
  causes of, 128–129; consequences of,
  employees as targets, xiv, 77, 121,
  130–131, 147; consequences of,
  management, 127–128; consequences
  of, witnesses, 130; customer service,
  119–120, 122–123, 128, 134–136, 196;
  definition and features of, 121–122;
  forms of, 123–130; gender and cell-
  phone texting norms, 155; intervention
  programs for, 195–198; mainsplaining,
  109–110; management strategies,
  132–137; microaggressions in, 106;
  reciprocity and spirals of, 126–127,
  131; statistics and magnitude of, 6, 122
WSPU (Women's Social and Political
  Union), 80–81

Xilinx, 190

"Yes Sir, No Sir" bill, 188
Yik Yak (mobile app), 147–148, 150
youth: age as civility influence, 69; cell-
  phone norms, 155; characteristics and
  personality descriptions, 69–70;
  communication styles of, 70; context
  and civility perceptions, 13–14;
  criticism of, 19, 69, 70; norm-shifting
  and perceptions of, 17–18, 70; social
  media and political criticism, 17; sports
  events conduct policies, 189;
  technology usage, 17–18, 71–72; value
  perception comparisons, 87
YouTube, 151